THE NOAH SYNDROME

Books by Laura Knight-Jadczyk

Amazing Grace – An Autobiography of the Soul
The Secret History of the World
High Strangeness: Hyperdimensions and the Process of Alien Abduction
9/11: The Ultimate Truth
The Apocalypse: Comets, Asteroids and Cyclical Catastrophes

The Wave series:

Riding the Wave
Soul Hackers
The Terror of History
Stripped to the Bone
Petty Tyrants
Facing the Unknown
Almost Human
Debugging the Universe

Laura Knight-Jadczyk

The Noah Syndrome

Red Pill Press
www.redpillpress.com

First edition.
Copyright © 1987–2012 Laura Knight-Jadczyk.
Research Sponsored by Quantum Future Group, Inc.
P. O. Box 5357 Baltimore, MD 21209

ISBN 978-1-897244-79-1

Design & layout: © 2012 Quantum Future Group, Inc., The Fellowship of
the Cosmic Mind, Inc.
Cover image: Nicolas Poussin (1594–1665), 'Winter (Le Déluge)', fragment.

Contents

Introduction   7

Chapter One   21
Chapter Two   43
Chapter Three   67
Chapter Four   79
Chapter Five   99
Chapter Six   119
Chapter Seven   129
Chapter Eight   145
Chapter Nine   159
Chapter Ten   179
Chapter Eleven   197
Chapter Twelve   221

Notes   229

Introduction

In October of 1984, my grandmother died. I was at the hospital when she passed, and afterward, the nurse left me alone with her to say my goodbyes. I wept long and bitterly while holding her now stilled hand, growing perceptibly cold as I pressed it to my cheek. I understood deeply that this flesh that was my grandmother was no longer my grandmother, no matter how dear and familiar to me she had been. Her body was like a glove that had been cast away after it was worn and threadbare. But still, her physical form was the only such representation of her I had, and I knew that this moment was the last I would look upon her in the natural state, so I must look enough to last me the rest of my life.

Without animation, her beloved face was almost unrecognizable, her glorious, clear blue eyes were closed forever, but her hands were still the same hands that I remembered from my childhood. Those hands had never been still; they had always been busy stroking away my hurts, or covered with flour from baking some special treat. My grandmother had beautiful hands with long, graceful fingers, and elegant nails. For a long time I sat there, holding and examining her hand, until finally I was urged to leave.

Since my grandmother had been an omnipresent part of my life up to that point, and I was then 32 years old, it produced a huge sense of 'object loss.' It is fairly simple to deal with this aspect of grieving since those who have experienced loss know that, over time, a new 'history' is created of which the absent loved one is no longer a part. After a time, even if the wound is deep, it is covered with a scar, and the new 'history' becomes the new way of being; the loss is no longer acutely painful. One becomes accustomed to not expecting to hear a certain voice, to not expect to see a certain visage on a daily basis, and to not interact with that individual in a dynamic way. And this new 'custom' becomes the reality as though the universe in which one now exists is not the same universe as the former one in which the loved one was present.

There was another aspect to my grief, however, that was not so easy to deal with and this formed itself into a question: what happens to the love between people when one of them dies? Where does it go? How can it be that such a bond, that may be assumed to exist in Platonic noumenal terms, seems to just suddenly end?

If we understand that the idea of a chair or an apple or any other concrete object is the only truly lasting thing about it, and we then decide that conceptual things like love and kindness that exist only as ideas, are more 'real' in some realm of abstraction, when the dynamic in which those abstractions come to be ceases to be active, where does it go? In what realm does this world of ideas of engendered things, be they solid or only ideological, exist?

The answers that were offered by the Christian faith of my background suddenly seemed not merely unsatisfactory, but downright insulting to the memory of my grandmother and the bond that had existed between us. And for those who find comfort in Spiritualism or concepts of reincarnation, please do not confuse those ideas with my issue here which is, again: for what purpose is love engendered, and where does it go when the interaction comes to an end?

It's easy to say that 'love never dies,' and that love continues to exist between us and our loved ones who are no longer with us in some 'astral' plane or place of the dead; or that we will meet the dear departed at some end-time resurrection of the dead. But when actually faced with it, and these facile and glib answers are offered, I'm sorry - they just don't cut the mustard. I was not satisfied with 'The Lord gives and the Lord takes away; blessed be the name of the Lord.' Even worse was: 'It's not for us to understand God's ways; it's a Mystery.'

I didn't buy it.

To say that I became rather desperate while contemplating this problem is putting it mildly. It became the lens through which my entire life as a seeker of Truth was focused on the singular issue of the concept of 'Eternal Life' and its dual pillars of Salvation and Faith.

At this point in time, I attended church one Sunday and listened to a stirring sermon based on the Book of Revelation from the New Testament. I listened carefully, trying to find some solace in this message about the Resurrection, but it seemed to be nothing but a fear-inducing rant designed to bring the Christian to his knees in supplication and self-abasement. What did that have to do with Love?

The Pastor ended his monologue with a quotation, and I am sure that it was intended to strike fear in the hearts of the congregation, but on me, it had quite a different effect. The quote was: *"But when the days come that the trumpet call of the seventh angel is about to be sounded, then God's mystery — His secret design, His hidden purpose — as He announced the glad tidings to His servants the prophets, should be fulfilled."*

Now, of course, the entire Christian perspective, in whatever denomination you find yourself, teaches that they know what this 'mystery,' or this 'secret design' and 'hidden purpose' is. But it struck me forcibly that, if this was so clearly known, why was John, the author of Revelation, saying quite clearly that there was something we were not being told that would *only* be revealed at 'the end?'

Just exactly what was it that was not being told? What was it that would only be revealed 'at the last trumpet?' More than that, could it have anything to do with my question? Hearing this was like being handed the end of the thread of Ariadne, and I began to pull on it by asking questions and digging for answers.

At the time my grandmother died, I was pregnant with my fourth child who was born in the spring of 1985. The entire pregnancy was spent mourning for my grandmother, and it was especially poignant because this would be the first baby I could not bring home and put directly in Grandma's arms for her to love and rock and sing to. She was the main member of my 'support team,' and the organizer and leader of the 'baby fan club' in our house. My babies were wonderfully enriched by her devotion to each of them.

It was an extremely difficult delivery for both the new baby and me. My heart ached for my poor little baby who had been injured in the process. When she was finally laid in my arms, I began to examine her and right away I noticed her incredible little hands — exactly like my grandmother's. In fact, so much like them that I felt that it was almost like a message from her. Not only that, but the baby had a strawberry hematoma on her left ankle. My grandmother had broken her left ankle when I was a child, and it had required surgery to repair it. Ever afterward, it was swollen and red in exactly the same place that my baby's hematoma was situated.

My baby had also suffered a broken left collarbone during delivery, which made it impossible for her to use her tiny arm for several weeks. My grandmother had undergone a radical mastectomy on the left side that made it impossible for her to use her left arm. Grandma had died of lung cancer, which meant that she essentially drowned in her own lung fluids. At birth, my baby had been unable to breathe or cry because her lungs were full of a thick, sticky fluid. It was a couple of very tense minutes while the hospital staff worked frantically to clean out her lungs and get her to breath. She was so weak in her lungs that she cried like a little kitten mewing for several weeks after her birth, producing many anxious moments for me.

At about the same time that the collarbone healed, the strawberry hematoma disappeared, and her lungs improved so that I no longer sat up all night making sure she was breathing. And today, her hands are her own. But for that time, when I was most desperately grieving that my grandmother was no longer present to greet the new baby, I had received some small comfort from these 'signs' of Love that never dies.

As a result of the injuries I had received during the delivery, I was bedridden for many months. I had four little children to care for and I couldn't even walk. My oldest child was only 7, and the responsibility for the care of her brother and sister, as well as her mother and the new baby, fell on her. She was smart, talented, and a real trooper, but it was clearly not a healthy situation and I was frustrated and irritable at not being able to do anything about it. When I realized that my frustration and irritation was hurting my family, I faced myself and decided that I had to make some changes inside. Since I could no longer maintain my very active participation in life in a physical way, I was forced, by the universe, as it were, to find other outlets for my energy. I decided that this would be the perfect time to master the art of meditation and, prompted by the little 'signs' that appeared during this birth, I felt compelled to investigate this question of Eternal Life.

Without going into details about the meditation experiments, suffice it to say that a lot of strange things began to happen around me. After my regular meditation exercises, I would sit up in the bed, surrounded by piles of books and notebooks, reading and writing notes on what I read. As I did so, I would stop and think about questions that were occurring to me as I read, and the instant these questions were framed in my mind, thoughts would simply pour into my head so fast that I thought my brain would explode. These thoughts always and only came in response to the questions that I would pose mentally about whatever I was considering at the moment in my studies.

The urge to write these thoughts down was so overwhelming that I would spend literally hours a day, filling page after page in longhand, until I felt that I was completely drained mentally and physically. I still have these notebooks. There was a curious aspect to this experience: if

I didn't write the thoughts down, they would stay there; they would sort of 'back up' like dammed-up water and as soon as I had begun to write again, it was as if there had been no break in the flow of thoughts whatsoever; they picked up right where they left off.

At some point, I decided that I must find out if these ideas that were coming to me had any basis in fact whatsoever. I most definitely needed more input! The answers that 'came to me' pointed me in the direction of certain studies that otherwise might not have been part of my experience.

Those who know me understand fully that, even though I have studied it all my life, I have always been a skeptic about the 'paranormal,' including such things as 'channeling'. I have rarely read any so-called 'channeled material' that wasn't just glib and facile word salad. Sure, there are a lot of high-sounding phrases that seem to convey encouraging concepts and useful information, but when you really analyze it, you find that it could just as easily be composed by a computer program that puts certain words and phrases together in certain pre-designated patterns, with nothing new or really innovative ever being said. Also, as a hypnotherapist, I have spent too many years digging around in people's heads and finding all kinds of things there, to not know fully the mind's capacity for self-deception.

Thus it was that, as these ideas came to me, I was compelled by my rational and reflective nature to research each concept to discover if there was any way it could be supported scientifically and objectively. I subscribed to a library service by mail, and soon began ordering and reading book after book on subjects that ranged from geology to physics, from psychology to theology, from metaphysics to astronomy. As I read, I found many pieces that fit in the framework of the information that was pouring into my head relating to these very subjects. I was both surprised and energized to find that the answers I was getting weren't so crazy after all!

As I pulled on the thread of Ariadne, it seemed that the entire fabric of my religion unraveled and there, concealed behind the facts and ideas of science, was an idea so amazing that it took my breath away. The idea was Cosmic Metamorphosis in Quantum terms.

How did I come to this when I started out trying to discover the noumenal existence of Love?

Well, actually, it's quite simple. As I followed the thread through the labyrinth of material, going from the very large to the very small, with a lot in between, it became clear to me that the Hermetic maxim 'As

Above, So Below,' could be applied in any number of useful ways. In the end, the search for the true meaning of Love was the same as the search for Salvation and Faith and, in the end, all of it was ultimately the search for the meaning of Eternal Life. The fact is that the 'Great Mystery of God' that was to be revealed at the 'Time of the End,' prompted me to gather together all that I could on this eschatological theme.

In Matthew 24, Jesus gives a discourse on the 'End Times;' that period in which the last trumpet will sound and the Mystery of God will be revealed. He remarks *"... as were the days of Noah, so will be the coming of the Son of Man. For just as in those days before the flood they were eating and drinking, marrying and being given in marriage, until the day when Noah went into the Ark, and they did not know or understand until the flood came and swept them all away, so will be the coming of the Son of Man."*

This event, the End, the time when 'God's mystery — his secret design, his hidden purpose — as he announced the glad tidings to his servants the prophets, should be fulfilled,' was compared to the 'Days of Noah.'

Well, what's so 'mysterious' about a flood? What's so happy about most of the population of the planet being wiped out of existence? How can you call that 'glad tidings?'

The key seemed to be held in the concept of the Ark. My search for the true meaning of Love, Salvation, Faith and Eternal Life was, essentially, a search for the meaning of the Ark.

Metaphorically speaking, there is no better expression of this search than the story of Noah and the Ark. All of the quests of life and love and existence can be expressed in this story of a man, faced with the destruction of his world — and in this case, it was literally destruction of the entire world, or so the story goes — and he set about building an Ark.

Clearly, 'building an Ark' was considered to be an aberration in the time of Noah. His behavior was obviously looked upon askance by those around him. A syndrome is a group of signs and symptoms that collectively characterize or indicate a particular disease or abnormal condition, and I thought about this in two ways: first, the signs and symptoms of our reality that tell us that the body of the cosmos is not well; and second, the signs and symptoms of those individuals who are, in a microcosmic way, reflecting this same syndrome.

In another sense, a syndrome can also describe certain insects who, when they have achieved a certain stage of growth, begin to manifest a group of signs and symptoms that cause them to 'build a cocoon' in which metamorphosis takes place. Those who feel that the reality is 'right' or 'well,' will naturally think that those who believe otherwise are 'diseased' in their minds or souls. And such 'infected' people, who undertake to act in terms of 'building an Ark,' whether it is spiritual or material will most definitely be seen as experiencing the syndrome of the cosmic disease in themselves. It will not be recognized that their extreme discomfort and dissatisfaction with the world, as it is, is the syndrome that precedes cocooning. Thus, the Noah Syndrome characterizes both the conditions of the planet as well as the experiences of those who 'sense' the impending Metamorphosis.

This issue of 'clothing' was also brought up in Matthew 24, when Jesus notes, *"Let him who is in the field not turn back to get his overcoat."* John expands on this issue by talking about those who are 'naked' and who have no spiritual 'clothing.'

The question then becomes, exactly what is this process of Metamorphosis, and exactly what constitutes an Ark?

The book you are about to read is an effort to come to some ideas about these questions.

While assembling my notes and ideas, it was important to me that I present the information in such a way that I could include notes from more 'mainstream' sources that supported what I had written, or expanded the idea, or, at the very least, gave it plausibility. The reader will find this feature to be uncommon in the realm of 'channeled' books. If the 'inspiration' was not supported by observation or scholarly opinion, if only indirectly, it was not going to be discussed.

As it happens, the whole series of information streams did turn out to have a wide array of support, and I was forced to severely limit what I included for the sake of brevity.

I finished *The Noah Syndrome* on December 16, 1986. By this time, I was able to walk to a limited extent, though I still was in pain all the time. Nevertheless, I went out and bought an old manual typewriter and began to type up my book, which had been written in longhand. In fact, it soon became apparent that the fact that I didn't know how to type was going to really slow me down, and I decided that I had better learn how quickly. By the time I was done with the manuscript, I was a real hotshot on that old manual typewriter!

As I typed, I began to have some very strange impressions. I could 'sense,' or 'see with the mind's eye' a couple of very funny old men looking over my shoulder as I wrote, consulting with each other, telling me where I needed to make corrections or additions, and even chuckling with glee when I wrote certain comments. I knew that one of them somewhat resembled Albert Einstein, but it wasn't until quite a number of years had passed that I saw a photograph of Immanuel Velikovsky and recognized the other old gentleman.

To this day, I am not sure if they were simply figments of my overworked imagination, or if it was an actual experience with some form of discarnate 'guidance.' All I know is that they were hysterically funny in their remarks to one another as they oversaw my project, and they would jovially clap one another on the shoulder when I would finally 'get it' in regards to a particular point.

It took me about 3 months to get it all typed (including much retyping to get it as perfect as possible), and as soon as this phase was completed, I started to think about how to go about getting a book published. I was certain that, of all books, this one needed to be published. (Doesn't every author feel that way? I was so naive!)

I checked out a book from the library that claimed to tell the reader how to get a book published, and it included a list of literary agents. I selected one who seemed rather a likely prospect, a Mr. Scott Meredith, and wrote to him about *Noah*. I received a fee schedule in reply. I was nonplussed (in addition to being naïve), to discover that it was going to cost a rather tidy sum just to have the guy read it. But, feeling rather sure that what I had written was important, I borrowed the money from a friend and sent off a check with the neatly typed pages.

After a number of weeks of anxious checking of the mailbox every day to see if there might be a reply from Mr. Meredith, it finally came. It was dated September 1, 1987. The bottom line was, as Mr. Meredith wrote:

> ... At the same time, unfortunately, there are major flaws present in this manuscript as well from a market standpoint. These flaws strike deeply into the basic structure of the work — so deeply, in fact, that they make it impossible for me even to suggest any sort of revision, this time around. There is simply no way of revising these flaws, or of revising them out, without at the same time just revising the entire manuscript itself right out of existence as well. And it is the presence of these flaws, I'm afraid, that forces me, very regretfully indeed, to return 'The Noah Syndrome' to you as unsalable, despite all of the good work that you have indeed done with this one.
>
> ... I wish that I could have had better news for you on this one... you can write and explain your positions with great clarity. But, as you can see, the basic flaws I've been pointing out here are really inherent in the structure of the work itself; no revision, no rewrite at all, is going to be

able to remove them successfully... I do have to advise you, then, most un-happily, to put 'The Noah Syndrome' behind you as a work for the mass market...

Since he was an expert, I took his advice and put Noah on the shelf. That was 25 years ago.

Since then, I have found it very curious that many of the ideas and concepts that were 'given' to me at that time, are subjects of major discussion and/or acceptance in both scientific and metaphysical circles. If ever there was validation of 'channeled' material, the amazing series of confirmations of what I wrote then has to be outstanding.

Ten years after the writing of *Noah*, some of my later work, also partly 'channeled,' came to the attention of an internationally known Mathematical/Theoretical Physicist, Professor Arkadiusz Jadczyk, Head of the Department of Nonlinear Dynamics and Complex Systems, at the Institute of Theoretical Physics, University of Wroclaw, Poland, who had been researching along the same lines of Cosmic Metamorphosis. Two years later, we were married.

It is truly strange, in retrospect, that my efforts to 'find my Ark' ultimately led to being 'found by my Ark' ... my husband, Arkadiusz.

And, I should note here that, even though my husband is a physicist, he is in no way responsible for anything that was written in *Noah*, as it was done many years before we met.

Noah is now, finally, published in book form. Ark has gone through it, checked my statements and added commentary throughout the text from the point of view of an expert, so the book version will not be an ordinary sort of 'channeled book.' Now, even though this book, *The Noah Syndrome*, has been read and annotated by an 'expert,' thereby falling into a unique category of literary effort, almost none of the original text has been altered. And here, you will read it as I wrote it 26 years ago.

Many readers will be aware that some of these ideas are now common currency. The important thing to remember is when I wrote it.

Do I still think the ideas are important?

Yes. Time has already validated much that I wrote then, though the main thesis of Cosmic Metamorphosis will require much more theoretical work to be adequately demonstrated. Suffice it to say, we are working on it.

Of course, in 25 years, my thinking has also expanded a great deal, and if I were to write *Noah* today, I would probably add a lot of corollary material along other lines. For example, my understanding of the Bible —

who wrote it, when, and why — has changed a great deal, and is a subject I have dealt with at length in my book, *The Secret History of the World*, and will return to in my next book, *The Horns of Moses*. It has only been in the last 25 years that many of the misconceptions and assumptions about the history of the Bible have been overturned. The same goes for catastrophism. Velikovsky's work has been confirmed time and again, even if he was off in some of the details. And the idea of a companion sun is looking to be more and more likely, contrary to what I wrote in *Noah*. And, of course, the September 11th 2011 attacks have 'changed everything,' and many of the prophecies dealt with in this book, and my analyses and predictions relating to them, seem starkly prescient in retrospect, again, even if some of the details are slightly off.

With that said, as a historical document, as a thesis that was based on ideas that have later come to be commonly accepted, I think *The Noah Syndrome* deserves fairer treatment now than Mr. Meredith gave it back in 1987 when I was dismissed because I wasn't 'famous' and my 'opinion' meant nothing. As to whether I found the answer to my original question, I would have to say 'yes.' Not only that, but I found that, indeed, Love is Eternal.

I am inserting here the rejection letter from Scott Meredith because it is also a kind of 'historical' document of the stages of development I have passed through.

September 1, 1987

*   *   *

RE: THE NOAH SYNDROME

Dear Ms. Martin: [this was my former married name]

Thanks very much for allowing us to read, and to evaluate in market terms, this interesting and very well and carefully written volume on the Last Days, and, of course, a very warm welcome to this agency. As you may know, it's our agency policy to actively seek out newer writers, since we can only survive, as an agency, by placing their work — and that policy, I'm glad to says bears especially fine fruit when we come across a writer who can display the sort of talent you've been able to show us here. (In writing you to this effect, I don't want you to feel that we are in any way denigrating either your outlook or your con-

clusions as expressed in THE NOAH SYNDROME; we're not. But those conclusions, however important they may be to any of us as individuals, can't have great effect on us as literary agents; it's no part of our job to judge of the correctness of the statements our clients make, but merely to discover whether the works in which those statements are made are salable in terms of the current mass market, and, if salable, to take them out and place them for the authors at the best possible terms. It's that job we're called upon to do here, and, in this report, it's that job I'll be doing.) Your writing, then, is full of a great deal of very real clarity, and a lot of emotional flexibility as well; you have avoided equally the overshrill tone and the overly earnest approach, and have made your case with balance. All in all, Ms. Martin, there's a great deal of good to be found in 'The Noah Syndrome' (no pun intended, I assure you!), and you've done a lot of good work here of which you can quite honestly be proud.

At the same time, unfortunately, there are major flaws present in this manuscript as well from a market standpoint. These flaws strike deeply into the basic structure of the work — so deeply, in fact, that they make it impossible for me even to suggest any sort of revision, this time around. There is simply no way of revising these flaws, or of revising them out, without at the same time just revising the entire manuscript itself right out of existence as well. And it is the presence of these flaws, I'm afraid, that forces me, very regretfully indeed, to return 'The Noah Syndrome' to you as unsalable, despite all of the good work that you have indeed done with this one.

In order to find out just exactly what it is that's gone wrong with this manuscript, then, it's best to begin with a detailed picture of precisely what it is that's required, these days, of any mainstream non-fiction book, so here's a rundown of the criteria that publishers utilize when they're evaluating the chances for any new book's publication.

Publishers have found that it's most convenient to think of a non-fiction book as falling into one of three distinct categories, which correspond to different audiences and to different reading needs. These headings, and their ideal characteristics, include:

1) Information. Books in this category emphasize the factual, and usually the practical. Included in this grouping are the more serious social, political, sociological and scientific studies that are intended for the major markets, and the entire range of "How-To" guides. Criteria for evaluation include accuracy (of course!), clarity, developmental interest, and appeal to an identifiable readership.

2) Entertainment. This is the widest of the categories, and it's generally been proven to be the most popular one of all, as well, including any works which

have diversion as their primary goal. Humor books obviously fall into this category, as well as general works on sports, fashion and the arts, and any celebrity biography. Criteria include freshness, timeliness, readability and general flow, as well as potential appeal to an identifiable readership.
3) Opinion. This category includes editorial material, reviews, critiques, tracts and so forth. Publishers have stressed persuasiveness, timeliness, the provocativeness of the thesis, and author credibility. Due to this last criterion, this field is generally closed to newcomers.

It's clear that your work falls into this third category — which may require a bit of explanation. I do see that what you mean to do here is to provide information to your readers. But, in general, any religious book (or a book which, like yours, deals with religion and eschatology) is going to fall into the third category as a work of opinion — simply because (as a natural enough result of the First Amendment) the average reader is going to be perfectly willing that you believe whatever it is you say you believe, but most unwilling to be told, even by implication, that he has to believe it as well. This isn't some sort of flat rule set up by publishers, but just a description of the way a reader is going to look for a given sort of book; it's a publishing rule and, like most publishing rules, one set up to conform to what the readers want.

As a work of opinion, then, it runs into immediate trouble because of two words I've utilized in categorizing this sort of work: "author credibility".

All that the phrase means is that the average reader is very likely to have his own opinions on any subject which is of interest or importance to him, and that, therefore, he is most unlikely to want to pay out money for someone else's opinion, unless that opinion can be shown to be in some special way important to him. That demonstration is generally made in one of two ways.

The first way might be exemplified by a book on a given subject by someone who is recognized as an expert in that subject: a physicist writing on physics, for instance, or a politician writing on a political subject. Here the vital fact is that the author can be shown to have special information — due to his degrees, his position, his life experiences — which the average reader can't get on his own. These bits of information are utilized in forming the opinions stated, and it is this which makes those opinions special and important for the reader.

The second way might be exemplified by a book by someone famous — let's say a book of opinions by Bruce Springsteen. He does seem to be so very famous just now that his opinions on virtually any subject might well be salable; the reader might buy such a book, always curious about anyone so completely in the public eye, in order to find out a bit more about the author just from reading his opinions on a variety of subjects.

This second way, of course, isn't open to you; you are just not that famous. But the first way offers difficulties as well.

You've had experiences which you regard as revelations. I'm not attacking that position at all; I am saying, though, that for the average reader these experiences can't take the place of proven background in a given area, since anyone can claim to have had them at any time — the reader has no real reason to believe in them, from his standpoint. The book's authority has to be built on something else.

You quote heavily from Jeane Dixon, from Edgar Cayce, from our client the late Immanuel Velikosvky. But of course works by all of these authors (and many, many works about them as well) are available to the average reader now; he can feel no real need to buy your book in addition. You feel that Cayce and Velikovsky, in particular, tend to tie up in discussing many things, and you've quoted from both works to support this — but, again, where the works themselves (and other works by students of Cayce and of Velikovsky, of course) are available, this extra quotation isn't going to be a major impetus to make the reader buy your work.

The interpretation of Revelation, as well, is something that has been done many, many times in print, and in your interpretation there are a few stumbling blocks Which are going to impair the reaction of any reader. If, for instance, a comet is going to strike the Earth within the next few years (at one point you give 1988 as a possible date), then a struggle between countries, as in the US-USSR struggle you depict for a bit further on, isn't really going to be possible: a strike such as the one you suggest would do so much damage that any communication at all among countries (and the very existence of many count-ties as coherent entities) might not be possible.

At other times, you'll provide a common explanation as if it were the only one available to compete with the explanation you've developed from your own years of study:

> The question became: What is the Word of God? It was obvious that there were contradictions within the book we call the Bible. These contradictions are generally explained as meant to confuse the unworthy and allow revelation only to those for whom it is meant — those baptized with the Spirit. (Page 100)

Well, this is one explanation. There are a good many others, some dealing specifically with one contradiction at a time, some covering (as the one you have utilized here does) the entire field, anything perceived as a contradiction anywhere within the Bible. But what is clear is that the explanation you pro-

vide as the one with which you are going to do battle is not the only one available — and the average interested reader is likely to know this, I'm afraid.

Further on, you state about Revelation:

> Most people who read Revelation assume that it is either the vision of a mystic which can only be understood by another mystic, or that it is the ravings of a spaced-out hermit who had eaten moldy bread. (Page 129)

Once again, these are two possibilities. And of the two, you clearly fall into the first, since your own mystic experiences (seeing the pastor of your church with the head of a wolf, for instance, or awakening with the word 'calculate' in your mind) would have to fit you for the title of "mystic" in a real sense. But others do feel that the book can be understood as a rational set of statements; again you haven't covered the alternatives.

I wish that I could have had better news for you on this one, Ms. Martin; you can write and explain your positions with great clarity. But, as you can see, the basic flaws I've been pointing out here are really inherent in the structure of the work itself; no revision, no rewrite at all, is going to be able to remove them successfully.

I do have to advise you, then, most unhappily, to put 'The Noah Syndrome' behind you as a work for the mass market. That won't be easy, I know; it never is, for any writer. But it can be done.

And, once it is done, I hope you'll be able to turn your hand to a fresh project, with a Clear mind and with a solid understanding of the actual needs and demands of the real market.

If that can be done, as I am very sure that it can be, then your new project can certainly be the solidly salable and successful one we can expect from you, the one your talent and application certainly do deserve; and I'll be most anxious to be able to see it.

Meanwhile, then, until I do hear from you again, my best wishes. Sincerely,

(signed)
Scott Meredith

Chapter One

You never know how much you really believe anything until its truth or falsehood becomes a matter of life and death. It is easy to say you believe a rope is strong as long as you are merely using it to cord a box. But, suppose you had to hang by that rope over a precipice? Wouldn't you then first discover how much you really trusted it?

— C. S. Lewis.

The End of the World is an idea that has fascinated man for all of recorded history and perhaps beyond. In every religion, philosophy and mystery teaching, there are hints, allusions or outright claims to knowledge of this purported end to man's current status on the earth. Some teachings say that the earth itself will cease to exist, others that man will cease to exist in material form; still others claim a great judgment day in which the wicked are wiped from the face of the planet while the 'saved' are rescued in some miraculous fashion to return and inhabit a new, heaven-like 'City of God.' The persistence of these ideas and their prevalence is centered around the idea that man began somewhere, sometime, somehow, and will therefore come to an end somewhere, sometime, somehow.

This assumption is born of the conscious mind's tendency to think in linear terms. Scientific materialism has carried this tendency to the ultimate heights — 'The world must have been born; therefore, it must die.' And scientific materialism claims nothingness before birth and nothingness after death.

Scientific philosophies refer to the 'accidental mechanicalness' of the universe and teach us that the only meaning to life is no meaning at all. 'Eat, drink, and be merry for tomorrow you may die' and then — oblivion. Within the narrow empiricism of science, little room can be found, and even less sympathy, for the loosely-lumped-together orphans of psi, including prophecy.

In the East, prophecy is a natural concomitant of the Oriental view of the cyclical nature of time. In the West, we tend to think of time as long or short — linear terms — and find greater difficulty, as a society, in accepting the experience of precognitive vision.

By whatever means prophecy occurs, which we will discuss further on, there seems to be considerable difficulty in expression and interpretation. How is the prophecy perceived by the prophet? How is it verbalized? Does the individual reading or hearing the prophecy understand the terminology? Any ordinary conversation between two people loses some of its meaning by the many variables involved in speech. Does the person speaking have sufficient vocabulary to express himself accurately? Does the person to whom he or she is speaking have the exact same understanding of the words used? It is rather like the children's game where one person at the end of a line whispers a sentence to the person next to him who then whispers it to the next person — and on down the line. By the time it gets to the last person, the sentence bears little resemblance to the original statement.

And, if this is the case, we must admit that the 'Divine Inspiration' of the scriptures may be little more than a vague idea that there is some purpose and meaning to life, which man has tried to express — and often, not too well!

Every age of prophets and prognosticators has tended to interpret all former prophecies in terms of their own realities — or at least their understanding of their realities. In this day and age, the idea of the end of the world could be said to be archetypal and based upon some great ego/superego conflict. And, the average man tends to interpret all possibilities in terms of his own experience — he is concerned with bombs, fall-out, and his children in the Nuclear Age.

The End of the World: A mushroom cloud billows in slow motion, opening like an obscene flower to blot out the Sun and illuminate the landscape in surrealistic, ghostly relief. A hurricane blast of unimaginable heat sweeps out in all directions, turning to ash everything in its path. The half-formed thought — vague surprise, sudden regret, piercing anguish — hangs suspended in time as the blood begins to boil the matter of the brain and the flesh melts from the bone. Judgment Day: The distant vision of hellfire immolating loved ones who waited but a moment before — loving husbands and wives; trusting, laughing children; aged and helpless parents — lives, like fragile candle flames, snuffed out in the whirlwind of political passions.

The Day of the Lord. Armageddon. The Final Battle. The Ultimate Solution to man's inhumanity to man. Cauterization of the oozing corruption blighting the planet; those not vaporized instantly to diminish and writhe away in torment, finally and totally covered by the scar tissue of regenerating vegetable matter or dunes of windblown sand.

Planet earth: The glittering sapphire of the solar system, spinning peacefully, at last, in the velvet blackness of the void; hearing only its own sighing winds — stately and elegant in its ponderous self-consciousness.

And Man? What is Man that Thou art mindful of him?

Is this the scenario of the final act of prophetic revelation? Is this the 'End of the World?'

Or, is this Henny Penny crying, 'The sky is falling! The sky is falling!' Shall man evolve to adapt to a continuing series of dissolutions, only to finally fade away billions of years from now as the Sun burps and expands to become a red giant sautéing the revenant hold-outs of humanity?

These concerns tend to affect given individuals in one of three ways: The first is the way of the Pragmatist. This person is very practical and feels that life should be lived, such as it is, with no worries about things beyond one's control. These people live as though they were in a trance — hypnotized by material concerns. Their vision and energies channeled towards mundane duties, they rarely consider anything outside of this realm. If they do, they seriously doubt that things would get that far out of control; and if it did, who could stop it anyway? They putter through their lives, getting their thrills from the latest TV show, or newest acquisition; annoyed if some person or event forces them to the arduous act of thinking. Bertrand Russell commented upon this: *"Men fear thought as they fear nothing else on earth — more than ruin, more even than death."* [1] But these people constitute the greatest portion of mankind!

Slightly more aware are the Realists. Realists can be subdivided into two categories: the religious realist and the material realist. Both of these types believe that a final holocaust is a real possibility. They see the planet besieged by greed and avarice. They observe the suicidal tendency of man to ignore history and his failure to learn from the mistakes of the past. They see society spiraling downward faster than we can hope to correct it even if our governments put forth exceptional efforts. Thus, the material realist bases his belief upon logical analysis of facts and political issues, and sees only hopelessness and helplessness in the face of man's own evil. The religious realist projects these issues into concepts of good and evil and sees the triumph of good and hopes for his own salvation. Both of these types react to their beliefs in much the same way. The latter pursues his God to anesthetize his pain of realization of impotence. The first also pursues his God — materialism — to anesthetize his pain. Very often these two reactions combine in any number of interesting activities as evidenced by numerous scandals of note in recent times!

There is however, a third way: The Way of the Man of Faith. This man integrates the best of the other two and adds a third dimension — true faith. Being practical, he functions within the world system; being realistic, he perceives the dangers, and acts in whatever way he can to ameliorate the suffering he sees and to prepare himself — and those who will listen — for the potential of survival.

Acting in faith, absolutely sure of purpose in life, he strives to attain the conditions necessary for understanding truth; he searches diligently — often finding himself obligated to give up what he formerly held as true in order to receive deeper truth; hoping to find the meaning of 'salvation' in literal terms — and himself worthy.

In this sense I submit the experience of Noah as an example. Noah had a dream — a prophecy (who knows how God spoke to him) — and, seeing the evil of his day, he acted upon revelation in a very positive way — to the saving of himself and his family. Similar stories can be found in many other cultures the world over which gives one the idea that this revelation was well 'publicized.' Why did so few act upon it? Even to the person who gives these ancient tales no credence, the similarity to certain conditions in our society is quite interesting. The very name — Noe — means consciousness; and raising of consciousness has become a keynote of many groups growing larger and stronger every day.

Admittedly, down through history, the idea of the 'End' has surfaced as imminent on many occasions. As the year 1000 approached, all activity in the world of Christendom ground to a halt. The masses flocked to the cathedrals crying for mercy; cattle were turned loose in the countryside; generosity and brotherhood ran rampant. At the appointed hour — nothing happened. After a short time of confusion and reorientation, corruption resumed its normal course and Christians went on to massacre infidels in gratitude for their reprieve.

So, is there any reason to assume that the situation is any different now? What makes this second millennium after Christ the focal point of all the prophets of doom and gloom? Even the apostles of Christ were wrong in their belief that the end was coming any day. What is there about the present that has given rise to such a vast amount of literature proclaiming various scenarios of the End?

Could it be that all of the opposing views and doctrinal positions that specify different purposes and 'end-time schedules,' are all seeing the same thing, though from different perspectives? And, if we can examine the track records of the various prophets, can we establish some as being more 'in the know' than others and thereby find some concrete basis for speculation about the unifying elements of such prophecies? Can we figure out what the 'End' really means, if it is going to happen, and how?

As stated, the materialist interprets all phenomena in terms of his own experiences, including prophecy. The man of faith takes an entirely different view. And therein lies the very purpose of prophecy: to prepare the man of faith for positive action — to dispel the pragmatic and 'realistic' depictions of man's helplessness in the face of his own evil and self-denigration, and to clarify his place in the cosmos and the meaning of his existence in terms that will bring hope and anticipation. In other words, can we deduce from the very fact that prophecy exists — that it has existed in the past and has been demonstrated to be useful — that there is some unifying concept of consciousness — of Noe — which leads certain people to prepare, to build an 'ark,' and thereby ACT IN FAITH?

Carefully considered, the story of Noah is highly informative. The story does not tell us that some supernatural force prepared a place for Noah. On the contrary, Noah was told to perform certain tasks, which would ensure his survival as well as that of his family and certain animals. He had to work very hard. Had Noah done nothing, well, we wouldn't be discussing him now — we would never have heard of him.

Acting in response to a consciousness of impending disaster might be seen as a form of mental aberration — a syndrome not common to all of humanity — but a syndrome defining in very specific terms the 'Noe of the Elect' — the 'Chosen' — those moved to see the 'End' in terms of a beginning of a new order. And, as in the time of Noah, those not afflicted with this particular cast of consciousness will react to it with derision and ridicule.

But how does one acquire this kind of faith — this kind of consciousness? And what, exactly, is true faith?

The only hope we have to acquire this faith is to use reason. If we peel away the layers of personal interpretation and materialistic linear expectations, we may arrive at the truth. Simple truth is often intimidating for it provides no rationalizations in which to hide. The conflict between truth and tradition is due to the fact that man tends to put his personal expectations upon the phenomena around him, including prophecy. Considering this, and the historically proven tendency of man to repeat his mistakes, can we not safely assume that we may have done this very thing with the eschatological prophecies? Christians who consider themselves to be 'Spiritual Jews' would do well to remember that the most pious and sanctified men of their day brought about the crucifixion of Christ!

So, if reason is to save us, we must find a foundation for the giving, receiving and interpretation of prophecy.

For a long time matter and motion were accepted as the basis of reality and, to a great extent, continue to be. The 'Big Bang,' or Cosmic Firecracker theory is explained in these terms. A primal atom — matter, — of incredible density 'exploded' into motion. (Where the primal atom came from, how the space it exploded into came into being, and where the impetus for this event originated, are still on the drawing board.) And from this event, our universe and the life within it just sort of 'accidentally' happened. Man is the 'amoral end of a deadly biological evolution.' The mind and soul are inexplicable by-products of the struggle for survival. The Bible says, *"In the Beginning, God created the heaven and the earth."* Neither the Bible nor science have much to say about what happened before the beginning. St. Augustine was once asked the question: *"What was God doing before He created the world?"* The Bishop's rejoinder: *"Creating Hell for those who ask that question!"* put a period to such inquiries. Few have asked it since.

However, physics, the study of the deeper realities of existence, has failed to support the matter/motion theory. To the average person, a table, a chair, an orange, are real objects. They have dimension — three, to be exact — they are real. But are they? The physicist (and the knowledgeable lay-person) knows that the object is composed of atoms. And there lies the rub! The dissected atom (quantum particles) often displays some very disturbing properties.

Physicist Nick Herbert writes: *"Despite modern attempts to split it into finer bits, using energies a hundred billion times greater than those that hold the atom together, the electron remains steadfastly elementary. An electron, so it seems, simply doesn't have any parts."* [2]

One experiment shows that electrons are particles — another demonstrates wave properties. *"Some physicists conjecture that the electron is a point particle whose intrinsic size is zero!"* [3] So, having pursued reality to its farthest limits within human capability, man finds that his real world is made up of particle/waves, which do not exist except as a mathematical point!

Danish physicist Niels Bohr puts forth the theory that there is no deep reality. So, just what is matter? What is this estate in which we find our existence? Does the physical run out when it becomes invisible? Obviously not, as we cannot see electricity and other forces in the universe measurable only by their effect upon 'matter.' Do these forces run out when they become undetectable by our senses or by our instruments? Do the things we detect with the subtle mechanisms of our mind and emotions not exist simply because we cannot see or measure them?

Thus, there is a crisis in physics and a crisis in our world, for the prevailing cosmic view eventually filters down and influences our domestic, social and political patterns. Perhaps we have gone as far as we can with our materialistic orientation and this is reflected in our realities. Perhaps material reality, as we know it, has gone as far as it can go!

But, if science has failed us, how much more so has religion!

Some religions say that the only meaning to life is in spiritual self-improvement and creating a better future in the afterlife or in future lives. Other religions say that the meaning to life lies in working to dissolve the ego into nothingness.

One philosophy states that the true purpose of life is to align our self-created realities so that they become as one and thereby we may achieve a unified race which will survive beyond predicted cataclysms for a thousand years before things wind down into the usual state of decay. Naturally this effect can only be initiated and maintained by a group effort at consciousness raising.

There are other ideas and combinations of ideas similar to the above — all leading where?

"A religion contradicting science and a science contradicting religion are equally false." [4]

Surely there must be some way to reconcile the two! Are we, in fact, an accident of evolution in an accidental universe, on a race to nowhere except oblivion? Or, worse still, are our very minds — our desire for knowledge — our enemies; damning us for our lack of belief? The choice seems to be between a sick joke and a mistake — neither of which is conducive to faith.

But, help is on the way! In 1964, a man named John Stewart Bell, a theoretical physicist, constructed a proof that has since become known as 'Bell's theorem.' This theorem tells us that reality must be non-local. That is, anything happening anywhere whatsoever in the universe, instantaneously affects everything else everywhere else in the universe. He demonstrated that an atom's measured attributes are determined not just by events happening at the actual site of being, but by all events occurring in the entire universe simultaneously and instantly!

Notice the key word above — instantaneous. This means 'superluminal' or faster than the speed of light. But, since nothing can travel faster than the speed of light, this must mean that there is no actual distance separating events. Bell's theorem demonstrates the idea that all that exists — past, present, and future — are combined into a single entity whose farthest parts are joined in an immediate manner.

In other words, the world we perceive — the stars and planets; the land and seas; the trees, animals, buildings, people — are all manifestations of a single unmitigated force. But, remember, when physicists pursued reality down to the quantum level, they found that reality is composed of a no-dimensional mathematical point. But, we are three-dimensional, are we not? Aren't the table, the chair, the dog and the steak we had for dinner solid objects with length, depth, height and existence in time?

What exactly are these objects we perceive as existing solidly in space for varying periods of time? What is the space we define as separating the objects? How are they connected in time? If physics demonstrates to us that All is One, then what is it — what characteristic do we possess — that separates us from this deeper reality? And, what is the true nature of this reality?

We say that space is infinite — that it is illimitable in both scope and direction. (There may be some who postulate an outer limit to space, but what they propose as being outside that limit is an even greater difficulty than that of infinity.) Space, as we perceive it, has only three dimensions; length, width, and height. We define this condition as three independent directions — that is, each measurement lies at right angles to the others simultaneously.

But, this is a contradiction. For, if space is infinite, then it must possess an infinite number of lines perpendicular and not parallel to one another. Is infinity, then, a foolishness and does space necessarily have a limit? If it does have a limit, in what space does our space exist?

But, if space does possess an infinite number of lines perpendicular to one another, then we must ask why we can only perceive three. If we exist in a condition of mind that perceives only three dimensions, this must mean that the properties of space are created — or differentiated — by certain attributes within us. For some reason or another, the Whole is inaccessible to us.

This condition, I believe, is the 'death' described in Genesis — the 'Fall of Man.' Man originally existed as a true 'image' of God. The Bible says that God is a spirit — *"For that which is known about God is evident to them and made plain in their inner consciousness, because God has shown it to them. For ever since the creation of the world His invisible nature and attributes, that is, His eternal power and divinity have been made intelligible and clearly discernible in and through the things that have been made ..."* [5] Man was originally a spirit creation who could perceive the infinity and oneness of the universe.

I would like to suggest that the 'Fall' of man was not just a spiritual event, nor even just a cumulative activity wherein mankind became 'trapped' in the flesh, unable to recall his origins or reach his full potential, but that it was a quantum event of metamorphosis which I will discuss at length further on.

For a very long time, materialist science has recognized the existence of matter and motion — yet, in actual fact, matter and motion are unknown quantities x and y, and are always defined by means of one another. It is an absurdity to define one unknown by means of another! What this means is that science defines matter as that which moves and motion as changes in matter.

This is reality?

However, Bell's theorem shows us that 'All' simply is. Therefore, the changes must originate within ourselves.

Who has really seen matter or force? We think we see matter in motion, but physics has shown us that what we see is an illusion. When we try to focus on it, a quantum particle/wave is a one-dimensional entity incapable of being perceived, in that instant, as a three-dimensional body moving through space. When we look away, the quantum particle/wave acts like a wave of pure energy — invisible force.

Just exactly how bizarre this activity is, is described by Richard Feynman of Cal Tech as, *"a phenomenon which is impossible, absolutely impossible, to explain in any classical way, and which has in it the heart of quantum mechanics. In reality, it contains the only mystery ... the basic peculiarities of all quantum mechanics."* [6]

There are no comparisons we can carry over from our real world into the world of quantum mechanics, so we must just plunge in and tell it like it is. The central mystery is described in what is called the double-slit experiment which goes something like this:

Imagine a barrier of some sort such as a concrete wall, with two tiny holes in it. They can be elongated or round. On the one side of the wall is a screen with sensitive detectors on it, which are sensitive to whatever we are going to send through the holes. On the other side of the holes is a device that shoots quantum particles — photons of light, electrons.

In our everyday world we can observe how waves diffract through a wall by working with a similar set-up in a tank of water. A wave-making machine sends waves toward the concrete wall. The waves pass through the two holes and set up two identical little wave patterns on the other side. The intensity of each individual wave pattern, taken alone with one or other of the holes closed off, is expressed as H^2, or height (amplitude) squared. But, with both holes open, there is a very large peak intensity exactly in line with the two holes, which can be expressed as $I = (H + J)^2$. This means that the sum of the two wave intensities is not $H^2 + J^2$. At the points where the two daughter wave patterns touch each other, they set up an interference pattern. So, the extra term added into the equation is the contribution due to interference and accounts for all the energy whether negative or positive. So much for waves.

Now, if we take solid things, such as bullets being fired from a machine gun at the concrete walls, we would not find the interference term. We would find a lot of bullets in one spot on the other side of each hole. Period.

Now, what do you think is going to happen when we shoot quantum 'things' through the holes? It is natural to believe that each individual electron or photon must go through one hole or the other, particularly since we have slowed down our quantum gun to shoot one electron at a time. Guess again. When we block off one hole or the other, we get the usual pattern for single-hole experiments — that is, a whole bunch of electrons hit the same spot. But, when we open up both holes, we do not get the pattern we would get for bullets. We get the wave diffraction pattern. And, if we do the experiment a thousand times with only one electron released in each experiment, adding them all together we still get the wave diffraction pattern. A single electron or photon, on its way to the wall, knows whether or not the other hole is open and that it must obey the statistical laws. If we try tricking the electron by shutting or opening one of the holes while the electron is in transit, it doesn't work. The pattern is always exactly right for the conditions of the holes at the instant the electron passes through. When we try to observe to see which of the holes the electron goes through, we always see the electron at one hole or the other, never both at once. And, if we continue to watch, the pattern built up on our detector is exactly that as for the bullets. So, we can only conclude that the electron knows not only which hole is open, it knows if we are watching it! When we try to observe the electron as a wave, it collapses into a particle, but when we are not looking, it seems that it goes through both holes. It is as though the world keeps all its options open until the very last instant of observation. So, from an array of ghost, or potential, electrons, our observation crystallizes one and collapses the wave.

So what are we seeing and experiencing with our five senses? Could it be that each moment of reality is like a slice of the 'All' similar to the focus of a CAT scanner?

When we look at the table, the chair, the salad and the dog, they seem to be solid and stable, but the physicist can assure us that they are a dance of atoms ever moving into and out of being — the atoms making up the table a minute from now being perhaps an entirely different group from the atomic constitution a moment before.

So, we might say that reality is a continuous flow or invisible something passing momentarily into a focused object much like a light shining through a slide creates an image upon a screen. The light is ever flowing at 186,000 miles per second and the celluloid slide focuses the image creating and maintaining cosmic realities. The celluloid slide is our mind!

In this sense, archetypal images are extremely important, being the patterns of human, societal, and national interactions as conceived, and created by mass thought. And, it may be that these archetypal images — these racial thought forms — are viewed or perceived by those whom we have come to know as prophets.

Yet, the question must be asked: why have we created a world in which material extinction is a real possibility? Where has man gone wrong? Are we truly on the edge of an abyss, losing our balance, preparing to fall into a hole so deep and dark that we shall never come out of it? What is this mysterious gap between intent desire and physical manifestation? What darkness exists in our subconscious minds that has created a world so hostile and uncaring? What power separates us from knowledge of our inner creative selves and leaves us exposed to suffering and pain?

For, no matter how one defines reality — as a self-created manifestation, or as an accomplished fact thrust upon us — the reality of suffering must be seen as a consequence of this separation. And, if the world of matter is created and maintained by us, what brought this blindness into being? Is it a consequence of willful disobedience? If so, then man's being is a blight on the cosmos. And, if that is so, then what shall we do with man's lapses into goodness, nobility, brotherly love and reverent worship? From where has this duality originated?

If we accept that, for whatever reason, some aspect of creation has manifested the limited three dimensions in which our consciousnesses find themselves, how would we describe this condition and its potential for change?

In our geometry we define a point as an infinitesimal section of a line. A line is an infinitesimal cross-section of a plane and a plane is an infinitesimal section of a solid. Thus, our three-dimensional reality must be defined as a series of infinitesimal sections of a four-dimensional body. In other words, a quantum particle is the intersection of a four-dimensional body by the plane of our consciousness. This means that our entire reality is a section of a four-dimensional body — a realm of potential dimensions beyond three-dimensional contemplation.

We usually consider the past as no longer existing. The future does not exist either and the 'present' refers to the momentary transition of non-existence into non-existence! How absurd that is, but this is where material science and linear logic will take you.

But, it is true that only NOW exists. The problem is our concept of time. We regard time as linear — long or short — an endless line — a progression from past into future. But this creates an insurmountable problem. On a line, NOW is a mathematical point of infinitesimal smallness — it has no dimension! By scientific logic, it does not exist!

P. D. Ouspensky, the Russian philosopher, illustrates this for us using the example of a snail on a journey:

> "We know nothing about its inner life, but we may be sure that its perception is very different from ours." (Is it?) "In all probability a snail's sensations of its surroundings are very vague. It probably feels warmth, cold, light, darkness, hunger, and instinctively (i.e., incited by pleasure/pain guidance) it crawls toward the uneaten edge of the leaf it sits on, and draws away from a dead leaf. Its movements are governed by pleasure/pain" (good and evil?) "it always advances toward the one and retreats from the other. It always moves on one line — from the unpleasant towards the pleasant. And, in all probability it senses and knows nothing except this line. This line constitutes the whole of its world. All the sensations entering from the outside are sensed by the snail on this line of motion. And, these come to it out of time — from potentiality they become actuality. For a snail, the whole of our universe exists in the future and the past, i.e., in time." [7]

The snail is probably not self-aware — that is, aware that it is surging across the landscape, all of which exists simultaneously, of which the snail could be aware if it were possible to expand its awareness through some process of metamorphosis and lift it high above the garden to expand its scope. But, it only perceives the various phenomena — the leaf, the grass, the twig, the sand, the walkway — at the moment it interacts with them — and then only a little at a time. They are events of long or short duration, past and future, which come to pass as the snail inches along.

In the same manner do we experience our world; our five sense organs are merely feelers by means of which we touch and interpret the world through the mathematical constructs of our brains and in the limited terms of three-dimensional consciousness. Scientific gadgetry only lengthens our feelers a bit.

> *"Imagine a consciousness not limited by the conditions of sense perception. Such a consciousness can rise above the plane on which we move; it can see far beyond the bounds of the circle illumined by our ordinary consciousness; it can see that not only does the line along which we move exist, but also all the other lines perpendicular to it which we now cross"* (in our series of nows.) *"Rising above the plane this consciousness will be able to see the plane, make sure that it actually is a plane and not only a line. Then it will be able to see the past and the future living side by side and existing simultaneously."* [8]

There are two important considerations contained in the analogy of the snail. First, if our true perception is as limited, relatively speaking, as a snail's, why is this so if we do, in fact, possess inner knowledge and capabilities unknown to our waking, ordinary consciousness? Second, we must note the implications of the pleasure/pain principle.

But, before we endeavor to deal with those questions, let's return to the question of time.

> *"The past and future cannot be non-existent ... They must exist together somewhere, only we do not see them. The present, as opposed to the past and the future, is the most unreal of unrealities.*
>
> *We must admit that the past, the present and the future do not differ from one another in any way, that the only thing that exists is ... the Eternal Now of Indian philosophy."* [9]

The Alpha and Omega.

But, we do not see this — at least very few of us do — and then we only see imperfectly, 'through a glass darkly.' We are snails crossing the fields of flowers of the universe, aware only momentarily of the earth, the leaf, the flower, or the raindrop before us. At any given moment we are only aware of a small fragment of the universe and we continue to deny the existence of everything else — namely the coexistent past and future and the possibility of perceiving it.

There are two main theories of the future — that of a predestined future and that of a free future. The theory of predestination asserts that every future event is the result of past events and if we know all the past then we could know all the future. The idea of a free future is based on quantum 'probabilities.' The future is either only partially determined or undetermined because of the varied interactions possible at any given point. This idea of 'free will' says that quite deliberate volitional acts may bring about a subsequent change in events.

Those who support predestination say that so-called 'voluntary' actions are, in fact, not but are rather the results of incompletely understood causes which have made them imperative acts — in short, nothing is accidental. On the one hand we have 'cold predestination' come what may, nothing can be changed — on the other hand we have a reality which is only a point on some sort of needle named the present surrounded on all sides by the Gulf of Non-existence — a world which is born and dies every moment. Ouspensky unifies these views:

> "At every given moment all the future of the world is predestined and existing, but it is predestined conditionally, i.e., there must be one or another future in accordance with the direction of events of the given moment, if no new factor comes in. And a new factor can come in only from the side of consciousness and the will resulting from it." [10]

In other words, the snail can choose to change his direction by overcoming his instinctive urge for pleasure and avoidance of pain. But this can only come about by becoming aware of the probable course he is on. If his natural tendencies are leading him to an abyss which will plunge him into a blazing inferno below, then it would behoove him to learn exactly what it is he must do to avoid it.

> "In the past, in what is behind us, lies not only what was, but also what could have been. In the same way, in the future lies not only what will be but also what may be." [11]

All exists simultaneously — it is only we who, singly and collectively, can change the focus of our consciousness. So, we can understand that time is merely the distance separating events.

> "This distance lies in a direction not contained in three-dimensional space. ... (it is) a new extension of space.
> This new extension fulfils all the requirements we may demand of the fourth dimension ..." [12]

In other words, motion in space is merely an illusion of the brief illuminating light of our consciousness upon a given point of reality and time is the intersection of our perception with this point.

> *"... in time 'events' exist before our consciousness comes into contact with them, and they still exist after our consciousness has withdrawn from them."* [13]

Now we must ask the question: Why can we not perceive reality as it is? Why can we not enlarge our perception — why are we chained in this painful existence we call 'reality?' Can our consciousness get beyond the conditions of three dimensions without fundamental alterations in material existence? How long can we sustain it there? In order to live in that state of expanded consciousness, is it necessary for the fundamental nature of our reality to change dramatically? I believe it is.

Bell's theorem demonstrates that all that exists, past, present, and future, is combined into a single wave-form whose farthest parts are joined in an immediate manner. No field mechanism is required for this oneness. I ask you to take note of the term 'waveform.'

The study of wave motion is a precise science and all waves follow the same fundamental rules, which are clearly demonstrable both practically and mathematically. One of these rules states that a wave takes its character from what is doing the waving. Also, waves go through exactly determined cycles that have 'phases' which can be known or estimated. Since this is the case, what we perceive as reality is nothing more than the myriad oscillations of the Primeval Waveform. And, since it is implied in physics that a wave must have a waver, we might assume that our reality has a waver also.

Using the idea of understanding the macrocosm by means of the microcosm, let us look at a wave and see if it can give us an indication as to how our reality is perceived and why and how prophecy is a part of that reality.

A unit of light can be defined as a quantum wave/particle. Light can also be observed to have qualities as defined through a spectrum. At either end of this spectrum are expressions of light undetectable by the unaided eye. Let us suppose that 'All-that-is' expresses in our perceptual world in a similar manner — that is, only a limited portion is detectable by our senses. At either end of this spectrum of reality are portions of the waveform we are incapable of knowing except by the use of special equipment, or senses. These other portions could be, in part, simply phases of the waveform we perceive to be past ... or future. And, just suppose that reality consists of an infinite number of waveform oscillations which meet, intermingle, augment or restrict according to definite, fundamental behavior patterns; we might call some of these waveforms good and some evil.

This brings us back to who or what is doing the waving? We must perceive that man is an oscillation of the Absolute and, as such, has the potential of being augmented by other waveform expressions of energy and thus expanding, so to speak, his own self-consciousness. (It is also interesting to conjecture the relationship of the double-slit experiment to brain-wave augmentation.) Just as certain mechanical aids can augment the perception of certain ranges of light such as infra-red, ultra-violet, x-rays, and radio waves, so might personal energies be synchronized by psychic means, or even, at the very deepest level, move into phase with the Primal Wave itself! This is what I believe happens during mystical states of being which bring about enlightenment or during which prophecy is received. The descriptions of the greater reality beyond time and space are, of necessity, beyond words. In many instances, the individual receiving such information indicates the impossibility of explaining what they have experienced.

So, I think we can assume that the finite nature of our minds, is self-limiting in an absolute sense. And all the instruments we can create and build are also incapable of penetrating this mystery because of the simple fact that they are three-dimensional. The only material way we may be able to go beyond our reality is through mathematics, which seems to transcend time and space.

The brain is an instrument devised to focus reality in mathematical constructs — interpreting waveforms as material objects. The abilities of certain individuals to achieve such higher states of consciousness in the realms of physiological science is being documented by fantastic examples every day and we should understand that these abilities may extend even into the realms of perceiving the motions of the vast 'Universal Ocean' in other ways. These individuals might be able to perceive the effects of other waveforms and, depending upon the amplitudes and energies, predict the outcomes of certain motions, even, perhaps, in very precise terms based upon the direction which consciousness is taking. The new research in physics sounds provocatively like ancient mystical teachings yet I believe that the true nature of the reality behind our world is beyond quantum mechanics and theory. We may find that much truth was known by the peoples of the past and that they did, in fact, express deep, mysterious, realities in their poetic and obscure messages. Mystics and seers perceive quantum states that are demonstrably difficult to translate into language. Additionally, with the passage of time and changes in word usage, we find a very great barrier to understanding.

There are numerous instances in literature and history when individuals have claimed to have achieved just such an 'elevation' of consciousness — at least for periods of time. There is much information pertaining to how this state may be achieved, which in general involves great self-discipline and extended preparation, but under certain circumstances may occur spontaneously.

The experience of viewing simultaneous, cause/effect reality may be extremely difficult to maintain when one is constantly being bombarded by three-dimensional interpretation, and the difficulty of translating this into linguistic expressions may be even more difficult. Imagine the difficulty of explaining to a snail the expanse of an acre of ground! Mystics and seers have attempted to do just that for millennia with the result that the vast majority of mankind have absolutely and totally misunderstood these concepts. And, there is no worse lie than a truth misunderstood by those who hear it. The greatest lies are the dark and evil systems of religion created by those who do not understand.

In certain recent 'controlled' studies of elevation of consciousness, it has been made plain that faith and intent play a very important part in achieving a higher state of consciousness. In addition, as I will discuss later, certain spontaneous elevations of consciousness occur at times of great stress.

Until quite recent times, science has lumped all psychic or mystical states under the heading of pathological or unhealthy conditions of the mind. Many scientists still hold this opinion. There are conditions of 'pseudo-mystical' perversion, purely psychopathic states and conscious deceit — often manifested in churches and cults around the globe and have been so for centuries.

How do you separate the true from the false?

If a mystical state can be defined as cognition under conditions of expanded consciousness, what may the results be?

1. Mystical states give knowledge which nothing else can give.
2. Mystical states give knowledge of the real world with all its attributes.
3. The mystical states of men belonging to different ages and different peoples show astonishing similarity, and at times complete identity.

4. The results of mystical experience are totally illogical from our ordinary point of view.[14]

And, with these criteria in mind, we will begin to examine the results of mystical states by many peoples and in 'many times' and see if we cannot piece the puzzle together regarding these results — namely prophecies regarding the future of man and his place in the cosmos.

But, before we move on, I would like to pose another question to carry into the next section: Might not life be looked at in a different fashion? In the human being, the pre-birth life is as different from the after-birth life as life, perhaps, is from death. Does death mean annihilation? Surely not since we know that our material world comes into being from that which can be neither seen nor measured. And, if the real 'deeper reality' of the world passes into three dimensions as a phase, might we not assume that the world, itself, could do the same? That is, if our observation of the life of an individual human is a microcosm, perhaps the material world is a gestational state — a preparation for an existence of an entirely different order in quantum terms — preparation for a fundamental transformation of matter itself?

And, although there is a great movement toward transcendentalism, this movement cannot transform due to the fact that the fundamental forces of the world are antithetical to this physical reality. While we all might like to think we can transform our world by thinking positively, we must remember that there is a great deal of scientific evidence that transformations of the planet have repeatedly been cataclysmic. A philosophy that ignores this fact is, in fact, courting disaster. It may be that their focus upon a 'New Age' quite literally contributes energy to the dissolution of the current age in a manner which follows scientific principles. To think that the transition will occur by thought alone ignores certain very important scientific factors — a science which contradicts religion or a religion which contradicts science must be equally false. We are looking to find the threads of identity — the points of agreement in science, philosophy and religion.

Matter, as we experience it, seems to be opposed to spirit, otherwise we would easily be able to manifest and ascertain our spiritual natures from our present state of existence. Research will show that this is possible, but only on a very limited level, to very few people who work very hard and devote their lives to this pursuit. Therefore, in order to manifest the prophesied or projected UNITY of spirit and matter either the spiritual estate must become grosser and more material or the material estate must become finer and less dense and material. And, in order for either of these events to occur, macrocosmic quantum changes must occur according to the observable processes of microcosmic quantum mechanics.

In any event, the idea of the end of the world is essentially correct from many points of view — but the result is as unknown to us as adult life is to an unborn child.

The conclusion is that the fundamental three-dimensional nature of the universe is the defect which must be altered — the effect of the 'Fall.' It is this that must change in order for any of the prognosticated eschatological scenarios to manifest.

But, the understanding of this concept, if it is true, reveals a cataclysmic holocaust so soul-chillingly dreadful that the psyche reels in mindless denial. Prophetic truth, revealed as the time for fulfillment draws near gives birth to visions of primeval destruction beyond the most gripping and searing nightmare; concepts that make the obscenity of nuclear war seem like child's play.

But — not to those with the 'Noe' of the elect.

We must look at the concepts of 'Doomsday' — admittedly a violent and horrendous prospect — in an entirely new light. The end is, indeed, The End. The end of the world as we know it. And, I mean that in a very basic sense. Not just the end of a civilization — though it will be that, too — not just the beginning of the New Age — it will be that, also — but the end of matter as we presently know it and the quantum alteration of the universe according to observable scientific principles, which will enable the earth, life and the cosmos to manifest in the manner originally intended. Restoration of perfection and the Edenic state — the harmony of spirit and matter — the end that is the beginning.

Recognizing the pitfalls and the prideful collapses of those who have gone before, I humbly request the reader to suspend former interpretative beliefs for the duration and let the truth take care of itself.

"In the beginning was the Word, and the Word was with God, and the Word was God. ... In Him was life; and the life was the light of men. And the light shineth in darkness; and the darkness comprehended it not." [15]

Chapter Two

The most beautiful thing we can experience is the mysterious.
It is the source of all true art and science.

— Albert Einstein.

"Scientism: The word 'science' comes from the Latin word 'sciens' which means 'knowing.' Followers of scientism are called 'scientists,' a term which was first used by William Whewell in 1840. The study of science began as a hobby among Greek intellectuals. For centuries those who acquired scientific knowledge kept it secret and although this practice is less common today, there are still many scientists who believe that their knowledge would be misused if it were spread to non-initiates. From a small sect, scientism has risen to the heights of respectability and its basic principles are taught to school-children throughout the world.

Scientists believe that the order of the universe can be determined by systematic study and analysis. They believe that theirs is the only true path and that other paths are 'mere superstition.' Over the years scientism has split into over 1,200 sects, or 'fields', each with its own sacred texts. It is estimated that the worldwide scientific community has over 3 million members, although the number of believers is much greater." [16]

The foregoing tongue-in-cheek description of 'science' is, unfortunately, all too true. Aside from the fact that science has brought us numerous technical advances, it has done little to fulfill its self-designated function of explaining the 'order of the universe.' In this respect, a little story I heard years ago, a favorite of mine, will nicely illustrate the condition.

An eminent scientist was once conducting research, using frogs as subjects. The frogs were conditioned to jump on command. The scientist then cut off one leg of each frog. He commanded them to jump, which they did with some difficulty. He then cut off another leg and commanded them to jump. They did so, but with greater difficulty. These results were noted in the research log. The scientist then cut off another leg of each frog and commanded them to jump. With great difficulty the poor creatures managed a sideways lunge. Mercilessly, the scientist then cut off the last leg of each frog and commanded them to jump. They lay there gasping and blinking — unable to move — but did not jump no matter how loudly the scientist shouted at them. The scientist noted it all down in his research log. Some time later the scientist presented the results of his experiments to his colleagues. Before a packed auditorium he began to speak: 'It is eminently clear to me that cutting off a frog's legs causes profound deafness.'

There never has been, nor will there ever be, a shortage of such 'authorities' to provide us with rational explanations for the phenomena around us!

Many years ago I acquired a book about lost civilizations. It was large and lovely — filled with beautiful color photographs of ancient ruins all around the globe. Wondering what tragedies may have befallen such obviously magnificent cultural centers, I eagerly read each section. The speculations were many and varied, but no real consensus of opinion emerged except the assumption that the inhabitants had been either forcibly evicted or had migrated elsewhere.

The Golden Age of Greece gave way to the Roman Empire, which fell to the barbarians ushering in the dark ages. The Romans had running water and sanitary sewers — the later medievals lived in fear and ignorance and filth. Great civilizations even older than these are conjectured to have existed.

But at least in the case of the Greeks and Romans and medievals we have a continuing history — an understanding of the decline and advance to our present position. Many 'lost' civilizations simply disappeared without a trace — and no traditions nor knowledge nor hint of who they were and how they lived is actually known. So many elegant, advanced and obviously highly structured civilizations just simply gone — no traces — nothing.

I have tried to imagine what the structures of our civilization would look like after hundreds or thousands of years of abandonment. I had to admit that we have not created a very substantial environment. The prospects of providing future archaeologists with such elegant ruins is indeed remote! And, to assume that societies that did leave such sophisticated metropolitan centers were primitive in their technologies, and backward, compared to our own, seems to be the ultimate in absurd conceit.

So, when scientists found they could decipher a few written records of some of the ancient civilizations, they assumed a primitive mind-set simply because those peoples described their realities in terms different from our own.

In many instances when astronomical data was examined and certain discrepancies found, it was immediately assumed that the ancients had incomplete knowledge. And, when other records became sanctified as 'holy writ,' it was automatically thought that the language was 'figurative' or 'symbolic.'

All of this struck me as very strange and I wondered if science had been analyzing frogs again.

Nevertheless, this book awoke in me a great thirst for information relating to anomalies. Anomalies are things which do not fit in with the accepted, scientific explanations and are usually dismissed by the high priests of science as highly suspect, probably hallucinatory, or fraudulent.

This, however, does not prevent anomalies from existing in great number and variety. And, since the credibility of many of the witnesses of such things would be more than sufficient to stand in a court of law, and much of the evidence a great deal more than circumstantial, I think that the time is long past for the adherents of scientism to admit the possibility of error and open their minds to new ways of looking at things. Science has always tried to understand nature by breaking things into their parts but it is becoming overwhelmingly clear that we cannot grasp the nature of reality until we cure ourselves of our pattern blindness — our inability to see relationships and detect meaning.

One particular little bit of information stuck in my mind and you will later understand why:

> "During mining operations in 1851, at Dorchester, Massachusetts, blasting threw out a bell shaped vessel from its bed in formerly solid rock. It was made of an unknown metal and was decorated with floral inlays of silver." [17]

There have been found and preserved: a human tooth imbedded in coal estimated to be 10 million years old; imprints of shod human feet fossilized in rock estimated to be 300 to 600 million years old; skeletons of apparently 'modern' humans found in rock formations estimated to be at least 100 million years old; and on and on. Tools, skeletons, artifacts — all have been found in sufficiently great numbers to raise serious questions about the narrow theoretical framework of science.

The easiest — and the usual — way the scientific community deals with these anomalies is to dismiss them as frauds. But, consideration of the facts makes this even harder to believe than accepting another explanation of the 'order of the universe.'

Very often anomalies are discovered or experienced by ordinary, honest people who suffer nothing but ridicule and harassment for their insistence of authenticity. (It makes one wonder how much may have been withheld for fear of such reprisals.) And, to suppose that many of these anomalies are the work of pranksters begs credulity. Admittedly, such hoaxes have occurred. But, generally, the circumstances of many anomalies make them a work of such magnitude as to require vast expenditures of time and money — to what purpose? Most often the individuals involved have had their lives ruined and their credibility destroyed by scientific 'smear' campaigns.

The average person — even the average educated person such as a teacher — has no idea of the controversies that rage in the ivory towers of science among the high priests. Darwin's theory of evolution by chance mutation and survival of the fittest has proven hopelessly inadequate to account for a great many observations in biology.

And so, just as the Church fell from authority in matters pertaining to 'knowledge of the order of the universe,' and Newton's physics followed to make way for Einstein's shocking new theories, we can see a large paradigm emerging to replace our understanding of the phenomena around us.

In each period of history when great advancement takes place, there are always examples of the forms from the past and it takes time for the one to give way to the other. And, just as there is a Flat Earth Society and other aboriginals still with us in this day of supersonic transport and moonwalks, so will the new order of thought coexist with outdated science. Unfortunately, the old gives way only by great struggle and sacrifice. The Catholic Church forced Galileo to recant and burned a few others at the stake, which is a witness to how dearly illusion is held. But, eventually, despite persecution and repression, truth emerges in place after place. Science is beginning to resemble the cartoon character trying to catch water from dozens of leaks with a single pot which he frantically moves from one spot to another, not realizing that, in the downpour, the dam has collapsed and he will soon be swept away!

I mention all of these things preparatory to introducing the theories of Immanuel Velikovsky. Although I think we can understand the attitudes of most scientists, in that they have staked their entire lives and reputations upon what they have been taught to believe, and to admit error would be tantamount to academic suicide, still, the reaction of the scientific community to the work of Velikovsky is an outstanding example of scientific demagoguery of the most reprehensible sort. This is particularly deplorable in light of the fact that Velikovsky has drawn the most sensible and logical conclusions from a massive collection of data relating to the 'order of the universe.' He has, in fact, observed that the frog cannot jump because it has no legs!

In 1950, Immanuel Velikovsky published *Worlds in Collision* in which he argued:

> "*Several times during the 15th and 8th centuries B.C., the earth was convulsed by near collisions with other celestial bodies. These cosmic brushes caused a series of catastrophes that altered the course of ancient history.*
>
> *A host of ancient myths and legends offer clues as to what happened during these catastrophes. Further written evidence is contained in the Old Testament Book of Exodus and also historical and astronomical texts inscribed on papyrus and on stone and clay tablets.*
>
> *The planet Venus originated in a violent disruption of Jupiter. Venus must be exceedingly hot.*
>
> *The universe is not a vacuum populated only by celestial bodies. Rather, it is crisscrossed by charged particles and riven by magnetic fields.*"[18]

Millennia after being ejected from Jupiter, the cometary Venus was thrown into an elliptical orbit around the *Sun*. Along that orbit, it intersected the orbit of the earth. Mankind watched in terror as the sky seemed to catch fire. The Babylonians called Venus the "bright torch of Heaven."[19]

The Chinese wrote that Venus spanned the heavens, rivaling the *Sun* in brightness. An ancient rabbinical record said that Venus "Blazes from one end of the cosmos to the other."[20]

Velikovsky theorized by following the trail of Venus through worldwide myths and legends, that Venus intersected the earth in its orbit sometime during the middle of the fifteenth century B.C. This event was recorded in the Bible as the plagues of Egypt and the means by which the Jews escaped from bondage.

Searching for verification of his theory, Velikovsky spent weeks trying to find an Egyptian account of the events of the Exodus. Finally he discovered a translation of an Egyptian papyrus that contained a description of a great catastrophe including the plagues of Egypt. It was called 'Admonitions of a Sage,' or the *Ipuwer Papyrus*. Let us compare it to Exodus.

EXODUS	IPUWER PAPYRUS
7:21. [T]here was blood throughout all the land of Egypt.	**2:5-6.** Plague is throughout the land. Blood is everywhere.
7:24. And all the Egyptians digged round about the river for water to drink; for they could not drink of the water of the river.	**2:10.** Men shrink from tasting — human beings thirst after water.
7:21. [A]nd the river stank.	**3:10-13.** That is our water! That is our happiness! What shall we do in respect thereof? All is ruin!
9:25. [A]nd the hail smote every herb of the field, and brake every tree of the field.	**4:14 and 6:1.** Trees are destroyed. No fruit nor herbs are found...
10:15. [T]here remained not any green thing in the trees, or in the herbs of the fields, through all the land of Egypt.	**6:3 and 5:12.** Forsooth, grain has perished on every side. Forsooth, that has perished which yesterday was seen. The land is left over to its weariness like the cutting of flax.
9:3. [T]he hand of the Lord is upon thy cattle which is in the field ... there shall be a very grievous murrain.	**5:5.** All animals, their hearts weep. Cattle moan.
9:19 and 9:21. [G]ather thy cattle and all that thou hast in the field. And he that regarded not the word of the Lord left his servants and his cattle in the field.	**9:2-3.** Behold, cattle are left to stray and there is none to gather them together. Each man fetches for himself those that are branded with his name.
10:22. [A]nd there was a thick darkness in all the land of Egypt.	**9:11.** The land is not light...
12:29. And it came to pass, that at midnight the Lord smote all the firstborn in the land of Egypt, from the firstborn of Pharaoh that sat on his throne unto the firstborn of the captive that was in the dungeon.	**5:3, 5:6, and 6:15.** Forsooth the children of princes are dashed against the walls. Forsooth, the children of princes are cast out in the streets.
12:30. [T]here was not a house where there was not one dead.	**2:13.** He who places his brother in the ground is everywhere.
12:30. There was a great cry in Egypt...	**3:14.** [G]roaning ... throughout the land, mingled with lamentations.[21]

The events recorded in Exodus and the *Ipuwer Papyrus* were also written in many other records the world over. The same things happened, written in the Mexican Annals of Cuauhtitlan, indicating a global rather than a local disaster, when *"the sky rained not water, but fire and red hot stones."* [22]

In addition to the plagues brought on by the dust, gases, and stones in the tail of the comet, an interaction with the head of the comet brought even greater disaster. As the earth pursued its course through the gloom it became caught in the gravitational grip of Venus. Suddenly a violent convulsion ripped the earth; it tilted on its axis and cities were destroyed, forests were leveled, mountains tumbled, the seas were tossed in violent fury and most of the earth's population was destroyed.

The tradition of the Cashinaua of western Brazil says,

> *"The lightnings flashed and the thunders roared terribly and all were afraid. Then the heavens burst and fragments fell down and killed everything and everybody. Heaven and earth changed places. Nothing that had life was left upon the earth."* [23]

Rivers were reversed and the earth was swept by an incredibly fierce hurricane wind. The Chinese wrote about the seas, which *"over-topped the great heights, threatening the heavens with their floods."* [24] With each convulsion of the earth, the axis tilted until it reached an equilibrium with the comet's gravitational pull. The earth was suddenly frozen in space. Part of the world was in extended darkness and part in a seemingly endless day. The Persians and the Chinese wrote of a single day which became three before turning into a night which lasted three times longer than usual. The Chinese said that the Sun did not set for three days while the earth roasted.

The terrible exchanges of electrical potentials between the head and the tail of the comet seemed to the peoples of the earth as a great battle between the gods. The Babylonians, the Egyptians, and the Hindus recorded this battle. At the point of closest approach, a great discharge of electricity was exchanged between the earth and Venus and it was at this point that the seas inundated the Egyptian army. For weeks Venus agitated the earth and the Israelites marched after the receding comet as a pillar of fire by night and smoke by day. Throughout the world, small groups of people survived the disaster and even they might have perished had it not been for the gift of the comet: Manna.

The hydrocarbons in the comet's tail that had saturated the earth were now being slowly changed within the earth's atmosphere into an edible substance. It made survival possible. In Iceland, India, Greece and other places all around the world, there are legends of the ambrosia, manna, madhu, and sweet dew, which fell from the heavens to the earth.

The earth also suffered another effect — the reversal of the direction of the earth's axis. This caused to Sun to appear to set in the opposite direction. Herodotus quoted Egyptian priests who said, *"four times in this period ... the sun rose contrary to his wont; twice he rose where he now sets, and twice he set where he now rises."* [25]

Seasons were changed: In China the emperor sent scholars to locate north, east, west and south and to create a new calendar. For forty years the earth was shrouded in clouds — the 'Valley of the Shadow of Death.' The Israelites wandered in the desert in this darkness.

The question is: What do the theories of Immanuel Velikovsky have to do with the prophetic revelations relating to the 'End of the World?' I intend to show through an analysis of Velikovsky's theories as compared to other prophecies, that said prophecies are couched in the same terms as past prophecies which have already been fulfilled as interpreted by Velikovsky. Further, that these terms which express cataclysmic events brought on by extraterrestrial contact between the earth and another celestial body, are terms which describe literal events — a shattering upheaval of the entire surface of the globe, bringing about the death of nearly the entire human race; establishing a 'new heaven and a new earth' in the sense of a reorientation of the polar axis, a new orbital path and position; and material changes in the atomic structure of the earth and its atmosphere which will qualitatively affect the life — in terms of manifestation — of the survivors; that this cataclysm is necessary for the restoration and replenishment of the planet. I further intend to show that survival of this cosmic holocaust is promised and possible, but only by those who have the Noe — the consciousness — to be aware of the impending events and to prepare themselves physically, mentally and spiritually.

Also, I wish to examine the idea that this cataclysm is predetermined, inevitable, and necessary for the restoration and renewal of the planet, and that without it, the earth, as well as all life on it, is doomed to inevitable extinction; the planet becoming a barren and atmosphereless wasteland.

Who is Immanuel Velikovsky? What is his background? What makes his theories so important?

Immanuel Velikovsky (1895—1979) was a Russian-born Jew; educated in Moscow and graduated from Medvednikov Gymnasium with full honors. He later studied in France and Edinburgh. In addition to receiving a degree as a medical doctor, he studied natural history, law and ancient history. He co-founded *Scripta Universitatus*, a compilation of major works by Jewish scholars around the world to which Albert Einstein was a regular contributor. He practiced medicine in Palestine for 15 years before traveling to Vienna to study psychiatry. Velikovsky authored a controversial paper describing the existence of pathological brain-wave patterns characteristic of epileptics which was well received within the scientific community.

It should be apparent to anyone that Dr. Velikovsky was a man of wide interests, learning, and talent — certainly not a publicity seeker, nor a crackpot.

Velikovsky's theories relating to scriptural prophecies and events arose out of his studies in psychiatry. During the course of research into the supposed mythical figures of Moses, Oedipus, and Aknehetan — characters figuring prominently in the writings of Sigmund Freud — he conceived the idea that these tales were narratives of actual events and were not, in fact, symbolic nor figurative. He began to search for corroboration in the myths of other cultures.

Being admirably suited for this broad overview with his background in natural and ancient history, as well as psychiatry, he waded through one of the most astonishing collections of literature ever sifted and studied by one man. Fitting all of the pieces of the puzzle together he wrote *Worlds in Collision*.

Dr. Velikovsky's conclusions, based upon a unique ability to see patterns (as well as the fact that physics has uncanny parallels to ancient poetic and mystical descriptions of nature), were irreconcilable with the traditional assumptions of the scientific community.

Velikovsky spent four years trying to be heard in established scientific circles, meeting with total failure. Those who supported him suffered ostracism and academic blackballing. The editor who had handled the publication of his book was dismissed and, under pressure from the scientific establishment, the publication rights were transferred to another publisher.

The scientific community worked long and hard to discredit Velikovsky and the *Encyclopedia Britannica* Yearbook for 1950 does not even mention that *Worlds in Collision* was a bestseller for that year.

What in the world did Velikovsky say to engender such censorious reactions? Surely if they simply disagreed with him they could write their refutations and allow all to be heard in open forum? Why did they work so hard to silence this book? In the morass of differing scientific opinions, why did this one engender such a near-unanimous outcry of 'Foul?' In his own role as psychiatrist, Dr. Velikovsky analyzed the reactions of the scientific community as being similar to the response of a psychotic who has been told that his problems stem form the repression of desires to rape his mother and kill his father; the patient has erected elaborate defenses against this unbearable truth, and it manifests in disorder, which all operate to conceal from him his true desires. And, while he may know that it is the truth, he lashes out in violent fury against the one who has deprived him of his elaborately constructed defenses, which constitute, in fact, his personality.

Velikovsky's theories are troubling for other reasons as well; they assault our deepest feelings of security, our prejudices against change. Psychologists have constructed charts that itemize events leading to stress, giving each a point value. Apparently, collision between the earth and another celestial body is off the scale. A thought such as this affects us deeply even if we are speaking of things that may have been experienced in ages past. We want to feel that our homes rest on solid foundations and that the blue sky above us is a benevolent firmament. *"What good is a house,"* said Thoreau, *"if we haven't a decent planet to put it on?"*

What has become of Velikovsky's theories since the time of their publication?

"All of (his) works contain challenges to modern science, questions to be reexamined, tests to be conducted, ... since the first publication of Worlds in Collision, *many of these tests have been conducted with very impressive results... Professor H. H. Hess, former chairman of the space board of the National Academy of Science, commented to the doctor that, while all of his predictions were made long before proof that they were right was at hand, 'I do not know of any specific prediction you made that has since proven to be false.' Among these correct prognoses: the extremely hot surface temperature of Venus, (owing to its recent birth), the hydrocarbonaceous content of its atmosphere and its disturbed rotation; the electromagnetic nature of solar flares; the existence of the Van Allen radiation belt; strong remanent magnetism on the moon, evidence of its recent heating, and the presence there of carbides and aromatic hydrocarbons; and radio emissions from Jupiter... Just a few days before he died, Einstein learned that radio noises had been detected from Jupiter, he offered to use his influence to arrange other experiments on Velikovsky's behalf. Albert Einstein died with* Worlds in Collision *open on his desk."* [26]

"In 1967, a Russian space probe, Venera 4, and the American Mariner 5, arrived at Venus within a few hours of each other. Venera 4 was designed to allow

*an instrument package to land gently on the planet's surface via parachute. It
ceased transmission of information in about 75 minutes when the temperature it
read went above 500 degrees F. After considerable controversy, it was agreed that
it still had 20 miles to go to reach the surface. The U.S. probe, Mariner 5, went
around the dark side of Venus at a distance of about 6,000 miles. Again it detected
no significant magnetic field but its radio signals passed to earth through Venus'
atmosphere twice — once on the night side and once on the day side. The results
are startling. Venus' atmosphere is nearly all carbon dioxide and must exert a pressure at the planet's surface of up to 100 times the earth's normal sea-level pressure of one atmosphere. Since the earth and Venus are about the same size, and
were presumably formed at the same time by the same general process from the
same mixture of chemical elements, one is faced with the question: which is the
planet with the unusual history — earth or Venus?"* [27]

And, I would like to point out that it certainly makes a lie of the idea
of being able to perform the same experiment twice with the same results. Either that, or we have two different processes here.

Dozens of space probes and robots were sent to Venus by Russia and
the U.S. It is now known that the clouds of Venus are not water vapor
but droplets of sulfuric acid. They are violent with storms, thunder and
lightning, and shed a perpetual downpour of acid rain. The air beneath
the cloud layer is almost all carbon dioxide. It is so soupy that the atmospheric pressure at the surface of Venus is the same as the pressure
3,000 feet beneath the Atlantic Ocean.

The clouds are so thick that sunlight never touches the ground, so
Venus is dusky even at noon. It is so hot you could melt lead on the surface, and the acid rains from the clouds boil, turn to vapor, and rise
again long before they reach the desert. At night, the rocks may glow a
dull red. Sounds pretty much like Hell to me!

When the space probes revealed this inferno, planetologists were baf-
fled by it, for the Venusian clouds reflect 98% of the light from the Sun
back into space, and only 2% filters down. It seemed strange that 2% of
the Sun's light should be enough to keep a whole world hotter than an
oven. The planet should be quite cool.

True, Venus is closer to the Sun than we are, but not enough to explain its temperature. Even Mercury, the planet nearest to the Sun, is
not as hot as Venus.

At first, some scientists thought the answer to this problem might be
Venus' spin. Venus takes 243 earth days to complete one rotation. The
direction of its rotation is also unusual; on Venus, the Sun rises in the

west and sets in the east. Oddly enough, Venus' upper atmosphere swirls around the planet at more than 200 miles per hour.

Carl Sagan suggested that the carbon dioxide traps the 2% of the sunlight and keeps it there.

The foregoing is the current scientific opinion of the enigma of Venus. No mention is made of the theories of Dr. Velikovsky even though he predicted that this would be the state of the Morning Star over 40 years ago. It should also be noted that Carl Sagan is one of the chief opponents of the theories of Velikovsky and once predicted, himself, that the moons of Mars were intelligently constructed satellites. So much for his ability to predict!

While Sagan's theory about the extremely high temperature of Venus is, to my knowledge, untested as yet, I find it stretches credulity to suppose 2% of the Sun's heat, even in a very good greenhouse, to be responsible for temperatures up to 900 degrees, particularly when the planet has one side in darkness for two thirds of a year at a time.

*   *   *

What were the series of events as described by Dr. Velikovsky, and how did he come to such startlingly accurate conclusions so far in advance of the scientific establishment?

Dr. Velikovsky begins *Worlds in Collision* with a presentation of the theories of geology, paleontology, archaeology, biology, cosmology, and so forth — all of which are expressed in Darwinian terms which state that change takes place slowly over eons, aided by gradual processes of natural selection, erosion, etc. James Hutton, founder of the modern view expressed it: *"No powers are to be employed that are not natural to the globe, no action to be admitted of except those of which we know the principle."* [28] It is a doctrine taken for granted within the scientific community. *"If nature were not uniform, then one could not use the results of one experiment to predict the outcome of the next; neither could one assume that laws founded on a thousand varied observations would remain true. Without uniformity in nature, doing physics, chemistry, and biology would be like traveling in Alice's Wonderland. Logic, science, and life itself would fall to pieces."* [29] (It is said that what Copernicus did for space, Hutton did for time. And, the majority of the scientific community continues to operate on the assumption that we are pinpoints on an extraordinarily long time line.)

Nevertheless, this view of the processes of the earth has been accepted as truth and taught as such for over a hundred years. The gradual layering of the various strata of sediment and fossils is considered to be absolutely orderly and forms the foundation of the various dating methods employed to support all other fields of scientific endeavor.

To suggest that this idea of slow and orderly process is, in its basic assumption, totally wrong, is a threat of the most disruptive event in the history of science. The dismissal of this as 'truth' would eclipse the furor that surrounded the denial of the earth as the center of the universe. As long as it was accepted that the Sun traveled around the earth, all other ancient errors held up as truth. In the same way, as long as the steady state of the solar system is the asserted dogma, all current scientific assumptions will hang together on this point.

However, there are very serious problems with these supposed truths upon which popular theoretical extrapolations have been intricately constructed. These problems have been pointed up in the anomalies I have mentioned and further complicated by other very vexing problems which science does little to satisfactorily explain, or ignores entirely.

Dr. Velikovsky pointed out some pretty obvious ideas:

> "The process of raising the mountains is supposed to have been very slow and grad-ual. On the other hand, it is clear that igneous rock, already hard, had to become fluid in order to penetrate sedimentary rock or cover it. It is not known what ini-tiated this process, but it is asserted that it must have happened long before man appeared on the earth. So when skulls of early man are found in late deposits, or skulls of modern man are found together with bones of extinct animals in early deposits, difficult problems are presented. Occasionally, also, during mining op-erations, a human skull is found in the middle of a mountain, under a thick cover of basalt or granite... Human remains and artifacts ... are found under great de-posits of till and gravel, sometimes as much as a hundred feet." [30]

> "Not many thousands of years ago, we are taught, great areas of Europe and of North America were covered with glaciers. Perpetual ice lay not only on the slopes of high mountains, but loaded itself in heavy masses upon continents even in moderate latitudes. ... Traces have been found of five or six consecutive dis-placements ... Neither the cause of the ice ages nor the cause of the retreat of the icy desert is known...

> Many ideas were offered... Some supposed that the sun at different times emits more or less heat... Others conjectured that cosmic space has warmer or cooler areas... A few wondered whether the precession of the equinoxes or the slow change in the direction of the terrestrial axis might cause periodic variations in the climate. ... Still others thought to find the answer in the periodic variations in the eccentricity of the ecliptic... Some scholars thought about the changes in

the position of the terrestrial axis. ...it could have shifted up to ten or fifteen degrees in a very slow process. The cause of the ice ages was seen by a few scholars in the decrease of the original heat of the planet... Others supposed that dust of volcanic origin filled the terrestrial atmosphere ... (and) contrariwise, that an increased content of carbon dioxide ... obstructed the reflection of heat rays... Changes in the direction of (ocean currents) ... (etc.)" [31]

The currently accepted theory of what caused the ice age is, more or less, a conglomerate of the ideas about the precession of the equinoxes, the orbital variations of the earth and the positive feedback effect of ice accumulation due to increase in albedo — or the tendency of a body to reflect the heat of the Sun back into space; which is exactly what Venus does, except that it makes Venus hot in that theory. Elaborate calculations have been performed by computer based upon assumed dating of core samples, which come 'very close' to matching the calculations of perturbations of the earth's orbit. The scientific establishment claims that this theory and evidence fit like lock and key.

One problem: All of the foregoing theories lack one essential element and Velikovsky fearlessly points out the obvious:

> *"In order for ice masses to have been formed, increased precipitation must have taken place. This requires an increased amount of water vapor in the atmosphere, which is the result of increased evaporation from the surface of the oceans; but this could be caused by heat only. ... in order to produce a sheet of ice as large as that of the Ice Age, the surface of all the oceans must have evaporated to a depth of many feet. Such an evaporation of oceans followed by a quick process of freezing, even in moderate latitudes, would have produced the ice ages. The problem is: What could have caused the evaporation and immediately subsequent freezing?"* [32]

Well, obviously, since the scientific community has painted itself into the corner of 'slow and gradual change,' it has no adequate answer for this one. And, to further complicate the mystery, it should be noted that the ice sheet covered most of North America, to the basin of the Mississippi, and Europe, while the north of Asia, currently the coldest area on earth, was not covered, but rather shows evidence of a sub-tropical climate. Flora and fauna once lived in this frigid region that cannot exist there now. Since the end of the last ice age, the climate in Siberia changed so suddenly that the mammoths of this area were frozen solid, immediately. It is patently obvious that if the drop in temperature had been gradual, these beasts, superior in every way to elephants, which continue to exist as a species, would have migrated to an area of milder temperature and more abundant food supplies. The fact that the carcasses found in ice were not in a state of putrefaction bespeaks the fact that the ice precipitated upon them within a very short period after death, or was, itself, the cause of death.

The inhabitants of the earth have written records that stretch back five or six thousand years. These consist of documents, stone carvings, clay tablets and papyri, recording everything from bills of sale to astronomical calculations. The scientific community has always been quick to assume error on the part of the ancient observers if the observations did not mesh with the current order of things, which is often the case. Modern science does not admit the possibility that, at some time in the recorded past, the order of cosmic as well as terrestrial phenomena could have been quite different.

The ancients described several 'world ages,' each of which had been prophesied and was termed variously 'the great and terrible Day of the Lord,' 'The Day of Judgment,' 'The End of the World,' and so forth. The same themes and stories can be found in cultures the world over, separated by vast oceans and communication barriers. Science, itself, has made certain recent observations that bear heavily on this subject and many recent psychics and prophets have dealt with this idea at length.

Dr. Velikovsky concluded from his research into the ancient manuscripts that the planet earth was totally devastated at the time of the Exodus and that this event was chronicled by all the various cultures of the world. This devastation was caused by a comet passing very close to the earth; and, that this comet originated from the planet Jupiter and ultimately, after terrorizing the peoples of the earth (those who survived) for hundreds of years, was precipitated into a planetary orbit after a final dramatic encounter with the earth and the planet Mars. This comet became the Newcomer, the fallen Morning Star, the Planet Venus.

If some recent observations of science agree, at least in context, with the statements of the ancients and the more recent psychics, considering the fact that, until recently, the ancients and psychics stood alone in these descriptions, might we not assume that science is only just now catching up with things that have been known by other means for ages? And, if the ancients and the psychics are so much in advance of science in these demonstrable ways, might we not also conjecture that they may be more accurate in their statements regarding future events?

* * *

One of the primary methods used in dating rock samples involves measuring radioactive decay of certain elements. In a laboratory, one can measure the quantity of the element in question against the quantity of the element it decays into over a known period of time. Knowing, theoretically, the rate of decay, one can calculate the age of the material being dated.

There are two problems with this system immediately apparent. The first is that it depends upon knowing precisely the ratio of the determining element in the earth's atmosphere at the time the rock was formed or hardened. Secondly, one must consider if any other events could accelerate or retard the rate of decay and if those events may have occurred. It becomes obvious that this dating technique, as with most other scientific theories, rests upon the same premise — defining x in terms of y and y in terms of x — as well as the assumption that the earth's processes have changed little since it began to cool and life took hold on its surface.

It is assumed that man is the product of slow and orderly evolution and his present hope for three-score and ten years is a great advancement, since recorded history indicates to us that during other periods of history, when more hostile conditions prevailed, man had a much reduced lifespan.

Can we not conjecture that a fundamental reordering of things might have appreciably changed conditions detrimentally in times past? Obviously many creatures have lived upon the earth that can no longer live here. Must we assume that the ancients did not understand time as we know it when they claimed to live hundreds of years? In this regard, some observations about dinosaurs are pertinent.

Dinosarus have been found — remains in 'bone-yards' — that had shoulder blades 11 feet long. The towering Brachiosaurus, an herbivore, stood up to 50 feet tall and weighed perhaps a hundred tons. How could it have sustained itself? One hundred tons is about 15 times the weight of an adult African bull elephant — an animal that consumes 300 to 600 pounds of fodder every 24 hours and spends up to 18 hours a day feeding! It seems totally out of the question to imagine this 'Super-saurus' feeding itself.

If Brachiosaurus was warm-blooded like an elephant, it might have been unable to eat enough to keep itself alive. But, even as a cold-blooded animal, there is doubt that this gargantuan creature could have eaten enough with its small mouth and teeth. We are taught by orthodox science that the dinosaurs were failures — colossal failures. There is a litany of 'couldn'ts' recited about them. They couldn't walk on land because they were too heavy. They couldn't eat anything but mush because their heads were too small. They couldn't run fast because their joints were imperfect. They couldn't be warm blooded because their brains were too small. They couldn't compete with smaller, warm-blooded animals. Yet, when dinosaurs began to emerge as the dominant group, there were many other animal types, which had equal opportunity to dominate. For five million years, the dinosaurs were on equal footing with the other inhabitants of the ecosystem. But then, the dinosaurs showed that they were the fittest and survived into absolute domination of the globe. During their rule, there was no non-dinosaur larger than a turkey. The dinosaurs monopolized the planet for 130 million years. As they spread into every area of dominance, they drove out and/or destroyed very advanced clans that had been evolving and adapting for tens of millions of years. During their long reign, other clans threatened — each time, the dinosaurs showed that they were there 'firstest with the mostest' in terms of adaptive vigor.

The class Mammalia emerged fully defined just as the dinosaurs began their expansion. But, obviously, being a mammal wasn't so great during that time. Dinosaurs evolved quickly, changed repeatedly, and maintained their dominance until some terrible event brought their rule to an abrupt end.

> "No one, either in the nineteenth century or the twentieth, has ever built a persuasive case proving that dinosaurs as a whole were more like reptilian crocodiles than warm-blooded birds. No one has done this because it can't be done. ... So hundred-year-old dinosaur theories live on without being questioned, and too often they are assumed to be totally correct. Even when such a theory is caught in an error, it's likely to be excused. ...
>
> The sudden extinction of dinosaurs is one of the most popularized topics in paleontology. Why, after all, did the last dynasties finally end in total extinction? In reality, however, the dinosaurs' history contains the drama of much more than a single death. They suffered three or four major catastrophes during their long predominance, each one thinning the ranks of the entire clan. And after each such fall, they recouped their evolutionary fortunes, rising again to fill the terrestrial system with yet another wave of new species and families of species. The final complete extermination did not come until sixty-five million years ago, at what geologists label the 'Time of Great Dying,' the greatest evolutionary disaster of all time. ... Our view of evolution must take into account the profoundly disorienting blows struck by the environment during these world-wide extinctions." [33]

There are many theories put forth to explain these problems but, as is the usual case with Darwinian thought, they are highly unsatisfactory and leave too many questions that require fantastic cerebral gymnastics to answer.

Might it not be more reasonable to assume that the earth was a different place at the time the dinosaurs walked? They may have obtained a portion of nourishment from the act of breathing itself. Additionally, a different level of gravity would have greatly reduced the energy needs and a more salubrious climate would have further eliminated the energy expenditure for heat regulation. At the same time, a soupier atmosphere would have shielded the inhabitants of the earth from the harmful radiations of the Sun and would have been more conducive to extensive lifespans, which may have been the means by which the dinosaurs grew to such fantastic sizes.

Robert T. Bakker, author of *The Dinosaur Heresies*, makes an excellent case for the warm-bloodedness of dinosaurs, as well as the superiority of the clan in terms of evolutionary processes. He notes:

> *"Any attempt to analyze the events of the extinction of the dinosaurs runs into the fundamental difficulties that hinder the investigation of any of these mass murders of species. Most fossil bones owe their preservation to quick burial by sediment right after the death of their owner. But generally most spots in the terrestrial biosphere suffer erosion, not deposition."* [34]

But, suppose cataclysmic events repeatedly struck the earth, thinning, and finally destroying the dinosaurs; this would easily explain why cemeteries of dinosaur skeletons exist, such events resulting in mighty terrestrial upheavals that would have created vast bone-yards entombed for future speculation.

And, returning to the idea that the earth may have been an entirely different place in terms of total environment, concomitant with such effects would have been the benefits to man himself; for there is evidence that man existed alongside the dinosaurs.

What could be the oldest fossil footprint yet found was discovered in June 1968 by William J. Meister, an amateur fossil collector. If the print is what it appears to be — the impression of a human sandaled foot crushing a trilobite — it would have to have been made 300 to 600 million years ago and would be sufficient either to overturn all conventionally accepted ideas of human and geological evolution, or to prove that a shoe-wearing biped from another world had once visited this planet.

"Meister made his potentially disturbing find during a rock and fossil-hunting expedition to Antelope Spring, 43 miles west of Delta, Utah. He was accompanied by his wife and two daughters, and by Mr. and Mrs. Francis Shape and their two daughters. The party had already discovered several fossils of trilobites when Meister split open a two-inch-thick slab of rock with his hammer and discovered the outrageous print. The rock fell open 'like a book,' revealing: 'on one side the footprint of a human with trilobites right in the footprint itself. The other half of the rock slab showed an almost perfect mold of the footprint and fossils. Amazingly the human was wearing a sandal!'" [35]

Trilobites were small marine invertebrates — relatives of crabs and shrimps — which flourished for some 320 million years before becoming extinct *280 million years ago.*

Humans are currently thought to have emerged between 1 and 2 million years ago and to have been wearing well-shaped footwear for no more than a few thousand years.

"Meister took the rock to Melvin Cook, a professor of metallurgy at the University of Utah, who advised him to show the specimen to the university geologists. When Meister was unable to find a geologist willing to examine the print, he went to a local newspaper ... the curator of the Museum of Earth Science at the University of Utah, James Madsen, said: 'There were no men 600 million years ago. Neither were there monkeys or bears or ground sloths to make pseudohuman tracks. What man-thing could possibly have been walking about on this planet before vertebrates even evolved?' ...

On July 20, 1968, the Antelope Spring site was examined by Dr. Clifford Burdick, a consulting geologist from Tucson, Arizona, who soon found the impression of a child's foot in a bed of shale." [36]

There are many, many instances of similar finds and others even more mysterious. Although the documentary evidence seems to have been strong in most cases and the witnesses reputable and intelligent, the scientific community has interesting ways of dealing with such things: *"The rock in which the prints were found ... (was) destroyed by vandals... Some of the bones were sent to the American Investigating Museum in Philadelphia, where they seem to have disappeared... They were lost in a flood... The mummy disappeared... The professor never made public any test results; he left his position for another in a different state..."*, and so forth. It is apparent that experts have a way of dismissing unpalatable finds rather than admit that the frog cannot jump because he has no legs.

One conclusion to be drawn from all of this is that perhaps we have not evolved as the best adaptation for our planet. Perhaps things were better and different in the past. Perhaps we are just barely hanging in there now, in a hostile environment rapidly becoming more hostile every day. If this is the case, then it is also possible that this condition could change. Perhaps all the dinosaurs did not die on one day in a cataclysm — perhaps some of them did pass through a change and then fade away, unable to adapt to the new environment. Perhaps there were other human types on the earth that also could not adapt and we are a remnant — like crocodiles and alligators, elephants, and Gila lizards. The Bible says: *"There were giants in the earth in those days..."* [37] What a suggestive idea!

*   *   *

Returning to Velikovsky's ideas, he described in great detail the mechanics of the extraterrestrial interaction. During the initial contact with Venus, the earth might have been knocked out of its orbit and into a new one, and then again when the comet reappeared some fifty years later (which it continued to do for several centuries). These near misses caused worldwide earthquakes, tidal waves, volcanic eruptions, hurricanes, emergence and submersion of land masses, sudden changes in the polar orientation as well as the boiling of the seas, and shadowing of the earth in cometary dust as well as incendiary products of volcanoes. Forty years of darkness following the initial contact, and other periods of darkness, brought on the rapid cooling which destroyed many species of plants and animals. The excessive heating of areas of the oceans brought on the destruction of many marine animals.

During these contacts, massive discharges of electrical potentials between the earth and the comet, and the comet and its tail, brought about considerable alterations in the earth's atmosphere as well as possible alterations in its atomic structure. These cosmic displays left an indelible imprint upon the suffering inhabitants of the earth and long after cultural prowess was lost, time after time, they continued to memorialize them in song, myth and legend.

As the comet approached the earth, the gravitational attraction between it and the earth held the seas in suspension as the rotation of the earth slowed. A great discharge of electricity broke the attraction and the seas fell, followed by a great rain of rocks and debris from the tail of the comet. Velikovsky conjectures that all of this occurred at the time of the Exodus, which was a crucial period in the history of the Jewish people. Though many of them undoubtedly perished, the retelling of this event — which was the means of their deliverance from bondage, and was therefore interpreted by them as an act of a god favorable to them — glossed over the loss of life on their own side and glorified the destruction of their enemies and former masters.

When fully considered in all its ramifications, this theory accounts for many problems science has had no success in dealing with. It would adequately account for the disappearance of many of the earth's mystery cultures — perhaps they fled in terror or were swept away or died from any number of cataclysmic events; it also easily explains the extinction of numerous species including the dinosaurs; admits reasonable explanations for anomalies — violence of this extreme nature would undoubtedly stir up and turn over and melt and redeposit many portions of the earth's crust; it would radically alter the earth's dating chronology as well as method, since we cannot be sure what quantum changes may have occurred during massive electrical discharges or other unknown forces; accounts for the recent heating and cooling of the moon — during these interplanetary contacts, the moon flowed and bubbled with lava which cooled rapidly due to the lack of atmosphere; the moon also bears many more scars of these events due to the fact that it has not the atmospheric protection the earth has nor does it have the involved system of plate tectonics which serves to heal and efface evidence of such encounters on the earth's surface.

This theory also easily accounts for the extremely unusual conditions found on the planet Venus. Venus, born from the planet Jupiter, violently expelled, running amok in the solar system, engaging in war with both the earth and Mars, passing close to the Sun; Venus is HOT!

This theory explains mountain and canyon formation and would account for the tremendous flooding that must have taken place in the Badlands of America, carving the fantastic rock formations found there. It accounts for the now-established fact that the magnetic orientation of the earth has changed many times. This theory explains why the ancients had a different map of the bodies of the solar system in both number and relative position; as well as the troubling idea that they 'did not know east from west.'

As Velikovsky shows, it is entirely possible that the earth was flipped over like a spinning billiard ball and when the dust and debris cleared from the skies, the Sun was seen to rise from the direction opposite to the former position!

Each time the planets interacted, changes occurred in the earth's orbit, orbital velocity, axial position, atmosphere, etc. These events were recorded as the 'changing of the times and the seasons,' a 'new heaven and a new earth,' the 'Day of the Lord.'

Thus, if we accept Velikovsky's hypothesis of possible periodic interactions between the bodies of the solar system — or even bodies or energy sources from deep space — we make our task of explaining the order of the universe a great deal broader in scope and potential. This is not to say that this theory solves all problems, but it certainly works far better than the present concepts of uniformitarianism. As Dr. Velikovsky pointed out, many tests need to be devised and performed to determine the operations of many aspects of this idea.

And that is not to say that we must be entirely convinced of the exact chronology as he presents it, but I believe it is most important to look at his analysis particularly as it relates to terms and concepts of the order of the universe and the purpose of life. These concepts are inextricably involved with one another, for to know our past we may conjecture about our future. And to know our future is to be able to divine our purpose in a cosmic sense. And, having done that, our priorities my be ordered accordingly so that we will no longer groan under the weight of feeling cast adrift in an uncaring and hostile universe — orphans of the cosmos — playthings of the gods.

Chapter Three

There are two kinds of truths: those of reasoning and those of fact.
The truths of reasoning are necessary and their opposite is impossible;
the truths of fact are contingent and their opposites are possible.

— Baron Leibniz.

For decades scientists have conjectured about the death of the dinosaurs. Most of these theories, thankfully, have died as well. However, a recent event in the scientific community gives one hope that all do not believe that the emperor is fully clothed.

In 1978, Walter Alvarez, a geologist from the University of California at Berkeley, was working in Italy. He was trying to find ways of identifying the layer of sediment formed immediately before the Cretaceous Period ended.

The idea was to provide a yardstick for comparing sequences of geological events. Alvarez inspected a thin layer of clay in a deep gorge near Gubbio. The reddish clay layer was just a half inch thick, but it stood out clearly because below it the limestone gorge was white, and above it, grayish-pink. This red clay was right at the boundary between the Cretaceous and the Tertiary periods. This meant that it had been laid down just at the time the dinosaurs had died.

Walter's father, Luis, a Nobel Prize-winning physicist, decided to try and determine just how long it took this layer to accumulate. The idea was to find out how much of the element iridium was dispersed through the clay. By comparing this with an average year's accumulation they would be able to determine how long it took to form the layer in question. It should be noted that iridium is an element that the earth has in only trace amounts and an average year's accumulation comes from comet dust as the earth spins through space picking up small amounts from the meteorites that penetrate our atmosphere, or that which is simply floating in space.

The results of this analysis were unexpected, to say the least. The clay layer in question contained huge amounts of iridium — as much as 10,000 times more than an average year's accumulation!

Tests were performed on samples from other places around the globe and the results were consistent. The two scientists, in attempting to account for the comet dust layered over the globe at the time of the extinction of the dinosaurs, finally were forced to the conclusion that a comet must have collided with the earth, shadowing the planet in comet dust, which then brought about the death of many of the living beings on the earth.

Walter Alvarez's theory has gained a number of converts because a giant collision could explain part of the peculiar selectivity of the great extinctions. It also lends credit to the idea that the dinosaurs were warm-blooded. Cold-blooded animals could wait out the freezing darkness because their low metabolisms would permit long fasts with no problem. The survival into our own era of crocodiles and turtles, meat eaters, could then be explained. Many mammals died out, and many did not. This is because, so the scientists say, some mammals burrowed and hid and huddled for warmth — coming out only to eat the carcasses of the dinosaurs which succumbed.

If the dinosaurs were, in the main, plant eaters, this would have been against them as well, for in the darkness most species of plants would have died leaving only those with seeds, spores and underground tubers and bulbs. This idea also explains why the extinctions exacted such a heavy toll on the oceans.

Considering the fact that it is estimated that about 96% of all known animal species have been killed off in the history of the earth, many simultaneously at specified points in time, it is apparent that some event other than 'uniformitarianism' is responsible.

Nevertheless, most geologists do not care for the Alvarez theory. Science is abysmally slow in both its methods and change. Perhaps the current scientific process is the only area where 'slow and gradual change' and 'survival of the fittest' actually applies. The continental drift theory was also poorly received, but has now been widely accommodated.

The reasons for this resistance have to do with what scientists contemptuously call 'catastrophism.' To the average scientist, catastrophism is fantastic and violently lurid. It is unacceptable in the hallowed halls of sober and respectable science where the quiet hush of slow and gradual changes dominates. It is only recently that such rude barbarity has disturbed the domain of narrow empirical rigor. *"It is interesting how much of our thinking about the Earth is shading toward catastrophe theories,"* Clark Chapman notes in *Planets of Rock and Ice:*

"Once, for instance, we spoke of the Grand Canyon as having been eroded by wind, weather and water, day by day and grain by grain. But some time ago, Eugene Shoemaker, the man who proved the Arizona Meteor Crater to be a meteorite impact, (a catastrophe theory if ever there was one), retraced the route of the first scientific expedition through the Grand Canyon, and he re-photographed all the outcrops and cliffs from the same point of view the 19th century scientists had used in making their meticulous etchings. Shoemaker was surprised to find that in most places the Grand Canyon's walls were essentially unchanged by the passage of 100 years. But here and there, in a sudden, rare torrent, a whole facade had caved in. He concluded that the Grand Canyon is not carved so much grain by grain as landslide by landslide. Catastrophism again." [38]

Paleontologists Stephen Jay Gould and Niles Eldridge have proposed a revision of Darwin's theory of evolution. Darwin believed that species evolve smoothly and slowly. One of his mentors, geologist Charles Lyell, saw the development of the earth in the same way — as a process of slow, smooth changes proceeding at a uniform rate.

"Nature does not make jumps," Darwin said. But the fossil record does not really bear this out. Try as they might, Darwinists have found very few fossils that show smooth transitions from one form to another with hundreds of small, intermediate steps, as the master expected.

Perhaps nature does make jumps. Many species stay more or less the same for long periods of time, and then undergo relatively sudden bursts of evolution in perhaps only a few hundred generations — too short to have left a continuous record in rock layers. Catastrophe theory yet again.

But these ideas are causing a furor similar to the uproar over *Worlds in Collision*, and for much the same reason. And this reason is actually deeper and more fundamental than Velikovsky's own analysis of the reactions of the scientific community: Catastrophism snatches the rug of security from beneath our feet. It violently ravages our deepest feelings. No matter how materialistic the scientist or deeply faithful the religious person, no one ever wants to confront the remote possibility that the planet which gives us life might not be as securely hung in space as we think. The scientist's intricate extrapolations relating to the slow, gradual changes and the exquisite balance of forces that holds everything together is his defense — his protection against the prospect of annihilation. For even the most hard-core atheist achieves some immortality in the idea that the earth will spin for billions of years, inhabited, perhaps, by some of his descendants. And, if you peel away the layers of doctrinal wrapping from the faithful, you will find that often they are just practicing their religion to hedge their bet — better to believe, just in case, than not believe and be sorry.

In the controversy over the new Alvarez theory, counter-theories have sprung up all over to combat the idea of the earth being hit by an extraterrestrial body. One such idea was that the iridium-saturated clay was of terrestrial volcanic origin. One scientist with such an idea took a sample to test it. What he found was that the clay layer also contained silt-sized grains of quartz that were like nothing with which he was familiar. He checked around and discovered that some few other scientists had run into such formations in rocks from the moon and at the sites of nuclear explosions. Identical grains had also been found at the site of the Arizona meteor crater.

This discovery only strengthened Alvarez's theory. And, another interesting piece of the puzzle was soon to come forth. It seems that one researcher had compiled a list of all the extinct species and supposed times of their extinction and fed his data into a computer. He wanted to see if there was some biological pattern of dying out. The computer spit out rather disturbing results — not only is there a pattern, there is a very definite cycle!

Some of these 'Great Dyings' were more widespread and devastating than others, but it was unmistakably *a regular pulsing of extinction*. This is not, to put it mildly, a pleasant thought. Formerly, extinctions were thought to occur because a lot of things just coincidentally got bad all at once. The idea that the Dyings are a regular, cyclic thing implies *"a single, powerful, and awesome cause, recurring like clockwork."*[39]

Naturally, there was quite a bit of scurrying about to find an explanation for this that was sufficiently remote and far in the future so that the scientific world could go back to bed and get some rest. This sort of thing could definitely keep one up at night!

What they came up with was this: Far outside the edges of our solar system there is a ring of comets which circles around and around like good little comets should. Supposedly these are bits of matter which did not have sufficient impetus to amass into a planet or are remnants of a planet or planets which were broken up billions of years ago. Also, spinning around somewhere past the far reaches of solar system is a dark star which swings close to this little band of comets (called the Oort Cloud), and the force of the Death Star's gravity sends billions of them spinning through our solar system and, of course, a few of them smack into the earth.

You will notice that this explanation does several important things. First, it maintains the steady state of our solar system — an outsider is the culprit. And, secondly, it makes the event chancy enough that we might escape if we are lucky.

Based upon the dating of the extinct specimens, it is said that this event occurs once every 26 million years or so — give or take a day.

While science is looking for the Death Star, which, I reiterate, is only a theory, and waiting for it to brush up against the Oort Cloud, which is also only a theory, I would like to make several pertinent remarks.

In the face of all the evidence in the cosmos, why does science continue to cling so tenaciously to the slow evolutionary process and seek to interpret and explain all phenomena in these terms? Are we, as a species, repressing a collective archetypal experience of world catastrophe in the same fashion as an individual represses and forgets painful memories of childhood? Do we seek in every expression of our culture to deny cataclysmic world upheavals? And then, do we project these troublesome repressed elements onto a vague religio-spiritual event called Judgment Day? Or, worse, does the repression express itself in societal sickness — self-fulfilling prophecies of Doomsday expressed in self-destruction of all sorts?

I would like to suggest that the psychic records support the idea of the Great Dyings, and, in fact, they were the first to do so. The main area of difference at this point is timing. Science has pushed everything off into the outer limits of time in both directions. According to them, not only did the cataclysms of the past happen so long ago that no human being could possibly have been a witness, but any future events will be so far in the future as to be inconsequential to us all.

Well, since they are just coming to an acceptance of the idea in its most basic form, while the ancients and mystics have known about it all the time, I suppose we must be patient with them until they finally come up with some concrete evidence — since that is the only kind they will accept — that their methods of dating are desperately in need of revision.

And, speaking of the ancients and mystics; most readers of the Bible and other ancient literature think it speaks of only one great cataclysm — the Flood of Noah. But, I believe that careful analysis will show that other events were actually cataclysms which each, step by step, brought the earth from one state of existence — quantumly speaking — to the present.

The 'Fall' of Adam and Eve could be such an incident for it does speak of an 'angel' with a flaming sword set to guard against re-entry into the

Garden. Velikovsky suggests that the 'Angel of Passage,' represented to the Hebrews as a pillar of smoke and fire, was, in fact, a comet. Could it be that the moon is the 'angel' set to guard the entrance of the garden, an acquisition at the time of the first great cataclysm when matter became more dense? An object necessary to maintain the quantum density of matter?

And, the Tower of Babel: Could this be the story of the breaking up of a land mass and consequent separation of the indigenous inhabitants? Ignatius Donnelly wrote about this in the last century as an allegory of the destruction of Atlantis.

*   *   *

The story of Noah is fairly straightforward. Or is it? Science has been puzzled for a long time over the fact that there must have once been great quantities of water on the planet Mars as evidenced by the massive erosion in many areas. Where did this water go? Is it locked up in the soil of the planet as permafrost as Carl Sagan suggests, or did the earth have an encounter with her near companion and steal its water and atmosphere? The Bible stated that it had not rained upon the earth until the time of Noah; that a mist watered the garden. Could this be a description of a water vapor canopy, or thick, soupy atmosphere, which protected the earth from the harmful radiation of the Sun? As noted earlier, such a condition, coupled with a different axial orientation, rotational velocity, and orbital position might have been contributory to the great sizes of the dinosaurs as well as a factor in the fantastic longevity the ancients claimed to achieve.

If there had been a thicker atmosphere, a water vapor canopy, *"The waters above and the waters below,"* it would not have been noticed if another body of the solar system were drawing close. But, the agitation of the planet would have caused the 'fountains of the deep' to burst forth and surface tension between the two planets broken by electrical discharge might have caused any water present on Mars to vaporize and overload the terrestrial atmosphere, possibly with molecular combinations in different proportions to what had existed until then, the consequence of which was a rain falling for forty days and forty nights. The Bible notes that the Lord caused a great wind to blow, which dried up all the waters. This is written as though wind were an unusual event. A prior perpendicular axial orientation combined with a water vapor canopy would have equalized atmospheric temperatures to such an extent that the earth would not have suffered the high pressure and low pressure systems common today, which are the impetus for massive air flow from one location to another. A sudden disruption in this stability would have caused violent winds. The Bible also notes the appearance of the rainbow. This would have been a new thing if the skies were suddenly cleared of a thick, soupy atmosphere. It is worth noting that the Bible denotes the time subsequent to the flood of Noah as the point which mankind was allotted a lifespan of three score and ten years. If mankind were suddenly exposed to a new level of UV radiation, one of the consequences of this event would have been a sudden shortening of lifespan.

The numerous 'Days of the Lord' mentioned in the later portions of the Bible could have been, as Velikovsky suggests, the earth's interactions with an untamed Venus — a 'Queen of Heaven' bent on destruction.

* * *

Edgar Cayce (1877—1945), the great American psychic, spoke often of three Atlantean upheavals and mentioned others relating to even more distant civilizations. The three Atlantean upheavals were described as massive earthquakes in which entire continents were broken up and subsided beneath the sea while other landmasses rose or grew in size. Cayce mentioned that a partial reason for these disasters was the misuse of powers — perhaps atomic — and the unleashing of forces by a giant crystal that operated along the line of today's lasers.

Referring to future cataclysms, Cayce spoke rather grimly, but when pressed for details as to why or precisely how these events would take place, he was maddeningly reticent.

* * *

Getting back to the new 'Cometary Impact Theory' of Walter and Luis Alvarez, I think we should ask what finally happened to Velikovsky, the originator of this idea and so many others, which have proven to be astonishingly correct?

He remained an outcast from the scientific community until his death in 1979. In the recent reviving of the cometary impact theories, I have yet to read one single reference to Velikovsky in any serious scientific article. Fortunately he was not threatened with death like Galileo, and I suspect he is till saying, 'But it happened!'

The conclusion we can draw from all of this is that we might find our-selves in a better position in all respects if we give credence to those who have the better track record in explaining the order of the universe to us. In a way, scientists are like dinosaurs — they proliferated rapidly with many variations, grew very large and dominated the landscape. But their very size, number and nature shall make it impossible for them to pass through the coming cataclysm in thought, if not in fact.

*   *   *

Did Immanuel Velikovsky draw any conclusions from his research that we can examine and project into the future?
He did.

> *"When physicists came upon the idea that the atom is built like a solar system, the atoms of various chemical elements differing in the mass of their suns (nuclei) and the number of the planets (electrons) the notion was looked upon with much favor. But it was stressed that 'an atom differs from the solar system by the fact that it is not gravitation that makes the electrons go around the nucleus, but electricity' (H.N. Russell).*
>
> *Besides this, another difference was found: an electron in an atom, on absorbing the energy of a photon (light), jumps to another orbit, and again to another when it emits light and releases the energy of a photon. Because of this phenomenon, comparison with the solar system no longer seemed valid. 'We do not read in the morning newspapers that Mars leaped to the orbit of Saturn, or Saturn to the orbit of Mars,' wrote one critic. True, we do not read it in the morning papers; but in ancient records we have found similar events described in detail, and we have tried to reconstruct the facts by comparing many ancient records. The solar system is actually built like an atom; only, in keeping with the smallness of the atom, the jumping of electrons from one orbit to another, when hit by the energy of a photon, takes place many times a second, whereas in accord with the vastness of the solar system, a similar phenomenon occurs there once in hundreds or thousands of years. ...*
>
> *If the activity in an atom constitutes a rule for the macrocosm, then the events described ... were not merely accidents of celestial traffic, but normal phenomena like birth and death. The discharges between the planets, or the great photons emitted in these contacts caused metamorphoses in inorganic and organic nature."* [40]

As Dr. Velikovsky points out, we do have written records of such events of the past. We also have prophecies for the future couched in identical terms.

According to the cometary impact theory formulated by the Alvarezes, the last Great Dying took place approximately 13 million years ago and they have projected the next to occur about 13 million years from now. If we take Velikovsky's interpretations of ancient records to be correct, as well as numerous psychic references from sources with proven track records, then we have a real problem reconciling the time element. The key to this discrepancy may lie in the idea of metamorphosis. If, at the time of any interplanetary interaction, fundamental atomic changes take place, it would obviously invalidate any atomic dating method in use.

If there have been repeated metamorphoses, and if we are truly in the dark scientifically regarding time and perception then it is entirely possible that another Great Dying is just ahead of us in the immediate future and that this is the true hint, or vision of the prophets of gloom and doom as well as the religious configuration of 'The Day of The Lord.'

And, if it is true, as the recent work in quantum physics seems to show, that our deepest realities can only be perceived in an altered state of awareness, should we not look to persons who have demonstrated an ability to achieve this state for explanations of the order of the universe? More, should we not follow the dictum of Jesus and look within for our *kingdom* — a kingdom promised to come into being on a worldwide level, but which may be experienced on a limited level as an inward journey of the soul: *"Thy kingdom come, thy will be done, on earth as it is in heaven..."*

There are numerous aspects of these ideas to examine in order to arrive at a more complete understanding of the events which are in our world and in our future, and I believe that we can find a common denominator within all of them which points to another Great Dying — and the cause.

I intend to show that we are facing an extraterrestrially caused global catastrophe which will initiate metamorphosis and a New Heaven and a New Earth.

Judgment Day.

Chapter Four

The sum of things is unlimited, and they all change into one another.
The All includes the empty as well as the full.
The worlds are formed when atoms fall into the void and are
entangled with one another; and from their motion as they
increase in bulk, arises the substance of the stars.

— Leucippus (c. 450 B.C.).

At this point I want to discuss metamorphosis as it applies to 'atomic' interactions between bodies of the cosmos. The single most important statement made by Immanuel Velikovsky is:

> *"If the activity in the atom constitutes a rule for the macrocosm, then the events described were not merely accidents of celestial traffic, but normal phenomena... The discharges between the planets or the great photons emitted in these contacts caused metamorphoses in inorganic and organic nature."* [41]

As we can surmise from the data analyzed in the Alvarez theory, this event recurs like clockwork and must represent a single, powerful cause. I would like to suggest that this cause is not a 'death star' which approaches our solar system every so many millions of years, sending comets hurtling towards the earth.

This is too chancy a hypothesis. Considerable odds exist against the earth being directly in the path of such a phenomenon at the time of each such event.

No, the cause must be specific to our solar system. There must be found some quality or aspect of the solar system's existence that acts as the catalyst or initiator of such events; something that generates, at regular intervals, such an excess of energy that the result causes a fundamental imbalance in the orbital paths of the planets so that interactions between them take place. At times, these interactions could take place between other bodies without directly involving the earth except to create conditions that bring about magnetic changes and moderate lithospheric disruption. At other times, more direct contacts might be made with accompanying exchanges of matter and concomitant cataclysmic disruption.

I believe that the clues to the source, or catalyst, of this activity can be found in scientific observations of the Sun, which is not to say that current theories relating to these activities are in any way complete or satisfactory.

The processes which turn a planet into a magnet are poorly understood. It has been assumed that this magnetism, a concomitant of electricity, is generated by motion. In the Sun, it is conjectured that this motion is of gases. The same is assumed for Jupiter. In the case of earth, it is assumed that the motive generator is the molten core eddying beneath the lithosphere. If this is so, then we have problems with Mercury, which has an axial rotation period of 59 days (approximately), much too slow to generate electricity, yet it has a magnetic field. Additionally, this poses a problem with Saturn, which is spinning quite rapidly, yet evidences no apparent electromagnetism. (This, of course, may not be true and may only reflect observational deficiencies.)

Nevertheless, Venus has a dense, rapidly swirling gaseous envelope — and no appreciable magnetic field. And, due to the heat of Venus, it may be assumed that it has a molten core. However, the axial rotation of the planet is very slow — about 243 days. Mars, on the other hand, rotates on its axis at about the same rate as the earth. It has very little atmosphere, possibly just CO_2 — and no appreciable magnetic field.

If magnetism is concomitant to electricity, then we must consider another factor — consumption. In order for an electrical charge to maintain a continuous flow, it must be consumed. There must be a continuing situation wherein the negative electron flow passes into a positive deficit condition. There must be a *contact potential difference*. In addition, heat can affect the force attracting electrons to atoms. I would like to suggest that the planet Venus does not act as a magnet for the simple reason that it does not possess a contact potential difference. Mars also does not *consume* electricity. But what about the other planets?

The question is: Could it be possible for the electromagnetic force of any of the bodies of the solar system to be increased to the point that instability in their orbits occurs? Could they then be drawn together for an exchange of energy such as the exchange of photons between charged electrons?

When two electric particles approach each other, they come under the influence of their mutual electromagnetic fields, and forces operate between them. These forces cause the particles to deviate in their motion and the disturbance that one particle inflicts on the other must be transmitted in the form of photons. The exchange causes the two particles to scatter apart. Inside the nucleus of an atom, protons and neutrons are glued together by pions flitting back and forth between them. Normally they go unseen because no sooner are they created than they are absorbed by another particle within the nucleus. However if, somehow, energy is pumped into the system, a pion can fly out. Pions are violently unstable and rapidly decay into light particles called muons, which are identical to electrons in all ways except mass.

Niels Bohr, a Danish physicist who completed his doctorate in the summer of 1911, began to concentrate on the puzzle of the structure of the atom in 1912. He envisioned the atom as a miniature solar system with electrons moving around orbits in accordance with the laws of classical mechanics. However, this model could not be stable according to classical laws.

Einstein had already established the idea of quanta, though it was not generally accepted. Patching together some quantum theory and classical theory, Bohr concluded that electrons could not spin inward out of their orbits emitting radiation because they were only allowed to emit whole pieces of energy — quanta — not the continuous radiation required by classical theory. It is rather like an automatic teller machine that can only dispense money in specific denominations. It is not that one dollar and fifty cents doesn't exist; it is that the machine is not programmed to dispense that sum.

Each atom emits or absorbs energy with a very precise frequency and when they do this the electron jumps from one energy level to another. A jump from one state to another can occur either up or down. But just as energy that is admitted must be admitted in terms of definite quanta, so must these jumps be very precisely determined.

The energy levels of an atom can be thought of as a flight of steps. The depth of each of the steps is not equal in terms of energy. The top steps are closer together than the bottom ones. A transition from one level to another requires that an electron take in exactly the amount of energy required to move that step.

There is no in-between step and there is no way the electron can emit less than its quantum of energy.

The decay of an atom from an excited energy state to a state with less energy is very similar to the radioactive decay of an atom. No reason for radioactive decay or atomic energy transitions has ever been found. It seems that these changes occur entirely by chance on a statistical basis. An electron doesn't move from one energy level to another at any particular time for any particular reason. The lower energy level is more *desirable* for the atom statistically, so it is more likely that an electron will make such a move sooner or later, but there is no way to tell when.

An atom with three protons in its nucleus and three electrons outside the nucleus will have two of those electrons more tightly tied to the nucleus and one left over. This is because electrons form around the nucleus in something like energy 'shells.' The first shell stabilizes with two electrons. In our three-electron atom, the next shell with one electron is less stable. The innermost shell is full with two electrons; filled shells are more stable. Atoms *like* to have filled shells. The next shell level is full with eight electrons. If it is a carbon atom it only has four electrons in the outer shell but the shell *likes* to be full, therefore, the carbon atom likes to combine with other atoms and share electrons with them in its outer shell. (This is the reason that the carbon atom is the fundamental building block of life, chemically speaking.) In the case of hydrogen the single electron naturally sits in the lowest energy state available at the bottom of the quantum staircase. If it is excited by a collision it may jump up a step and then fall back, emitting a quantum of radiation. But when more electrons are added to the system, they do not all fall into the ground state; they distribute themselves up the steps of the staircase. The new electrons go into the shell with the least energy until it is full.

In the summer of 1925 a group of physicists wrote a joint paper discussing quantum variables — the equivalent in the quantum world of momentum and position. Werner Heisenberg did some inspired work with the mathematics, and was then joined by Max Born and Wolfgang Pauli in producing a definitive work describing these aspects. This work established that the mechanics must be described in dual terms, and that it was important in which order the terms were arranged. It was the beginning of what is known as *matrix mechanics.*

Matrices were totally unfamiliar to most mathematicians and physicists in 1925. However, the related equations included Newtonian mechanics. The significance of this occurred to a young theorist, Paul Dirac, who had turned to physics after his graduation in engineering. Unlike the other physicists of his time, he knew of mathematical quantities that behaved in the fashion of the matrix math, which was being developed to explain the behavior of the atom. The mathematics in question had been developed by William Hamilton a century earlier and had been used to calculate the orbits of bodies in a system, such as our solar system, where there are several interacting planets. The equations developed by Hamilton, which proved so useful in quantum mechanics, had their origin in a 19th-century attempt to unify the wave and particle theories of light. In one mathematical framework he set up equations that could be used to describe both the motion of a wave and the motion of a particle. It is interesting to conjecture that since these equations were used to calculate the motions of the planets, as well as the activities of the atom, that it may be precipitate to assume that the atom bears no resemblance to the solar system. In this sense, we may look at the bodies of the solar system more truly as quantum particles and evaluate their activities in similar terms. That this fact has not occurred to accepted contemporary schools of physical theory seems rather limited. Just as we have discussed the collapse of the wave function, which makes the electron 'real,' so might our entire solar system be attributed to the collapse of the wave function on a grand scale. If this is the case then it is entirely likely that electrons/planets can move from one level of energy to another. And as Velikovsky points out, relative to the size of the bodies of the solar system, this event would occur thousands of years apart. In keeping with the theories of quantum mechanics this event would be 'statistically probable' but not necessarily absolutely determined. An electron absorbing energy traps a free photon and becomes more excited. It then 'wants' to move to a less excited state and release the energy.

The equations of wave mechanics can be used to make predictions on a statistical basis. If we make an observation of a quantum system and get the answer to our measurement, then the equations can tell us what the probability is of getting other answers if we make the same observation a certain time later.

According to Einstein the energy of a particle that has mass M and momentum P was given by $E^2 = M^2C^4 + P^2C^2$ which reduces to $E = MC^2$ when the momentum is zero. But, what most people don't realize is that E can be positive or negative.

Electrons ought, according to theory, to fall into the lowest unoccupied energy state, but even the highest negative energy state is lower than the lowest positive energy state and vice versa. So why don't all electrons fall into the negative energy levels and disappear? Obviously because all of those states are full. A negative energy electron promoted into the real world would be normal in every respect but would leave a hole in the negative energy sea. Such a hole should behave like a positively charged particle. And, by the same line of thought, if the earth had been metamorphosed into an extremely low-level negative energy state in the distant past, wouldn't it be possible for it to have transformed several times in the direction of the positive energy levels, as evidenced by cataclysms of the past, with the final jump before us in which we move into an entirely different state of being — that of the positive state? Or, perhaps we started at a low-level positive energy state, have moved up several steps by absorbing energies, and are preparing to release all of this in a big jump to the lowest level where we are at rest?

A large nucleus can be thought of as wobbling in and out, changing from a sphere to something like a fat dumbbell and back again. If energy is put into such a nucleus, the oscillation can become so extreme that it breaks the nucleus into two smaller nuclei and a smattering of tiny droplets — alpha and beta particles and neutrons.

For some nuclei this splitting can be triggered by the collision of a fast moving neutron with the nucleus. A chain reaction occurs when each nucleus fissions in this way producing enough neutrons to ensure that at least two more nuclei in its neighborhood also fission. Each fission releases about 200 MeV of energy and each one sets off several more. Left to run away exponentially, this is the process of the atomic bomb.

*　*　*

There are traces of all the elements that are the building blocks of our earth (and our bodies) in the Sun. The Sun, however, consists of about 90% hydrogen, which is not relative to the ratios contained within our bodies or our planet. The second most abundant element in the Sun is helium, which is the product of the thermonuclear reactions that result in the energy output of the Sun. The key to this energy conversion process is supposedly expressed in Einstein's theory of relativity. The amount of energy released by any given amount of hydrogen in the Sun is equal to that given amount multiplied by $186,000 \times 186,000$ per second. This means, according to current theories, that the Sun converts about 700 million tons of hydrogen into 695 million tons of helium each second, releasing 5 million tons of its mass as energy which is expressed as a multiple of the speed of light squared. Considering that the present ratio is 90% hydrogen to all other elements, this gives us a good indication of the mass and survivability of the Sun.

In addition to emitting photons of light in the thermonuclear reactions within the Sun, some of this energy is also emitted as plasma, or fragments of the Sun itself in the form of hot gases or charged particles. This plasma gusts through the solar system at speeds up to a million miles per hour — a continuing bombardment of electrons, protons and atomic nuclei. This solar wind crashes into our ionosphere and some of it is discharged to the planet as aurorae and other types of electrical storms. It is thought that some of it spirals in at the polar regions and accumulates within the planet. *This is, in effect, an electrical current flowing through space, which is being consumed by our planet.*

The Sun is most peculiar indeed! The core temperature of the Sun is estimated to be about 15 million degrees Centigrade while the surface temperature is about 5,000 degrees. At the same time, the temperature of the corona is nearly two million degrees. This translates into the figurative representation of a hydrogen bomb encased in ice with a fire burning on the surface of the ice. Very strange indeed

Additionally, the Sun pulsates, or oscillates. It is conjectured that sunspots are points of magnetic concentration and that they are also areas of *cooler* temperatures that contrast darkly with the light-emitting corona. On the other hand, solar flares, areas of greater heat and more intense radiation — a concentrated, violent explosion on the Sun's surface — are *also* estimated to be zones of intense magnetic activity. It is thought that somehow, magnetic lines of force become twisted in the swirling, boiling mass of the Sun's gasses, and concentrate, growing cooler and emitting less light. At a certain point, critical mass is reached and the energy is released in a massive explosion.

Sunspots and solar flare activity generally occur at regular intervals and have direct effects upon the activities of the earth's electromagnetic field. A solar flare, which occurred on September 1, 1859, so charged the earth's magnetic field that the aurora was seen in Kansas and Hawaii. At the same time, telegraph wires all over the globe tapped incoherently, spontaneously, and telegraph operators found that they could send messages without using their batteries due to the fact that *the atmosphere was so charged.* All this from a single flare.

The solar constant has been measured by satellite since 1980 and has revealed an average decline of .004% in temperature per year. It is too soon to make conjectures about this figure, but scientists are not letting that stop them. Some are already predicting an ice age. (Meanwhile, the greenhouse effect is supposed to roast us and melt the ice caps!)

A range of oscillations has been detected on the surface of the Sun. Some of these demonstrate periods of from 5 to 70 minutes. The eleven- and twenty-two-year sunspot cycles are widely recognized and demonstrate a multiplicity of frequencies of vibration within the substance of the Sun. There is a definite order and periodicity in this activity and I would like to suggest that somehow this relates to the solution of the cyclical Great Dyings. If the Sun has oscillations ranging from minutes to years in fluctuation, it would not be impossible for it to have major activity at intervals of thousands or tens of thousands of years. If this were the case, and the Sun were to somehow suddenly emit vast quantities of energy over and above the fluctuations we are aware of, this could affect the bodies of the solar system in many ways, including disruption of orbital paths and exchanging of energies.

The exact mechanics are uncertain — perhaps this excess of energy will stimulate a limited thermonuclear reaction on Jupiter, which would expel a mass similar to Venus. Jupiter is composed of primarily hydrogen and helium. Some astronomers have suggested that Jupiter is a still-born star — unable to achieve the size and temperature required to ignite a nuclear furnace. It could be that the great red spot is a storm over the caldera of a volcano beyond our imagining. Or perhaps the resultant excess of electromagnetic energy might pull Venus out of her customary orbit or cause any of the other planets to break out and run amok in the solar system.

To overcome Jupiter's massive gravity, an escape velocity of over 60 km per second would have to be achieved. Is this possible? The explosion of Krakatoa generated 10^{28} ergs of energy, which would have been sufficient to send a fairly large chunk of the earth into space.

"Jupiter is a planet of awesome energies radiating almost three times more energy than it gets from the sun. Pioneer 10 measured an enormously powerful magnetic field about the planet which held within its force-fields radiation belts of enormous energies; fluxes of high energy electrons in such vast number that they exceeded by a thousand times the most optimistic of earth-based predictions.

... Yet none of the newly discovered information about Jupiter surprise(d) Velikovsky, for he believe(d) it confirm(d) his predictions and neatly fit the demands of his theory.

Not the least of these predictions was that Jupiter's core would have a high temperature. This comment was made at a time when astronomy textbooks were asserting that Jupiter was an icy planet with a surface temperature about -150 degrees Fahrenheit.

Pioneer's temperature readings of -207 degrees F recorded at Jupiter's cloud tops seemed to bear that out, for the temperatures would tend to drop even more at the upper reaches of the atmosphere, where whatever radiant energies were stored at the core would be rapidly dissipated as they percolated through the 25,000 mile deep atmosphere. But as the space craft probed deeper it recorded a temperature of 260 degrees F, or 48 degrees above the boiling point of water, only 125 miles down into the Jovian atmosphere. Not much further down, on the night side, where no sunlight could reach, the temperature soared to 800 degrees. This discrepancy astonished the scientists analyzing the data, and some estimated that at its core Jupiter might have a temperature of 2,500 degrees F, or even as much as 10,000 degrees F.

As Pioneer 10 passed by Jupiter it clocked the turbulent, seething clouds of its atmosphere whirling around the planet at an incredible 22,000 miles per hour. Here then, according to Velikovsky, on a massive, seething planet where turbulent clouds triggered lightning discharges equal to the power of two exploding hydrogen bombs, where radiation 10 million times stronger than those girdling the earth fling unimaginable energy forces about, Jupiter, the emperor of the planets and the chief of ancient man's deities underwent a planetary convulsion and hurled a planet sized chunk of itself into space." [42]

While many scientists consider this theory impossible because of the unimaginable energy needed, Dr. Sergei Vsekhsvyatskii, Director of the Kiev University Observatory, argues that enormous energies are generated as planets eject pieces of themselves into space. The fact that the presence of ammonia-methane ice has been verified in comet nuclei and that the same ice mixture has often been found on earth, Mars, and some satellites of Jupiter leads him to the conclusion that *comets are eruption ejecta of the planets.*

If one looks at a table of the planets, we find the following relationships: In millions of miles, there are differences between the planets which are, in order, 31, 25, 47, 342, 403, 896, 1,043, 872. The numerical relationship between the distances of the planets from the Sun is explained by the Titius-Bode law which goes as follows: Take the series of numbers 0, 3, 6, 12, 24, 48, 96 — where each number (except the first and second) is twice the preceding number. Add 4 to each, and the result is the series 4, 7, 10, 16, 28, 52, 100, 200, 400, 800. Taking the earth's distance from the Sun as 10 units, this series gives, to a great degree of accuracy, the distances of the planets from the Sun. The planets Mercury and Venus fall at 4 and 7 respectively; Mars is at 15 (very close to the predicted 16), Jupiter at 52 and Saturn at 95 (close to the predicted 100). But there is no planet between Mars and Jupiter, at the value 28 predicted by the Titius-Bode law.

I hope you noticed right away that the law holds up *except* for the first and second numbers *and* the 4th and 7th, as well as the missing planet in space number 5. So, we have a 'law' for 7 bodies, which holds up only for only two of them! And, it is interesting that this 'law' is based upon arbitrary units of measure related strictly to a geocentric view of the Solar System. How convenient! If our solar system were to obey this law we would find Mercury at 37.2 million miles from the Sun; it is close at 36. Venus would be at 65.1 million miles; it is only off by 2.1 million miles at 67.1. Earth is, of course at the correct distance of around 93 (92.9), since *it is the unit of measure.* Mars should be found at 148.8 million miles, but somewhere lost 7.3 million miles at 141.5. There should be a planet at 260.4 million miles but there isn't. The asteroid belt actually begins at 200 million miles and extends for 100 million miles farther. Next, Jupiter should be at 483.6 but is actually at 483.4. Here we have a very close match considering the distances under discussion. Saturn should be found at 930 million miles and is actually at 886.7 — a difference of 43.3 million miles. Uranus should be at 1,882.8 million miles and is actually found 40.1 million miles closer. Neptune is causing a real upset in the law by being 514.1 million miles closer than the 3,208.6 million miles distant from the Sun it ought to be. And Pluto is a real problem having lost 3,513.5 million miles, crowding in at 3,666.1 million miles from the Sun. So, it can clearly be seen that the Titius-Bode 'law' is not a law at all, but merely a feeble attempt to explain a quantum state in classical terms. I think we need to look at this from a different perspective and, hopefully, someone will come up with something that works a lot better than what Johann Bode and Johann Titius came up with.

Looking at the problem strictly in terms describing the distances separating the bodies, we find several interesting points. *Except* for the distance on either side of Venus, all the distances *increase* dramatically until we come to Pluto. It is as though Venus were shoved in as an afterthought. This could represent a fundamental instability relating to 'energy shells' and could be an indication that a more natural, or stable order will be sought within our solar system. In fact, the inner planets could reflect the inner energy shell and the outer planets an outer shell. If this is the case, then we have what is, upon initial examination, an imbalanced state within both shells. However, this may not be the case. It would depend upon what relationships might be discovered in quantum terms relating to the bodies of the solar system. There may, in fact, be three shells: the inner planets, the Jovian pair of giants, and the outer planets. In this case, there are five bodies, including the earth's moon, in the inner shell. Jupiter and Saturn with their many satellites in the middle shell, and Uranus, Neptune and Pluto in the outer shell. Jupiter might be a more fruitful point of reference in determining where planets ought to be both inside and outside its orbit. Of course size and mass would be an important consideration in orbital placement. What seems abundantly clear is that, no matter what mathematics one uses, the present orbits are highly unstable and it would not take much to stimulate interaction between the planets. If two or more planets were to suddenly expand their electromagnetic fields, they might be initially attracted to one another for the purpose of exchanging energies, though they would not collide because the exchange would cause them to fly apart.

This, I think, while not perfect, may be a closer explanation of why and how there have been, and will continue to be, Great Dyings on the planet earth. And, there is a great deal of testimony to support this concept, or something very similar, as I will relate further on. And, in terms of the earth, specifically, such a surge of radiation could not only alter the quantum nature of matter, it could be the means by which genetic mutations take place — another key to punctuated equilibrium.

*   *   *

Science has postulated a slow and gradual evolutionary process and has striven with all its might to conform all data to that mold. That which does not fit is reinterpreted or ignored. It is assumed that not only have we evolved as human beings from some primate ancestor, but that we are evolving as a culture as well. Science has given us the space program, laser, television, penicillin, sulfa-drugs, and a host of other useful developments, which would seem to make our lives more tolerable and fruitful. However, we can easily see that this is not the case.

After three centuries of domination by science, it could be said that never before has man been so precariously poised on the brink of such total destruction. Our lives, as individuals and groups and cultures, are steadily deteriorating. The air we breathe and the water we drink is polluted almost beyond endurance. Our foods are loaded with substances that contribute very little to nourishment, and may, in fact, be injurious to our health. Stress and tension have become an accepted part of life and can be shown to have killed millions. Hatred, envy, greed and strife multiply exponentially. Crime increases nine times faster than the population. We swallow endless quantities of pills to wake up, go to sleep, get the job done, calm our nerves and make us feel good. The inhabitants of the earth spend more money on recreational drugs than they spend on housing, clothing, food, education or any other product or service. (This amounts to half a trillion dollars annually.) Multiplied millions of people are without adequate food or shelter. Two hundred forty million children will starve to death before the year 2000 while we pay entertainment idols millions of dollars to perform for us while we hustle to obtain the cream, soap or toothpaste that will make us sexy and appealing.

Is this the acme of scientific philosophy and achievement?

But, we are promised that all this will change. In practical terms, what could this mean?

Organic life on earth can be viewed as an accumulator of electrical potential, either positive or negative, depending upon the general conditions prevalent at any given time. These ideas were known to the ancients and they attempted to express them in terms of good and evil.

Everything living has been shown to generate electrical potentials, which can be measured by various instruments. But what about unknown types of energy? Nils O. Jacobson wrote in *Life Without Death*: *"We could picture the brain as a transformer station, a device which transforms 'low tension' physical energy to 'high tension' psychic energy, or the reverse."* [43]

It could be said that all actions and interactions of humans and animals and even plants and inorganic matter on the earth could, conceivably, contribute to the build-up of static potential. This potential, in the fashion of all electrical charges, must at some point be released.

However, if the Sun were to radiate a sudden surge of energy by infinitesimally expanding its surface as a result of cyclical oscillations, the earth would become so charged as an electromagnet that it might have an appreciable effect on the orbits of those bodies closest to it. It would, in other words, manifest this attraction and draw to itself an oppositely charged, or neutral body to effect this release. And, relative to the size of the bodies of the solar system, compared to the size of the parts of an atom, which effects such emissions in fractions of seconds, this event may take some time to manifest. In addition, it may go on for some time. And, as in the case of atomic interactions, this emission may have fundamental effects regarding alterations of quantum realities.

This idea may be considered far-fetched, so I would like to add that there is at least as much support of a factual nature for what I have stated as there is for any of a number of other hypotheses relating to this subject. In addition, there is considerable psychic evidence to support this thesis.

I Corinthians says: *"For since [it was] through a man that death [came into the world, it is] also through a Man that the Resurrection of the dead [has come]. For just as in Adam all people die, so also shall all in Christ be made alive. But each in his own rank and turn; Christ (the Messiah) [is] the firstfruits..."* [44] (15:20,23)

These verses centers the idea of metamorphosis upon the example of Christ. They also indicate that man existed in a very different state prior to the Edenic 'fall.' This 'fall' is the allegory of cosmic catastrophe brought on by energy states created in mankind through certain activities. Examining the evidence relating to the resurrection of Christ may give us some clue as to our condition after this metamorphosis as it is indicated that we shall be 'as He is.' Paul describes this estate quite clearly:

"Thus it is written, The first man Adam became a living being (an individual personality); the last Adam (Christ) became a life-giving spirit [restoring the dead to life]. But it is not the spiritual life which came first, but the physical and then the spiritual. The first man [was] from out of earth, made of dust (earthly-minded); the second Man [is] the Lord from out of heaven. ... But I tell you this, brethren, flesh and blood cannot inherit or share in the Kingdom of God; nor does the perishable (that which is decaying) inherit or share in the imperishable (the immortal). Take notice! I tell you a mystery (a secret truth, an event decreed by the hidden purpose or counsel of God). We shall not all fall asleep, but we shall all be changed. In a moment, in the twinkling of an eye, at the last trumpet call. For a trumpet will sound, and the dead will be raised imperishable (free and immune from decay), and we shall be changed. ... Now sin is the sting of death..." [45]

Here we have a clear description of metamorphosis. I would also like to point out that the references to the dead being raised are made clear in the line *"sin is the sting of death."* The original death was a loss of spiritual consciousness and ability to act at 'higher' levels of vibration. The story of the serpent's temptation and the eating of the fruit of the tree of knowledge of good and evil describes man's fascination with material existence. 'Eating' symbolizes partaking of, or assimilating within, the lower vibratory rate so that man could no longer communicate with God. When Paul says that the dead will be 'raised,' he means quite literally that the frequencies of those who have been existing in a state of 'death,' or lower vibration, will be elevated to the degree that they will once again be able to experience their full spiritual nature exactly as Christ did.

Edgar Cayce said that mankind was originally a spirit and that he became fascinated by the evolving creatures on the earth. In great numbers, spirit beings thrust themselves into physical bodies to revel in material experiences. By engaging in sexual activity, which exchanges energy designed to create on a physical level, they became identified with that energy and lost the ability, through the intensity of the activity, to freely move in and out of materiality. As the energy levels of great masses of souls were moved to higher *physical* energy states, quantumly speaking, much energy was consumed which built up into a deficit, which then brought on the first great planetary exchange. When *"God walked in the garden"* the writer was expressing an initial extraterrestrial interaction, which occurred while great numbers of souls were in bodies. The souls, having consumed energy through sexual activity, which then combined with and added to the electromagnetic potentials exchanged between bodies of the solar system, were no longer able to draw upon it to elevate their own levels and withdraw from the body. They became frightened, and *"knew that they were naked."* (This condition of nakedness will be discussed more thoroughly in a later chapter.)

The cosmic interaction at the time of the 'fall' is what brought to the earth our moon. This is the angel with the flaming sword barring return to the Edenic state. As long as the moon is closely associated with the earth, it assists in maintaining the more active physical vibratory rate. It is, in fact, a quantum particle of the solar system/atom.

The mechanism by which this metamorphosis is accomplished, as well as the potential abilities of the resultant 'glorified' body, are hypothesized in an essay by David Vaughan, author of *A Faith for the New Age.* Mr. Vaughn writes:

"Controversy over the purported resurrection of Jesus has particularly centered around the allegedly empty tomb and around the 'appearance' recorded in the Gospels and by St. Paul in I Corinthians, Chapter 15.

Sceptics have asked: Did the women and other disciples go to the wrong tomb on that first Easter Sunday? Or was the corpse removed from the tomb provided by Joseph of Arimathea either by Jewish guards, or Roman soldiers, or the gardener, or by a group of disciples? ... Did Jesus recover consciousness from a deep coma, somehow escape from the sealed tomb, and at least live long enough for some of his followers to claim that they had seen him risen from the dead?

Some scholars have suggested that the frightened, dispirited disciples so longed to see their dead Master risen again, as he had promised, that they suffered subjective hallucinations — some singly, some collectively — sincerely believing that Jesus had been miraculously resurrected by God. Some theologians and lay Christians believe that, in order to revive the morale of the disciples sufficiently to inspire them to found a new sect within Judaism that would soon burst forth as the Christian Church, either God himself or Jesus, from beyond the grave, induced objective hallucinations or apparitional experiences in many who had known the Master in the flesh.

Many today believe that the 'clean shroud' which Joseph purchased is the very cloth which was brought to Turin Cathedral in 1579, and whose whereabouts before that in France is precisely known as far back as 1353. There are strong but not conclusive historical links to identify that particular cloth with 'the shroud in which Our Lord was wrapped' that Robert de Clari, chronicler of the Fourth Crusade saw displayed weekly on Fridays at a Constantinople monastery in 1203.

Fr. Francis Filas, S.J., who in 1979, looking at the eye area of an Enrie negative of the Shroud, reckoned that he could make out four letters, UCAI, as from the inscription on a tiny coin placed over the right eye. In 1980 he claimed that the coin over the right eye was a lituus dileption issued in A.D. 24-25 by Valerius Gratus, and by 1983, that the coin over the left eye was a lituus dileption of A.D. 29-30 of Pontius Pilate. Dr. Robert Haralick's use of digital enhancement techniques seem to confirm these hypotheses.

The Gospels certainly refer to grave-clothes being found in the empty tomb...

The Turin Shroud bears a series of brownish marks now known to be the three-dimensional, negative image, frontal and dorsal, of a crucified man about 5 feet 11 inches tall, with all the wounds which the Gospels relate as suffered by Jesus.

... Scientists are agreed in ruling out the application of paint, dyes, stains, etc., by some medieval artist..." [46]

The suggestions from among the scientists studying the Shroud as to how the marks were made include *"some brief but intense burst of 'photographic radiation' involving heat sufficient to scorch but not burn the cloth, or a thermonuclear flash photolysis in a millisecond of time."* [47]

Mr. Vaughan goes on to conjecture that:

"... some 36—39 hours after death, Jesus returned to his tomb in his spiritual body. Then, either lying flush with, or standing tangentially at the feet or head of his corpse, he exercised his spiritual power of mind over matter to draw the molecules of the dead flesh into his spiritual body by mysteriously raising the 'frequency' of the substance of the former to that of the latter. In this process — strictly one of transmaterialization rather than of de-materialization — the atoms would have passed through the Shroud, imparting what Mr. Geoffrey Ashe has called 'a kind of radiance, or incandescence partially analogous to heat'.

The Shroud, itself would have been left empty and virtually undisturbed. Many Christians believe that what made the disciples 'see and believe' (Luke 24:12), was the position and state of the grave clothes, convincingly demonstrating that the corpse could not have been separated from them by any outside agent, but must have mysteriously evaporated or evanesced through the shroud, which now lay quite undisturbed but no longer enclosing a body.

Subsequently, Jesus would have been able mentally to lower the frequency of his dual 'resurrection body' in order to appear, speak, eat and even be handled in the presence of his disciples, or to raise it in order to vanish, as at the inn at Emmaus or at the moment of Ascension." [48]

And, as Mr. Vaughn says, so much for speculation. But, concerning the Shroud itself, and its possible importance as evidence for the reality of the resurrection and, as a clue to what might be the 'glorified state' of mankind, supposing an event of metamorphosis takes place, as I believe it will, we can make some logical deductions with a list slightly adapted from an article by Frank Tribbe.

1. *Scientists are agreed that they don't know how the image on the Shroud was made. Unless we accept a "spiritual event", we have no explanation.*
2. *Had Christ's opponents stolen the body, they would have used it to quell the activities of the early Christians.*
3. *"Considering the high percentage of martyrs among the early Church leaders, it is inconceivable that the Peters and Thomases would have suddenly switched from being deniers and doubters to become one of the bravest and most persistent groups of advocates the world has ever known."*
4. *Scientific research into the nature and uses of hypnosis make it extremely fantastic to theorize mass hallucination.*
5. *Unanimous opinion of the scientists studying the Shroud is that the numerous signs of rigor mortis in the Body of the man of the Shroud, make certain the fact that he died on his cross!*
6. *If we cannot accept the identity of Jesus as the Man of the Shroud, considering the evidence, then "We should bend all efforts of our civilization to identify the Man of the Shroud and put him in the place of Jesus the Christ?"* [49]

Since it is becoming increasingly apparent that Jesus must have meant what He said about metamorphosis and a coming 'kingdom,' perhaps we should make every effort to find out the details?

The seemingly obscure remark made by Jesus: *"Wherever there is a fallen body, there the vultures will flock together..."*, [50] becomes more comprehensible when considered in the context of the earth as an accumulator of electrical potential and this potential being communicated to the other bodies of the system as the stench of carrion. The events of the earth in terms of political oppression, ecological destruction and spiritual decay, create the energy imbalances which will attract the needed event to cleanse the earth and, at the same time, metamorphose those who are in a spiritual state suitable to make this change act upon them in a positive manner different from the 'lost.'

In this section I have examined a theoretical underlying principle that binds the many elements of prophetic literature together and makes it reasonable and somewhat comprehensible. The teachings of Christ, if followed, would serve to balance the physical electrical energy as received from the Sun. It is this consumption, this conversion of energies, which is defined in terms of good and evil. Evil is that which manifests as the wrong kinds of energies; good is defined as that which manifests the right kinds of energies. It is in this sense that Christ taught that the thought was the equivalent of the deed, for the brain manifests electrical impulses and may, in fact, be constantly converting one type of energy to another. It is established that certain wavelengths are produced in the brain at different times and during different activities. The most energetic of these relate to physical activity and certain thought patterns. The slowest waves relate to periods of sleep, deep relaxation, peaceful reverie and creativity.

It could be theorized that accumulation of these energies takes place either at some outer point of the atmosphere of the earth or within the earth itself. On the other hand, it could be a permeating effect that is location specific — in this sense, the site of a great massacre or a heinous crime would retain the energies, making that area more subject to potential exchange in terms of electricity.

In any event, there are energies interacting in our universe and on our planet about which we know nothing. We have observed the atom within limits and the solar system within limits. And knowing that the laws which apply to atoms apply in a larger sense to chemicals to compounds and to man himself, we must see that the same laws apply to the solar system, the galaxy and the cosmos itself. We do not know what 'knowing' is behind the quantum particles' ability to select a specific reality. We do not know what 'knowing' is behind our individual and group realities. But if observation is the key to the collapse of the waveform and thought is thereby the creator of our reality, then the accumulation of centuries of thought may act to create a specific probability. And those who believe that they can create a positive transition may find that their focus merely increases the force of this probability because it is necessary that any transition obey the laws of physics as we know them. Therefore in order for any major change to take place, cosmic energies must be exchanged. This will, of necessity, be cataclysmic.

Most nations are now faced with a future of shortages of virtually all the resources considered necessary for an industrial society to exist. The vast oil resources of the Middle East will be gone within thirty years at the present rate of use. Copper reserves are now in short supply. The planet is rapidly being deforested. Clean air? Clean water? Food? Such ultimate shortages are already a grim fact of life in most of the world. The situation can only grow worse. There are essentially no food reserves anywhere in the world. And there is nothing anyone can do about it. There is no, I repeat, no conceivable technological solution to the problems we face. We will either die from disease, decay or disruption or we will transform.

However, an extraterrestrial interaction between the earth and another body in the cosmos might act upon our planet in very beneficial ways. In addition to quantum alterations, we might capture additional resources. We will certainly reduce our population by about 90% and there may be other benefits of which we are not aware. It is entirely possible that our orbital orientation will be changed; we may move to a new orbital position. At the same time, we may acquire a different atmospheric mix of gases that would be far more beneficial to life and conducive to extremely long lifespans. We may even acquire another moon or lose the one we have.

So we may conclude with the words of biologist J. B. S. Haldane: *"the Universe is not only queerer than we suppose, but queerer than we can suppose."*[51]

Chapter Five

About the time of the end, a body of men will be raised up who will turn their attention to the prophecies and insist upon their literal interpretation, in the midst of much clamor and opposition.

— Sir Isaac Newton.

There has long been a great deal of confusing commentary on the part of theologians relating to the prophecies of the Old Testament. One or another group of them will attribute these pronouncements, without regard to obvious contradictions, to a single or 'multi-stage' end time event in our future. This trying to fit all of these confusing elements into one single event has given rise to various schools of thought defined variously as 'Pre-Tribulation Rapture Theory,' 'Mid-Tribulation Rapture Theory,' 'Post-Tribulation Rapture Theory,' 'No Rapture Tribulation Theory,' and on and on. Naturally, each group claims to have a 'hot-line' to God, and put forth their explanation as the one true revelation.

However, if Velikovsky is correct in his analysis, and there were actually numerous cosmic interactions during the times that the Hebrew people were solidifying as an ethnic identity, this would present us with a reasonable foundation for all this disparity. In other words, all the descriptions were, in fact, true in possibility due to the fact that the Hebrew prophets watched the skies and were aware of the regular return, and potential for destruction, of the errant Venus.

The prophets of the Hebrews were, undoubtedly, well versed in the lore of the stars — and we have evidence of this in their extensive Kabbalistic writings. But, even the secret traditions and practices were alluded to in the Bible, and it is unfortunate that this has been lost to the Christian Church, which generally tends to ignore Jesus' heritage as a Jew.

The book of Genesis states: *"Let there be lights in the expanse of the heavens to ... be for signs and tokens and seasons..."* [52] What is a sign but a portent and what is a token but an ideological representation of something? Ecclesiastes says: *"To everything there is a season..."* [53] which plainly indicates that a knowledge of the stars would help one to know the proper time to perform any act from birth to death. Psalm 19 further amplifies

101

the study of the stars: *"The heavens declare the glory of God; and the firmament shows and proclaims His handiwork. Day after day pours forth speech, and night after night shows forth knowledge. There is no speech nor spoken word [from the stars]; their voice is not heard. Yet their voice goes out through all the earth, their sayings to the end of the world."* [54]

Thus we may understand that the Hebrew prophets made their predictions based upon observation of planets and comets, the means by which God speaks to man; not necessarily the only means, but an accepted and accurate one — a science perhaps brought with Abraham from Chaldea, and surely a major field of study for Moses in the Egyptian court.

Every time the errant comet Venus returned, at approximately fifty-year intervals, the Hebrew prophets pronounced balefully upon the sins of their enemies, and the shortcomings of their own people as well. Sometimes the comet passed closer than others and the prophets had a 'hit,' literally; at others it was a miss and the people celebrated their deliverance. Thus arose the custom of the Jewish Jubilees. It also tended to give stature and power to the priestly class who undoubtedly claimed credit for averting the disaster.

At the same time the Hebrews were using their knowledge of the stars to keep the people in line, other peoples around the globe were doing likewise; sacrificing maidens and infants and strong warriors to appease the goddess in all her varied forms and identities.

After a final, dramatic and soul-searing encounter in the heavens between the cometary Venus and the planet Mars, Venus was precipitated into a stable orbit and the cosmic battle became the foundation for the legends and fables the world over.

Isaiah wrote: *"How art thou fallen from Heaven, O Lucifer, son of the morning! How art thou cut down to the ground, which didst weaken the nations!"* [55] Lucifer, or Light Bearer, is an allusion to the angel of passage, who went before the Hebrews as a pillar of fire and smoke — an obvious description of a nearby comet. And, as Velikovsky asks, what could there be about the beautiful Morning Star to make one equate it with terror and 'weakening' of the nations? (Decimation of population.) Why should it live in legends the world over as an evil power? It is interesting to note that Venus is never more than 48 degrees above the horizon — cut low to the ground, indeed!

The Bible clearly states that worship of planets and images representing them was common even among the Israelites. And, given the probable circumstances, we can understand why. The events of the

Exodus had such an incredible impact upon the Jewish people that it is mentioned dozens of times throughout the scriptures. It could be said to be the single most important event in the long history of these beleaguered people. It was the Exodus that saved them, as a nation, from assimilation, annihilation, and historical obscurity. It was the Exodus that planted the seeds of chosenness and knitted threads of national identity into bonds strong enough to withstand centuries of oppression and dispersion. And, since their national identity was created by this event — while the identities of many other peoples were obliterated from the face of the earth by the same event — who are we to say that this was not part of a great and noble intent on the part of the intelligence of the cosmos?

Thus, it is easy to see why, after the passage of years and many retellings of the events, the agents of transformation became anthropomorphized and took the forms we find today. The comet became an angel and Moses, the hero of the day, parted the Sea with his rod.

Is it conceivable that this event, recorded as unmitigated disaster by every culture of antiquity the world over, could be:

1. mythical;
2. localized disturbances exaggerated all out of proportion in the retelling;
3. hocus pocus — mass hypnosis used to dazzle and control ignorant slaves?

If one considers assorted other 'cataclysmic' events, it becomes immediately obvious that the tendency of man is to quickly forget disasters of even the recent past. Except for those who participated or who were witnesses, even World War II, an event merely fifty years past, has taken on a dream-like quality for the newer generations. The trials and tribulations of their elders are simply not relevant or important to them. There are many today who debate the authenticity of many of the events of this unspeakable abomination in our time! Who knows how future generations will perceive this 'War to End All Wars?' Naturally, the memories of the residents of Nagasaki and Hiroshima will differ considerably from the memories of the German people and even the Jews. One thing that seems to be forgotten already is that Hitler was responsible for the deaths of over forty-five million *other* people besides the Jews.

Thus we may understand how easily cataclysmic events may be rendered as subjective and subsequently mythologized. Also, we must acknowledge that these events must have been world-shaking — in a literal sense — to have received and retained the emphasis they still have. An annual flooding of the Nile, a solar eclipse, a severe hailstorm, would hardly have imprinted themselves on a world consciousness in the manner of the events of the time of the Exodus. (The eruption of Mt. St. Helens is 'ancient history' to the young people of today!)

The Jewish people saw in the extraterrestrial events at the time of the Exodus, the Hand of God, for it was the means of their redemption. It became a time of thanksgiving. Other cultures experienced only destruction and terror and their stories and rites express fear and foreboding.

With this understanding in mind, we can follow along with Velikovsky as he recreates the events of the Exodus — the drama of the earth on a collision course with a comet of immense size; the awesome spectacle of continents sundered and sliding; land masses buckling, and global tidal waves sweeping over mountain fastnesses — while, *at the same time comparing* these descriptions of past disasters with descriptions of *prophesied future upheavals* which are couched in the same terms. I will start with Revelation and then we will move on to more contemporary prophecies.

Nearly all of the scriptural writings may be interpreted in terms of archetypes — including the book of Revelation. The story of the Hebrews exactly parallels the experiences of the individual seeker. But, to interpret strictly in archetypal terms is to lose the sense that reality forms as an idea first — and then takes shape in our three dimensions.

Revelation is given in several parts. Much of it is obviously meant to be veiled esoteric instructions to the seeker, but its reality as pure prophecy cannot be denied. Each part is layered one upon the other similar to the process of applying color in lithography. It is also much like the broadcast of a sporting event — with various camera angles, close-ups, and a running commentary. With these things in mind, we can examine the Exodus as interpreted by Immanuel Velikovsky and compare it with the prophecies of the Book of Revelation and attempt to understand the possible true meanings.

The first of the plagues of Egypt is listed as the turning of the waters into 'blood.' This was a result of the earth moving into the tail of the comet, which contained particles of 'ferruginous' pigment. The Bible records that there was *"blood throughout all the land of Egypt,"* [56] and that all the fish in the rivers died and the land stank from their putrefying bodies. Here, we can recall that the clay layer, found and analyzed by Alvarez, and determined to be comet dust was red, and contained concentrations of iridium.

Revelation says:

"The second angel emptied his bowl into the sea and it turned into blood like that of a corpse, and every living thing that was in the sea perished." [57]

The second, third, fourth and eighth plagues consisted of verminous infestations. The second was a plague of frogs overrunning the land and every household. The Bible says: *"the dust of the land became biting gnats or mosquitoes throughout all the land of Egypt,"* [58] *"and there came heavy and oppressive swarms of [blood-sucking gadflies],"* [59] *"And locusts came up over all the land of Egypt."* [60]

Velikovsky comments:

"When Venus sprang out of Jupiter as a comet and flew very close to the earth, it became entangled in the embrace of the earth. The internal heat developed by the earth and the scorching gases of the comet were in themselves sufficient to make the vermin of the earth propagate at a very feverish rate. Some of the plagues, like the plague of the frogs ... or the locusts, must be ascribed to such causes. Anyone who has experienced a khamsin (sirocco), an electrically charged wind blowing from the desert, knows how, during the few days that the wind blows, the ground around the villages begins to teem with vermin.

The question arises here whether or not the comet Venus infested the earth with vermin which it may have carried in its trailing atmosphere in the form of larvae together with stones and gases. It is significant that all around the world peoples have associated the planet Venus with flies." [61]

This leads us to two fairly obvious lines of thought. The first is the possibility of some form of organic life on Jupiter, the speculated source of Venus. Spectral analysis of Jupiter reveals the presence of methane and ammonia, byproducts of organic decomposition. Jupiter is also relatively warm, radiating 1.5 times as much energy as it receives from the Sun.

Recent discoveries of extremely bizarre life forms at the very bottom of our oceans, where it was thought that no life could exist, make it entirely possible that some equally bizarre, verminous life forms exist on the Jovian planets, feasting and multiplying on chemical energy.

The second thought is the possibility that the earth is continually being contaminated by microbes from cosmic space. When one considers the fact that viruses are inert crystals when dormant, waiting for moisture and heat to waken them and stimulate them to invade and grow, the idea of 'plagues from God' becomes more than a mere metaphor.

Revelation 9 says:

"... locusts came forth on the earth, and such power was granted them as the power the earth's scorpions have. They were told not to injure the herbage of the earth nor any green thing nor any tree, but only such human beings as do not have the seal of God on their foreheads. They were not permitted to kill them, but to torment them for five months; and the pain caused them was like the torture of a scorpion when it stings a person. And in those days people will seek death and will not find it; and they will yearn to die, but death evades and flees from them. The locusts resembled horses equipped for battle. On their heads was something like golden crowns. Their faces resembled the faces of people. They had hair like the hair of women, and their teeth were like lions' teeth. Their breastplates resembled breastplates made of iron, and the noise made by their wings was like the roar of a vast number of horse-drawn chariots going at full speed into battle. They have tails like scorpions, and they have stings, and in their tails lies the ability to hurt men for five months. Over them as king they have the angel of the Abyss (of the bottomless pit). In Hebrew his name is Abaddon, but in Greek he is called Appollyon [destroyer]." [62]

Many theologians have interpreted these remarkable vermin to be some type of modern war machine such as armored helicopters. However, due to the clues that these locusts do not kill, but only torment, and that this torment is limited to flesh and does not attack plants, indicates that they refer to some type of carnivorous insect or to microscopic vermin borne in on the tail of a comet or the many pieces into which a comet might break. They obviously have wings and an exoskeleton, and, coming on the tail of a 'falling star,' it seems that John is describing the propagation of swarms — huge masses — of flying, stinging, extraterrestrial vermin. The reference to Apollyon, the son of Jupiter, may indicate the source of this affliction. This could either be another comet born of Jupiter, or some further contact with Venus due to as yet unknown celestial mechanics.

Exodus 9 describes another effect of the dust of the comet's tail: *"there shall be a very severe plague ... And it shall become small dust over all the land of Egypt, and become boils breaking out in sores on man and beast in all the land."* [63] Having already mentioned the possible presence of viruses and radioactive elements in cosmic dust, this verse becomes self-explanatory.

Revelation predicts: *"So the first [angel] went and emptied his bowl on the earth, and foul and painful ulcers came on the people who were marked with the stamp of the beast and who did homage to his image."* [64] *"[A]nd people gnawed their tongues for the torment [of their excruciating distress and severe pain] And blasphemed God because of the anguish and their ulcers..."* [65] (16:10,11)

All of these effects — the sores, vermin, bacterial and viral pollution, blanketing of the land with hematoid pigment — relate only to the initial effects of the earth encountering the tail of a comet. Entering deeper into the tail brought on more disconcerting and disastrous effects until the climactic event of 'potential exchange,' the discharge of great bolts of lightning between the earth and the comet. Comet dust gave way to gravel and meteorites. *"[T]he Lord sent thunder and hail, and fire ran down to and along the ground, and the Lord rained hail upon the land of Egypt. So there was hail, and fire flashing continually in the midst of the weighty hail..."* [66]

As Velikovsky points out, the word here translated as 'hail,' is *barad*, a term which is generally used to refer to stones or meteorites. The fact that this was not a hail of ice is shown by the repeated references to fire mixed with the hail. The thunder further expresses the din made by the falling fireballs. No doubt an awesome spectacle.

The falling fire which *"ran down to and along the ground,"* forms the basis for a fascinating hypothesis presented by Dr. Velikovsky. As he points out in *Worlds in Collision,*

"The tails of the comets are composed mainly of carbon and hydrogen gases. Lacking oxygen, they do not burn in flight, but the inflammable gases, passing through an atmosphere containing oxygen, will be set on fire. If carbon and hydrogen gases, or a vapor of a composition of these two elements, enter the atmosphere in huge masses, a part of them will burn, binding all the oxygen available at the moment; the rest will escape combustion, but in swift transition will become liquid. Falling on the ground, the substance, if liquid, would sink into the pores of the sand and into the clefts between the rocks; falling on water, it would remain floating if the fire in the air is extinguished before new supplies of oxygen arrive from other regions.

The descent of a sticky fluid which came earthward and blazed with heavy smoke is recalled in the oral and written traditions of the inhabitants of both hemispheres." [67]

Velikovsky refers to dozens of such accounts of 'flaming fire,' rivers of fire, and rivers of naptha from sources the world over. And, it is a fact that all of the countries that have a tradition of 'fire-rain' actually have deposits of oil.

Here we have another reason the scientific community sought to silence Velikovsky. According to the 'Darwinian' notion of slow and gradual change, oil and coal are formed over millions of years from the remains of plant and animal life; or from hydrogen and carbon being combined slowly, under great pressure and heat within rock formations.

And so, the numerous artifacts of modern human (that is, not primitive) types, found within solid beds of coal, are ignored or attributed to fraud.

In any event, the Biblical narrative of the wandering in the desert mentions frequent instances of fire springing out of the earth. This could show that the ground was soaked with petroleum and that flammable vapors floated in the atmosphere. The Promised Land was described as flowing with 'milk and honey.' Petroleum and water certainly make a milky looking mixture. And, until recent years of avaricious consumption of petroleum, oil could often be found by merely poking a stick in the ground.

Do we find meteorites, rains of fire, and darkness in our future as predicted in Revelation? Chapter nine describes an event that can only be a barrage of fiery meteorites:

> "So the four angels, who had been in readiness for that hour in the appointed day, month and year, were liberated to destroy a third of mankind. The number of their troops of cavalry was twice ten thousand times ten thousand (200,000,000); I heard what their number was. And in [my] vision the horses and their riders appeared to me like this: the riders wore breastplates the color of fiery red and sapphire blue and sulphur yellow. The heads of the horses looked like lions' heads, and from their mouths there poured fire and smoke and sulphur. A third of mankind was killed ... by the fire and the smoke and the sulphur that poured from the mouths of the horses." [68]

The descriptions of these 'horsemen' of a celestial army are interesting for several reasons. Virgil referred to the little satellites of Mars as 'steeds,' so it is a more or less contemporary allusion. (How Virgil knew that Mars had satellites is a mystery, which Velikovsky deals with rather creatively, but it is not pertinent to the present discussion.) Nevertheless, Virgil referred to two chunks of cosmic rock as horses — might not John have done the same with a great many more chunks of cosmic rock — an entire cavalry of celestial horsemen? John describes the heads of these cosmic critters as being like lions' heads. The most striking thing about a lion is the mane of the male. And, the word comet comes from the word coma, which means 'hair.' Thus, a comet is a hairy one — or something with a head like a lion!

Further, the sheer size of this army makes it very unlikely that this is a literal human army, though generations of theologians have attempted to so interpret this. The most recent have ascribed the abilities of these hordes to various types of modern armaments. However, the passage, in its entirety could only be a description of a bombardment of meteorites accompanying a celestial encounter.

The reference to four angels being in command of this 'army' is somewhat puzzling if we understand angels in the Hebrew Kabbalistic tradition — that is as representing planets. Perhaps this refers to four larger bodies which explode upon entering earth's atmosphere and give birth to millions of fiery chunks which rain upon the earth, and that these bodies are not necessarily planet size — just sizeable chunks. Or, this reference could represent purely astrological influences — a certain position of the planets, which would be noted prior to this event.

Immediately following the fiery hail, the earth approached the body of the comet at the time of the Exodus. This brought about a disturbance — a slowing of the rotation of the earth. An event such as this would result in several effects. First, the slowing of the body of the earth, while the atmosphere — less amenable to gravitational force — would continue to sweep and swirl about the planet with great violence, carrying gases, dust, cinders and smoke. These two events are recorded in Exodus 10: "And the Lord turned a violent west wind ... and for three days a thick darkness was all over the land of Egypt." [69] This darkness was described as thick — an indication of the impenetrability due to the concentrations of dust and smoke.

Revelation describes a similar stasis of the planet followed by darkness:

> "Then the fourth [angel] emptied out his bowl upon the sun, and it was permitted to burn humanity with heat. People were severely burned by the fiery heat...Then the fifth [angel] emptied his bowl on the throne of the beast, and his kingdom was plunged in darkness... Then the sixth [angel] emptied his bowl on the mighty river Euphrates, and its water was dried up to make ready a road for the kings of the east." [70]

If the motion of the earth were appreciably slowed, the Sun would seem to stand still in the sky and the additional heat from this increased exposure might be quite uncomfortable. Additionally, this passage may indicate a propelling of the earth into closer proximity to the Sun, a new orbital path.

The tenth and final plague in Egypt was interpreted by Velikovsky as an earthquake. *"The earth, forced out of its regular motion, reacted to the close approach of the body of the comet: a major shock convulsed the lithosphere, and the area of the earthquake was the entire globe."* [71]

The entire earth rotates with the same angular velocity. If, theoretically, it was stopped or slowed appreciably, and this action did not upset the equality of the angular velocity, the earth would survive. It could, conceivably, even be flipped over or reversed. However, the fluid parts — the air and the water — would certainly have their angular velocity interrupted and great tidal waves and earthquakes would sweep the earth as lands sink or rise, broad plains shove themselves upward into new mountains and rushing waters carve canyons and new river beds. Civilizations would be destroyed, but not the globe!

Additionally, the stresses of the sliding and shifting of the tectonic plates would create great heat, or this energy might be converted to other forms of energy, including electrical. A discharge of great electrical magnitude might then take place between the earth and another celestial body.

An important clue to the tenth plague, as Velikovsky pointed out, is the use of the word *nogaf*, which means 'smote,' and is generally used to refer to a very violent blow. In the narrative of the Exodus, it is said that the Angel of the Lord passed over in the night and 'smote' the firstborn of all Egypt. The word *bkhor*, meaning 'firstborn,' is very likely a corruption of the word *bchor*, which means 'chosen' or 'elite.' Dr. Velikovsky postulates that the Egyptians were harder hit by this event, while the Israelite slaves survived, due to the simple fact that the former lived in grand houses of stone which collapsed on them, while the latter existed in 'earthquake-proof' flimsy wooden huts in a marshy area. In this sense, the affluent Egyptians, the 'chosen,' would have been the ones to suffer the greatest casualties in this 'plague,' while the Hebrews would be 'passed over' to a great extent.

The very idea of the 'Angel of the Lord' passing over vividly illustrates the idea of the passage of a great comet.

Revelation predicts:

> *"Then the seventh [angel] emptied out his bowl into the air, and a mighty voice came out of the sanctuary of heaven from the throne saying, It is done! And there followed lightning flashes, loud rumblings, peals of thunder, and a tremendous earthquake; nothing like it has ever occurred since men dwelt on the earth, so severe and far reaching was that earthquake ... the cities of the nations fell. ... And*

every island fled and no mountains could be found. And great hailstones, as heavy as a talent [between fifty and sixty pounds], of immense size, fell from the sky on the people; and men blasphemed God for the plague of the hail, so very great was [the torture] of that plague." [72]

Islands fleeing and mountains falling are pretty definitive statements of global cataclysm. And, in case you didn't notice, John described it as the worst the earth has ever experienced. Assuming that John was, at least, psychically aware of previous cataclysms, his description of the future disaster as the worst, definitely gives one something to think about.

So, as a jumping-off point, we find that the prophecies of Revelation are very similar to the descriptions of the plagues of Egypt at the time of the Exodus. But, what other corroboration do we find in the Bible, as well as other prophetic literature from that time to the present? And, why should it take until now to begin to understand these prophecies?

In Revelation 10:3—4, John is told to 'seal up' the words — which he certainly did in extremely obscure language and images. The Old Testament prophet, Daniel, was also given a gag order and told to *"shut up the words and seal the Book until the time of the end."* [73]

Daniel is one of the Old Testament prophets who can definitely be said to have prophesied an end time event beyond the birth of Jesus. Enigmatically he predicts: *"And at that time Michael shall arise, the great prince who defends and has charge of your people. And there shall be a time of trouble, straitness and distress, such as never was since there was a nation till that time. But at that time, your people shall be delivered... And the teachers and those who are wise shall shine like the brightness of the firmament, and those who turn many to righteousness like the stars..."* [74]

Jesus discourses on the subject at length in both Matthew and Luke.

"For then there will be great tribulation (affliction, distress, and oppression) such as has not been from the beginning of the world until now — no, and never will be [again]. And if those days had not been shortened, no human being would endure and survive, but for the sake of the elect those days will be shortened. ... For just as the lightning flashes from the east and shines and is seen as far as the west, so will the coming of the Son of Man be. ... Immediately after the tribulation of those days the sun will be darkened, and the moon will not shed its light, and the stars will fall from the sky, and the powers of the heavens will be shaken. Then the sign of the Son of Man will appear in the sky, and then all the tribes of the earth will mourn and beat their breasts and lament in anguish, and they will see the Son of Man coming on the clouds of heaven with power and great glory [in

brilliancy and splendor]. And He will send out His angels with a loud trumpet call, and they will gather His elect from the four winds, from one end of the universe to the other. ... when you see these signs ... you may know ... that He is near..." [75]

The passages from Daniel and Matthew contain several important clues that bear close scrutiny. The first is Daniel's statement that *"Michael shall arise..."*

"'An old tradition, dating back to Gaonic times, had it that there are seven archangels, each of whom is associated with a planet.' 'The seven archangels were believed to play an important part in the universal order through their association with the planets and the constellations. There is some variation, in the different versions, in the angels assigned to the planets." [76]

"The celestial struggle at the Sea of Passage is depicted in the familiar image of the Archangel Michael slaying the dragon... He ... is the forerunner of Shehina or God's presence, but as Lucifer, Michael falls from heaven and his hands are bound by God. All these attributes and acts of the Archangel Michael lead us to recognize which planet he represents; it is Venus." [77]

It should be understood that the likelihood of Daniel being more than passingly aware of the relation between Venus and the Archangel Michael is highly probable, and this statement may give us a clue to the event that will precipitate the next Great Dying.

Revelation 2 says: *"And he who overcomes ... I will give him authority and power over the nations ... I will give him the Morning Star."* [78]

Jesus describes His coming as visible to all the tribes of the earth — appearing in brilliancy and splendor — and that this event is a source of great anguish: *"all the tribes of the earth will mourn and beat their breasts and lament in anguish..."* [79] What could evoke such global fright? Surely not an eclipse or a distant, passing comet? And, it is of paramount interest that Jesus describes his coming in terms of lightning — *electrical potentials.*

The prophecies of Revelation, Matthew, and Daniel could be construed to describe an extraterrestrial cosmic interaction between the earth and another body, and, for some reason, it seems that this event is unexpected. This unexpected aspect is described as the 'Thief Effect.'

Theologians have endlessly distorted the remainder of Matthew 24 to support an unfounded myth of being 'raptured' into the sky. (Note: only Christians who meet certain exclusive criteria based upon any number of variations in doctrine are eligible for the great airlift into the sky!) And, in more recent times, numerous psychics have jumped on the bandwagon claiming that certain persons will be saved from the 'axial shift' through the agency of alien visitors hovering about waiting for the word to 'beam them aboard.'

The passage in Matthew reads:

> *"As were the days of Noah, so will be the coming of the Son of Man. For just as in those days before the flood they were eating and drinking ... until the day when Noah went into the ark, And they did not know or understand until the flood came and swept them all away — so will be the coming of the Son of Man. At that time two men will be in the field; one will be taken and one will be left..."* [80]

To get the correct sense we must rearrange the sentence for our Western linear minds. 'The coming of the Son of Man, like the flood of Noah, will be sudden and unexpected, and will sweep away those who are not prepared.' It is obvious, in the context, that those who are 'taken' or 'swept away,' are the very ones who have not watched and kept ready, and that this is not a 'Stealing away of the Saints.'

Paul writes in I Thessalonians 5:2-03:

> *"For you yourselves know perfectly well that the day of the Lord will come as a thief in the night. When people are saying, All is well and secure, and, There is peace and safety, then in a moment unforeseen destruction will come upon them as suddenly as labor pains come upon a woman with child; and they shall by no means escape, for there will be no escape."* [81]

This last passage makes it obvious that the 'thief' is *unforeseen destruction*. Obviously, one who is ready and 'guarding his clothes' will not be looted by the thief nor would anyone expect a vigilant householder to go with a thief.

Paul also writes: *"But you are not in darkness ... for that day to overtake you by surprise like a thief... For God has not appointed us to wrath ... therefore let us be sober, and put on the breastplate of faith and love and for a helmet the hope of salvation,"* [82] which clearly associates the thief with wrath.

And in II Corinthians, Paul describes what kind of clothing we must have on in order to be prepared for this event:

> *"For while we are still in this tent, we groan under the burden and sigh deeply (weighed down, depressed, oppressed) — not that we want to put off the body (the clothing of the spirit), but rather that we would be further clothed, so that what*

is mortal may be swallowed up by life... For we must all appear and be revealed as we are before the judgment seat of Christ, so that each one may receive according to what he had done in the body..." [83]

And, the concept of the spiritual clothing that must be guarded from the thief is mentioned in Revelation:

"For you say, I am rich; I have prospered and grow wealthy, and I am in need of nothing; and do not realize and understand that you are wretched, pitiable, poor, blind and naked. Therefore I counsel you to purchase from Me gold refined and tested by fire, that you may be wealthy, and white clothes to clothe you and to keep the shame of your nudity from being seen, and salve to put on your eyes that you may see." [84]

These passages associate nakedness with spiritual impoverishment — which may be the realization Adam and Eve came to which caused them to feel shame. In this context, Jesus says in Matthew 24:17,18:

"Let him who is on the housetop not come down and go into the house to take anything; And let him who is in the field not turn back to get his overcoat." [85]

And so, we have an insight into the 'unexpected nature' of the event. If one's truly valuable possessions are spiritual clothing and deeds, it may be seen that these are not things that can be acquired in a short period of time. And, this leads us back to unified states of consciousness. Our personal waveform could be considered to be the three-dimensional manifestation of our spirit body — its clothes, in other words. And, if every thought we think, every deed we do, leaves its imprint upon this electromagnetic waveform, much as the videotaping of an event is arranged in terms of magnetism — then we can see that an individual who has worked to achieve a unified state, and who operates his life in terms of this broader view of reality may have an entirely different electromagnetic pattern than an individual who has limited the scope of both his mind and his spirit with concomitant limitations expressed in material ways.

A unified state of consciousness is harmonious, coherent and more nearly attuned to the primary level of reality — a realm of order and harmony. Achieving such a state of consciousness would be hampered by anger, fear, anxiety; and would be facilitated by love, empathy and peacefulness.

The redemption of man comes in and through his body and involves a total transmutation of that body. We are not our body — our body is part of us and whatever we do with and to our body is the measure of our spiritual development — our spiritual clothing. The idea that spiritual preparation for this 'Day of the Lord' is an important factor tells us something about the limited time we will have once it becomes apparent that an extraterrestrial event might take place. There are several possibilities revolving around this idea.

It is entirely possible that a body from deep space might pass into our solar system and swing close to Jupiter or Saturn, freeing one of the many satellites, and, as in a game of celestial billiards, send it spinning our way. Or, one of the many moons of one of the Jovian planets could collide with another through the myriad combinations and variations of their orbits and zip our way. There is a popular theory that a great earthquake will be caused by a multiple conjunction of planets, which will occur early in the year 2000. Anything which had the escape velocity to leave Jupiter would arrive in our area of the solar system in something like six months or thereabouts. A pretty short time indeed, particularly if the scientists were watching and calculating but decided not to cause a panic by telling anyone.

Another favored idea is that all of these effects will be caused by the shifting of the earth on its axis due to the extreme heaviness and consequent imbalance of the polar ice cap. This is very popular currently — as is the alien 'Rapture' — but conflicts with current scientific evidence of the melting of the polar ice caps due to the greenhouse effect.

So, before we form any conclusions or, at least, conjectures, let's examine more evidence from other sources and find if there are any common elements. The fact is, that whatever the cause, such an event as a worldwide earthquake stupefies the mind. Recent conceptions in regard to 'nuclear winter' are entirely applicable to this situation. And, computer models of the asteroid impact theory put forth by the two Alvarezes have yielded interesting results.

After an initial conflagration, dust and particles would shade and cool the earth and bring a sudden, brutal, winter, which would persist for a long time. Even if a billion or more people were killed instantly, the worst would be yet to come. With constant freezing temperature, rivers, lakes, and even the ground would be frozen. (It might, indeed, take seven years to bury the dead, as one prophecy forecasts!) The multiplied millions of people living in our vast metropolitan areas would suffer the most — if any survived. Dependent upon mass transportation for food and other essentials, they would be totally helpless. Knowing only the fantasy of television, they would be totally unprepared for the harsh realities of basic survival.

Most inhabitants in tropical regions — human, plant and animal — would perish, being unaccustomed to the bitter cold — a mass extinction of tropical and sub-tropical species. Death of the phytoplankton near the surface of the oceans would so disrupt the aquatic food chain that most of the fish in the seas would perish as well.

The greatest threat to our survival as a species is our belief that life will go on as always until some time in the distant future. It has been said that Satan's greatest weapon is that nobody believes in him. In the case of prophesied cataclysms, this is doubly true. Nobody really believes it.

The apostle Peter wrote:

> "To begin with, you must know and understand this, that scoffers will come in the last days with scoffing, [walking] after their own fleshly desires And [saying], Where is the promise of His coming? For since the forefathers fell asleep, all things have continued exactly as they did from beginning of creation." (Uniformitarianism?) For they willfully overlook and forget this [fact], that the heavens came into existence long ago by the word of God, and an earth also which was formed out of water and by means of water, Through which the world that then was deluged with water and perished. But by the same word the present heavens and earth have been stored up for fire, being kept until the day of judgment and destruction of the ungodly people... But the day of the Lord will come as a thief, and then the heavens will vanish with a thunderous crash, and the [material] elements of the universe will be dissolved with fire, and the earth and the works that are upon it will be burned up...
>
> But we look for new heavens and a new earth according to His promise, in which righteousness (uprightness, freedom from sin, and right standing with God) is to abide. So, beloved, since you are expecting these things, be eager to be found by Him [at his coming] without spot or blemish and at peace [in serene confidence, free from fears and agitating passions and moral conflicts]." [86]

Many people do not believe the prospect of global catastrophe. The greatest reality in their lives is the TV and the pursuit of the means of daily existence and accumulation of the accoutrements of material ideals. Many others think it is a probability, but they have decided that it is going to happen on their terms — a mystical or alien 'Rapture' or transformation by consciousness raising — and therefore place their reliance on something outside of themselves. And this explains the anguish of the tribes of the earth when the actual event occurs — it wasn't what they expected.

And, if the new conditions of the earth are different — in quantum terms — then even many who survive the initial cataclysm will be unable to adjust to the new atomic vibrational frequencies if they have not prepared themselves and 'clothed' themselves. They will be left with nothing — absolutely nothing — and no amount of wealth or position will buy them survival. The long period of planetary recovery would preclude growing and harvesting any sort of food, and once they have eaten what food may be available, or their pets, or, perhaps, each other, they will be doomed to a long, slow, solitary starvation in the dust and darkness of despair.

No haven, no help, and no hope.

Chapter Six

Be thou, Spirit fierce, My spirit! Be thou me, impetuous one!
Drive my dead thought over the universe
Like withered leaves to quicken a new birth,
And, by the incantation of this verse,
Scatter, as from an inextinguishable hearth
Ashes and sparks, my words among mankind!
Be through my lips to unawakened earth
The trumpet of a prophecy! O wind,
If Winter comes, can Spring be far behind!

— Percy Bysshe Shelley, 'Ode to the West Wind.'

Down through the centuries there have been numerous groups and schools claiming to possess methods and teachings that are designed to precipitate altered and/or unified states of consciousness. Most great world religions are corrupted offshoots of such groups. However, those who actually experienced such transformations were limited in number, and the 'inner' or 'hidden' teachings were shared only by small groups of 'Initiates.' The techniques used included disciplined mental, physical and spiritual exercises; but it can be observed that similar experiences have been known to manifest spontaneously — sometimes as a result of grave illness, creative efforts, deep stresses, intense inner struggles and so forth. Also certain individuals may be more susceptible to such inner transformation than others. This situation is reflected in the statement 'Many are called but few are chosen.'

All of the legitimate systems are designed to fine-tune the mind and body — thereby adding awareness potential — much like adding radar, sonar, and telescopic lenses to a vehicle. And, all of these systems lead to strikingly similar results. In recent times, laboratory studies of these states of consciousness are showing an actual physiological change in the brain's activity. Referring back to the unity of the cosmos as defined by Bell's theorem, we could express the attainment of such 'unified states' as a deliberate moving into phase with the 'Great Cosmic Wave.'

As noted in Bell's theorem, deep reality seems to be a unified, unmitigated waveform. Studies of wave motion show us that a wave takes its form from what is doing the waving. This implies that our reality must have a waver. We, ourselves, are electromagnetic waveforms — at least that part of us manifested in three dimensions. And, since the most elaborate gadget constructed within this three-dimensional realm can never, by its very nature of three dimensions, penetrate beyond, we cannot know in strictly scientific terms what is outside our reality. An idea, such as love, honor, or sympathy must be seen to be as real — if not more so — than a table or a chair. A table or a chair can also exist as an — one that eventually manifests in our dimension. But before it ever can, someone must think of it first. And, just as the chair comes into being from the realm of thought — a tangible manifestation of thought — so might we assume that a far vaster realm of thought may be manifesting in our reality, taken as a whole.

An example of this would be to imagine a two-dimensional Plane Being — a flat surface of infinitesimal thinness. A man approaches the Plane Being and places the tips of his fingers upon the surface. The Plane Being would only be aware of five circular phenomena introduced into his world. He would be totally incapable of perceiving the richness and complexity of the being and life of the man. And, if the Plane World were, so to speak, plastic — a film — and the man passed his hand through the Plane Being's world and then withdrew it, the phenomena would be perceived to change dramatically by the Plane Being and after the withdrawal of the hand, would be perceived to be at an end — though for the man, this would not be the case. We stand in a very similar relationship to our 'deeper reality.'

The brain can be defined as an instrument, which interprets myriads of waveforms in mathematical constructs — images of energy grids — and then must translate these into objects. When waveforms are perceived from a realm transcending time and space, these concepts are transformed into images which approximate concepts beyond our realm of understanding. These are extremely difficult to translate into words due to the fact that deeper reality is a whole and we are conditioned from birth to perceive ourselves and all about us in the terms of the Plane Being, so to speak. As entrapped 'Plane Beings' ourselves, we can only understand things broken into parts — point particles massed to 'create' a plane pattern. Deep reality is not linear — but we attempt to arrange it into properly translated subjects and verbs.

Despite this problem, prophets down through the ages have attained unified states of consciousness in some part of themselves and the resultant visions have then filtered through their clouded minds and been delivered in fantastic symbols and imagery. And, we should understand that we are as limited in our abilities to convey concepts as the ancients were in spite of the evolution of our highly technical linguistics. In fact, they may have been a great deal more creative than we are today. What we dryly call an atomic explosion, they would have called 'fire falling from heaven.' Our limitations will be even more apparent when you consider that it would be impossible to explain an atomic explosion to an aborigine — but the same aborigine would clearly comprehend 'fire falling from heaven' translated into his own language equivalent.

Therefore, it becomes very important to understand that we are not only limited by our linguistics; we are also hindered by our highly technical interpretations. Our scientific methodology and terminology have created a great barrier to understanding prophetic vision.

Our dream states are more nearly similar to unified states of consciousness than our waking, linear, conscious thought processes. In dreams we perceive deep realities, which come through as images or symbols of 'essences' or *noumena*. Some of these symbols are universal and some are highly personal and based upon an individual's early associations.

I was given a rather graphic lesson in the relation of symbols to reality and how the waking mind may distort these. In the early days of 1986 I was greatly troubled by a dream in which I found myself in a cold, barren, landscape, accompanied by my children. We were viewing what seemed to be a most peculiar tornado at a great distance. It was a loosely curled cloud of smoke, more like a stretched-out bedspring than a funnel. I was puzzled because it did not touch the ground, yet I knew it was killing people. I felt very sad in the dream and I was overwhelmed by the bleakness of the landscape. In the dream, I was reminded of Poe's 'Fall of the House of Usher.'

I commented to my children that we did not have to worry for there was no possibility of the tornado coming our way, but that we must pray for those we were seeing die.

I awoke immediately at the conclusion of this dream in a depressed state. On numerous other occasions I had dreamed flashes of disasters only to awaken and discover that something bearing strong similarities had occurred during the night somewhere around the globe. I expected to hear of a tornado striking somewhere and killing people, so I turned on the radio to catch the news. I was pleased to hear that I was up in time to view the Space Shuttle *Challenger* launch.

The children and I trooped out into the cold with binoculars and began to search the sky over the tops of the trees in the woods surrounding our house. We saw a bright flash, which we assumed to be the staging of the rocket, and I focused the glasses on the object. What I saw was the peculiar cloud of my dream and, at that moment I experienced an appalling sensation of sadness. I kept my eyes on the dissipating smoke as I listened to the radio announcer saying that some sort of problem was being experienced.

The only discrepancy between my dream and the actual event was the interpretation. I had interpreted my dream in terms of familiarity: a tornado — even though I had been puzzled by the peculiar antics of this dream tornado. I had no other experience with which to interpret other than that of tornados or waterspouts. I had seen a powerful, moving, death-dealing force in the sky — with cloud-like effects — which did not make contact with the ground, and which did not threaten me or my household. What I saw was, in fact, what I got! But, I had never seen a rocket blow up — or, at least, did not consider that to be a possibility. And, I might add, the central issue in the Poe story of the Usher family is premature burial. Did our astronauts go to their watery tomb alive?

And so we can see how symbols reflect actual potentials — even though our interpretations may be skewed by personal experience.

In the same way, it is not hard to understand that similar processes were in effect for the ancient prophets. In highly allegorical and culturally biased terms they described their visions and experiences. Thus heavenly bodies became angels, archangels — cataclysmic events were deliberate 'acts of God,' and stupefying groanings and thunderings of nature became the voice of God. And, all things considered, who are we to say that their perception of celestial beings and divinely inspired events are not more accurate than one would initially suppose?

The scenario created in the previous section, fraught with mindless horror and suffering, is supported and expanded by numerous other prophets and seers, who, I feel, have also been incorrectly interpreted not only by the prophets themselves — on occasion — but also in numerous expository theses.

I read in one such work by a Christian theologian: *"... It stands to reason that if scholars for centuries have not been able to 'crack the code' of even small portions of great Bible prophecies, it would not follow that books could suddenly appear in the last few years that explain everything."* [87]

However, that statement does not stand to reason. For many generations certain prophecies were fantastic and incomprehensible — particularly those describing modern technology, such as airplanes and automobiles. In recent times, though, such prophecies have become fully understood due to an increase in knowledge. The Bible itself prophesies:

"... in the last days, God declares ... I will pour out of My spirit upon all mankind, and your sons and your daughters shall prophesy [telling forth the divine coun-

sels] — and your young men shall see visions, and your old men shall dream dreams ... and they shall prophesy [telling forth the divine counsels and predicting future events pertaining especially to God's Kingdom]." [88]

Recall Daniel's statement:

"... shut up the words and seal the Book until the time of the end. [Then] many shall run to and fro and search anxiously and knowledge shall be increased and become great." [89]

This has often been interpreted as referring to the technological advancements of our society and the hustle-bustle of modern life (running to and fro). Taken in context, however, the subject of the chapter being prophecies of the end times, it can only refer to an increase in knowledge of Divine purpose acquired through diligent analysis and study of prophecy received through various sources.

Another question that needs to be asked in relation to prophecy is the question of timing. Everyone wants to know 'WHEN?' And many, many groups and individuals have really been embarrassed when setting forth an exact time only to wake up at the appointed hour to the fact that something must have gone wrong with their calculations. They usually deal with this problem by backtracking in pretty creative ways. One individual I can think of actually claimed that his 'Biblically-Inspired' calculations were thrown off by his inadvertent misplacing of a crucial decimal point. He then went on to push the event so far into the future that it was a certainty that he would be dead before he got egg on his face again!

One problem which has been created by this constant series of announcements of the time of the end that prove fallacious has been the tendency of most people to determine that no end will ever occur. It amounts to the same thing as the boy who cried 'wolf' losing his credibility.

The idea that the time of the end is an unknown variable and subject to numerous quantum probabilities in terms of course and duration is mentioned by various sources. Additionally, the fact that most people will have lost confidence in the idea that it will ever happen at all is part of the prophecies. *"... the Son of Man is coming at an hour when you do not expect Him,"* [90] and this has resulted in the tendency to interpret prophecy in allegorical or euphemistic terms. However, many clues are given as to 'times and seasons' in a general sense, and the dates given by various sources all reflect agreement within one or two years either way. The discourse given in Matthew 24 warns us that when certain signs are seen manifesting all together, that the final events will then transpire within a generation. A generation is generally taken to be 40 or 50 years, but we should note the exact wording of that passage: *"this generation will not pass away till all these things taken together take place."* [91] This makes the period of fulfillment within the given lifetime of a man — say 70 years at the outside. It also emphasizes that all of the clues must happen within a generation for validity.

The starting period has always been assumed to be the repatriation of the Jewish nation: *"From the fig tree learn this lesson: as soon as its young shoots become soft and tender and it puts out its leaves, you know of a surety that summer is near."* [92] The fig tree is the symbol of Israel and, if this is the case, we are looking at a timetable which has already gone past the half-way mark, counting from 1948 — the time of the repatriation of the Jews.

But, I think there is still a deeper meaning to this remark. The signs given by Jesus were: *"you will hear of wars and rumors of wars,"* an ever present condition throughout history; *"For nation will rise against nation, and kingdom against kingdom, and there will be famines and earthquakes in place after place,"* also fairly common throughout history. But, these statements contain a meaning that is not immediately apparent — **the fact that modern media makes the transmission of all of this type of information instantaneous.** The passage continues: *"For then there will be great tribulation such as has not been from the beginning of the world until now — no, and never will be again. And if those days had not been shortened, no human being would endure and survive; but for the sake of the elect those days will be shortened."* [93] And here we have another important clue: never before in recorded history has man possessed the technology to destroy the entire human race and never before in recorded history have we stood so perilously on the brink of chaos and self-annihilation because of the wanton destruction of the environment and concomitant creation of a vast host of ills and toxic substances which we take into our bodies daily.

Yes, there has been an increase, statistically, in the number and type of environmental disasters — but that could be merely cyclic. There have always been wars and famines — but we now hear about them all in graphic detail every evening at six. But, putting it all together, we have to see that the constellation of signs is the emerging of the bud of the tree, which shows that summer is near. And, if summer is the period of growth and ripening in preparation for the harvest, I think we are well on our way.

The next section will deal with the presentation of several prophetic views. In this I have attempted to remain as close as possible to the actual documentation and the four main elements of the eschatological thesis:

1. Geological changes,
2. Possible war,
3. The conflict between good and evil, and
4. Cosmic phenomena.

I intend to show how all of these elements may fit together and coalesce into the staging and effecting of the end result: Metamorphosis — a New Heaven and a New Earth.

Chapter Seven

The greatest thing a human soul ever does in this world is to see something and tell what he saw in a plain way. Hundreds of people can talk for one who can think, and thousands can think for one who can see. To see clearly is poetry, prophecy and religion all in one.

— John Ruskin, *Stones of Venice.*

In dealing with the corroboration that an extraterrestrial event is going to occur in the near future in the works of other, post-Biblical prophets, a complex and confusing undertaking at the very least, I have had to be somewhat selective and limiting in my examples.

The subject fills literally thousands of books. I have tried to deal with them in more or less chronological order, except when otherwise necessary. The reader should make every effort to read and study on his or her own.

St. Malachy

One of the earliest post-Biblical prophets of note was St. Malachy, a twelfth-century Irish archbishop, who made forecasts about the popes of the Catholic Church dating from 1143 up to, and just beyond, the present. At this time, there are two positions remaining on Malachy's list. These prophecies consist, primarily, of a motto, which has proven, in nearly every instance, to be remarkably apt. A few past examples will serve to demonstrate the ideology of St. Malachy.

Pope Adrian IV, Malachy described as *De Ruro Albo*, and was, in fact, an Englishman born at St. Albans.

Benedict XV was given the motto *Religio Depopulatea*, or 'Christianity laid waste.' He was pope during World War I.

John Paul I bore a most interesting motto: *De Medietate Lunae*, or 'of the half moon.' This pope was in office only one month and his tenure extended from one quarter to another; the 'quarter' position of the moon exhibiting only half of the moon's visible body.

The present pope, John Paul II, *De Labore Solis*, or 'of the toil of the sun,' is prophesied to preside over a lull, or quiescent period, before tribulation breaks out in full fury.

The two remaining positions are: *Gloria Olivae*[94] and *Petrus Romanus* — 'The glory of the olive' and 'Peter of Rome.'

In a certain sense these mottos reflect global conditions, as in that of Benedict XV, pope during the first world war. Christianity was certainly laid waste! In others, the motto is often very personal to the particular pope. It is hard to say whether the mottos of the present pope and the two remaining reflect any general effect on mankind, except that I do find 'The Toil of the Sun' to be most interesting in light of the predicted famines due to the changed weather patterns brought on by man's disregard for the environment. The Sun may indeed, in the next few years, become a toilsome thing.

The most significant factor in Malachy's predictions is that an end to the papacy is implied. This leads us into two lines of thought:

1. A total reorganization of the Catholic Church, eliminating the position of pope;
2. A complete end to the Catholic Church brought on by:
   a) political or military actions;
   b) an end to civilization as we know it.

Proposition number one is highly unlikely. It is hard to imagine the adherents of the Catholic faith countenancing such an idea. The Pope is the Holy Father and even if the cardinals or other members of the Church hierarchy did want to do away with the position, what would they do with the faith of the believers who rely on the Supreme Head of the Church to be their spokesman to God? There might be reform going on in the Church, but not that much!

Proposition number 2a is also equally unlikely. Even supposing a disastrous world war or the imposition of an anti-religious totalitarian regime, the Church would more likely go 'underground' and continue in its religious functions, retaining its hierarchy.

This leaves us with proposition 2b as the only possible explanation for this apparent lapse in the Catholic Church.

Nostradamus

Michel de Nostredame, or Nostradamus, one of the most acclaimed of post-Biblical prophets, has a very good record of 'hits.' Unfortunately, it is often difficult to determine how good due to the obscurity of his prophetic style. It is usually after the fact that his quatrains are discovered to be 'incredibly accurate.'

Nevertheless, Nostradumus' descriptions of modern events and technology, as well as his anagrammatic naming of specific individuals far removed in time from his period, is remarkable. He was extremely fond of puns and often used such ruses to conceal his meanings.

Much of the difficulty in interpreting Nostradamus and other prophets may lie in the attempts to mesh analysis with current scientific theories based upon Darwinian thought. This tendency is exemplified in a recent book of interpretations which claimed that Halley's Comet was the harbinger of the coming of the antichrist and the start of World War III.

Well, here we are, it is 1992, Halley's Comet has come and gone, and, while we are not exactly in a condition of perfect peace around the globe, we are not on the verge of a world war either!

To illustrate the difficulty in dealing with Nostradamus, here is a quatrain that is often interpreted to refer to the destruction of the west coast of the United States:

> *The Sun in twenty degrees of Taurus, (there will be) a terrible earthquake,*
> *The great theater (city?) and all in it will be destroyed.*
> *In the air and on land, darkness and trouble,*
> *When the infidel ignores God and the saints. IX.82*

Many have keyed the word 'theatre' to Hollywood and the word 'saints' to San Francisco and Los Angeles, thereby connecting this quatrain to the destruction of that portion of California. This area is, indeed, earthquake prone and everyone is waiting for the 'Big One.' However, unless this is a description of a comet, there is nothing in the aforementioned area which could bring darkness and trouble *in the air*, unless, of course, a volcano were to emerge from the land somewhere near this point, a not unprecedented event in other areas of the globe.

The month of May is, historically, a busy time for earthquakes and volcanic eruptions. The most recent of note was Mt. Saint Helen's — which is, indeed, a 'saint.' Twenty degrees of Taurus is approximately May 10, so the eruption of Mt. St. Helen's was not too far removed from the predicted time. But, a packed theatre or city was not destroyed during this eruption. In fact, there was very little loss of life at all due to the efforts of various agencies to warn and get everyone out of the area in time.

However, on May 8, 1902, the city of Saint Pierre, on the island of Martinique, was completely destroyed by the shattering eruption of Mt.

Pelee. Pelee, named for an infidel goddess of fire, rumbled and smoked and oozed lava for weeks before the eruption and the entire city was blanketed with smoke and soot (*"in the air and on land, darkness and trouble"*) long before the final blast. But, rather than evacuating, the residents remained — the city was full — and many of them toured the mountain as a Sunday outing; making expeditions to the crater as though it were a theatrical attraction. They entirely ignored the signs and when the mountain finally blew, rocks, sand and poisonous gases swept down upon the slumbering city and St. Pierre was entirely ablaze within three minutes. Also wiped out were the towns of Le Precheur, Manceau, and St. Philomene. The 'infidel' Pelee certainly ignored Le precheur of God and a couple of 'saints.' The blast was heard 300 miles away and the shockwaves were felt around the globe. This was, as Ed Sullivan would have said, 'A reely big shew!'

While there have been many earthquakes and volcanic eruptions in the month of May, none can, as yet, compare with the destruction caused by the eruption of the infidel Pelee which totally destroyed the city and the population of over 30,000 souls.

That is not to say that another event could not occur in the future on the prescribed date. As the first draft of this book was being written, there was news of an earthquake near Trinidad, south and east of Martinique, and I thought of Edgar Cayce's prophecy that Pelee must blow again before the West Coast of California is destroyed. It is entirely within the realm of possibility that another eruption of Pelee could set off a tectonic chain reaction leading to the destruction of the 'theatre' of America — Hollywood and surrounding environs. I, personally, think this verse refers to the blow of 1902 — but anything is possible.

There is another of Nostradamus' quatrains that may shed some additional light on this subject.

> *The earthquake shall be so great in the month of May,*
> *Saturn, Caper, Jupiter, Mercury in Taurus,*
> *Venus also, Cancer Mars in Zero,*
> *Then shall hail fall bigger than an egg. X.67*

In May of the year 2000, Jupiter, Saturn, Mars, Venus and Mercury will be in the sign of Taurus. The moon's north node will be in Cancer, but that is as close as I can get it.

Returning to our eschatological predictions, Nostradamus constantly repeats the themes of worsening conditions of the human race, war and political strife, and a great comet signaling the end of the world as we know it — and, the beginning of a new order.

In the year 1999 and seven months
From the sky will come the Great King of Terror,
Raising again the great king of the Mongols,
Before and after Mars reigns at his pleasure. X.72

The first event here is the coming of 'The Great King of Terror' from the sky. The ancients knew Venus as the Queen of Heaven and Mars as the King of Heaven or King of Terror — the god of war. There are several possibilities here. Either a great new comet could appear on the scene or this could denote an actual displacement of the planet Mars from its usual orbit. Or, it could be merely an astrological reference to an unusual configuration of Mars with another planet — or a time of particular brightness of the planet.

As far as I have been able to determine, there is no unusual conjunction of Mars in July of 1999. It will enter the sign of Scorpio on the fifth of July, but it transits Scorpio frequently with no ill effects. Nevertheless, this celestial event enables the 'Great King of the Mongols' to come forth. This is very interesting in light of a couple of other references.

"Then the sixth [angel] emptied his bowl on the mighty river Euphrates, and its water was dried up to make ready a road for the kings of the east." [95]

Edgar Cayce (who we will discuss further on) also pronounced a similar prophecy: *"If there is not the acceptance in America of the closer brotherhood of man, the love of the neighbor as self, civilization must wend its way westward — and again must Mongolia, must a hated people, be raised."* [96] It is indeed odd that Cayce used a similar term as Nostradamus — Mongols, while the Bible used 'Kings of the East.'

It is also within the realm of possibilities that the 'Great King of Terror' combines the idea of Mars, or war, with an atomic missile flying through the air. All three of these excerpts make it clear that the threat is from the Orient.

One of the oldest countries in the world, Mongolia reached the zenith of its power in the 13th century when Genghis Khan and his successors conquered all of China and extended their influence as far west as Hungary and Poland. In later centuries, the empire dissolved and Mongolia came under the suzerainty of China. At the time of the Chinese revolution, in 1911, Mongolia declared its independence. With Russian backing, a communist regime was established in 1921. Mongolia has changed from a nomadic culture to one of growing industrial and agricultural prowess with the aid of the Soviets. But, for many years, little has been heard from that area of the world.

The question is: do the references mean Mongolia proper, or simply the orient, such as China?

I would like to note that this last quatrain makes it clear that war (Mars) is in progress before the coming of the 'Great King of Terror,' so it is either an escalation to nuclear capabilities or an actual cosmic event while war is in progress. Another possibility is that, while other nations are at war — wiping each other out — Mongolia could be sitting quietly by waiting to take advantage of a situation not of its own creation.

One of the more interesting of Nostradamus' quatrains is the following:

Mabus will soon die bringing
Dreadful destruction of people and animals;
Sudden vengeance will be revealed,
A hundred to hand, thirst and hunger,
when the comet will pass. II.62

The first question is: who or what is Mabus? The next question is: why does Mabus' death reveal vengeance, bring death and destruction, thirst and hunger; and how is this all tied in with the passing of a comet?

The standard interpretation until recent times was that a world leader would die at the passing of Halley's comet leaving no strong leadership, which would then enable a cruel dictator to come to power who would use and abuse the population of the world and take us all into a war.

I have rearranged the quatrain so that it is more comprehensible to the Western linear mind: *When the comet passes, Mabus will die Revealing vengeance and dreadful destruction with a hundred dying at each blow. Those not killed will suffer thirst and famine.*

Knowing Nostradamus' penchant for puns and anagrams, I puzzled over the name Mabus for a long time. I noted that, with the exception of the insertion of the 'b' Mabus could be a combination of the names 'Mars' and 'Venus.' In many Latin root languages, the use of a 'b' or 'v' is interchangeable.

In the earlier reference from the book of Daniel in which he predicts the 'arising' of the archangel Michael to 'save' the people, and the connection between the archangel and the planet Venus, we can see that this places this quatrain in an interesting light related to the former quatrain about the coming of the 'Great King of Terror.'

Could it be possible that, at some point, either the planet Mars or another great comet passes close to the earth and disturbs the orbit of the planet Venus? Or, could some, as yet unknown comet come hurtling toward the earth to be deflected from destroying our planet by the fortunate orbital position of either Mars or Venus, yet with the impact sending great chunks of debris raining down on our planet killing hundreds of people at a blow?

Revelation predicts:

"The first angel blew [his] trumpet, and there was a storm of hail and fire mingled with blood, cast upon the earth And a third part of the earth was burned up, and a third of the trees were burned up and all the green grass was burned up. The second angel blew [his] trumpet, and something resembling a great mountain, blazing with fire, was hurled into the sea. And a third of the sea was turned to blood, a third of the living creatures in the sea perished, and a third of the ships were destroyed. The third angel blew [his] trumpet, and a huge star fell from heaven, burning like a torch, and it dropped on a third of the rivers and on the springs of water — And the name of the star is Wormwood. A third part of the waters was changed into wormwood, and many people died from using the water, because it had become bitter. Then the fourth angel blew [his] trumpet, and a third of the sun was smitten, and a third of the moon, and a third of the stars, so that [the light of] a third of them was darkened, and a third of the daylight was withdrawn..." [97]

And, this certainly meshes with the other prophecies so far. Recalling the turning of the waters into 'blood' recounted in Exodus and possibly explained by red comet dust found by the Alvarezes, this seems to imply a cometary impact of some kind, though sorting it out is a can of worms.

Is the coming of the 'King of Terror' a cometary event and, if it is, is this a further amplification of that event? What is the chronology?

In case the reader has not already figured it out by noting the quatrain numbers, Nostradamus did not arrange his verses in order of occurrence.

But, we can take heart! Apparently the destruction from this last event involves only a third of mankind immediately. But, it is implied by Nostradamus' references to famine and thirst that water is ruined and a darkening of the atmosphere would prevent the natural growing cycle and bring on famine as described in Revelation.

That both of these previous quatrains possibly refer to the same event — indicating cosmic activity between Mars, Venus, and a possible unknown comet may be indicated by the following:

The world is nearing its final period,
Saturn is late again on his return,
The empire will move toward a dark nation ...
Narbonne shall have her eye picked out by a hawk. III.92

Saturnalia, the celebration of the return of the lengthening of days and the beginning of the growing season, occurs on the winter solstice. An implied second delay to the return of the light indicates that some event has left the earth shadowed in wintry darkness for a considerable period of time. This gives credence to the repeated references to extreme famine. It may also, in fact, denote an actual alteration in the earth's orbit.

If the 'Dark Nation' refers to Mongols, this could be an additional indication that the greatest destruction is to take place in the West thereby bringing the peoples of the East to prominence.

Though not complete by any means, I feel that these interpretations of Nostradamus' quatrains, including the identity of Mabus, is entirely appropriate in light of the fact that Nostradamus took great pains to conceal names in anagrams and puns. It is in character for him to have employed this means, or ruse, to conceal such an obviously startling prediction.

In any event, I feel that the interpretation of Mabus as a global leader whose death leaves the earth open to unrestrained war is a little threadbare. One thing is certain, he was not 'revealed' by Halley's comet.

The next quatrain either amplifies the single cometary event with more detail, or describes an additional event. I hope it is the former because I am sure there are limits to how much a single afflicted planet can take. But, if the scientists are correct in everything except their timing, and the Oort cloud does shower us with billions of comets, then the latter explanation would stand.

After great misery for mankind, greater approaches,
The great cycle of the centuries begins renewal,
Rains of blood, milk, famine, war and disease,
In the sky, fire dragging a great trail of sparks. II.46

This verse echoes the previous ones as well as the events in Exodus and Revelation: rains of ferruginous pigment; rains of petroleum making the waters milky; famine, disease and war. The 20th century does not technically end until midnight, December 31, 2000, with the 21st century beginning January 1, 2001. So, this could actually be a separate event after much previous destruction. *"Fire dragging a great trail of sparks"* does not sound anything like a missile. It sounds like a comet. A missile does not become fire until impact.

The next quatrain is most interesting in that I feel it has long been a stumbling block to interpreters of Nostradamus. We must keep always in mind the fact that Nostradamus had a great fondness for playing with words in addition to the usual interpretative problem of dealing with archaic vernacular.

> *The great star will burn for seven days,*
> *The cloud will make the sun appear double,*
> *The big dog will howl all night,*
> *When the great pontiff changes his territory. II.41*

There are three elements to consider here: The burning star, which appears 'double'; the 'big dog'; and the traveling 'pontiff.' Most interpreters have depicted the pope fleeing by night while his dog mourns his departure during the seven-day passing of a comet.

First, does Nostradamus mean a flaming comet in his description of the burning star, or does the second line amplify that the Sun itself is in a state of expansion? Could it be that a comet is held in the embrace of the earth's magnetic field for a period of seven days, positioned in front of the Sun so that the Sun appears doubled in size? But, if it were a comet and those circumstances prevailed, the earth would be so blanketed with dust from the volcanic and earthquake activities that such a sight would be impossible from the earth's surface. Of course, if we were seeing a comet approach from the direction in which the Sun lies, at a distance, we could view it without disruption in the atmosphere until it gets much closer. And, it could take seven days for it to reach a point that it disrupts the orbital motion of the earth. Whichever it is, the second two lines are the result. And, not to be facetious, I don't think it would be at all significant that the pope changed his residence and left a broken-hearted hound if the earth were being shaken by a cosmic event!

The 'Big Dog,' considering Nostradamus' interest in astrology and astronomy — and his frequent use of such allusions — must refer to Canis Major ... Big Dog. That the dog howls all night after the residence change must indicate that Sirius, the Dog Star — one of the brightest in the heavens, is visible throughout the night — a new polar orientation. 'Pontiff' may very well be a play on words — *pont*, or 'point' — axial orientation. The traveling pontiff could refer to a shift of the axis of the earth toward the Dog Star as a result of a seven-day encounter with a great, burning star, or comet.

Of course, the description of a flaming star that appears double could refer to a supernova visible for seven days. But then, what would be the impetus for the axial shift? Of course, we could revert to the idea of a traveling pope who flees the Vatican at the same time Sirius explodes.

Before leaving Nostradamus, I would like to present a view from Alan Vaughan's *Patterns of Prophecy*.

> "*I first read Nostradamus' prophecy (about the Great King of Terror) in December 10, 1965 ... I pondered over the meaning of this strange image. The next day, I went to a nearby bookshop to try to find another book on Nostradamus ... It was not in stock ... as I was leaving the bookshop, my eye caught an absurdly titled book on a sale table:* My Contact With Flying Saucers, *by Dino Kraspedon. I opened the book to a prophecy that supplied an interpretation of Nostradamus' 1999 prophecy: Toward the end of this century, another sun would enter our solar system and form a binary star system with our own sun. It would not emit light until it reached our solar system. The orbits of the planets would be changed such that Mercury would move into the area between the present orbits of Venus and Earth. The Earth, in turn, would assume a new orbit where the planetoids are now. 'The earth will begin its new millennium with a new source of light to illuminate it... The Sun which is to come will be called the Sun of Justice. Its appearance in the heavens will be the warning signal of the coming of the One Who Will Shine even more than the Sun itself.*" [98]

Vaughan remarks that he regarded this prophecy as totally absurd. He went home and took a nap. While he was sleeping, something caused him to awaken and he opened his eyes to a strange sight:

> "*A miniature sun, its surface swirling as if it were alive, first appeared on the wall and then floated in the air about a foot away. I rubbed my eyes and opened them again. It was still there. The (vision) vanished as I went to answer a knock at the door.*" [99]

The knock turned out to be a friend inviting Alan to an artist's party. He went to the party and had an additional synchronous experience. At the artist's home he saw a painting of a sun in a blackened landscape. He was intrigued and inquired about it. The artist told him that he had had a vision that very day of nine lights. He reproduced this vision in a drawing, which Vaughn compared to a star map. Only one area coincided with the pattern of lights, with the addition of an extra light — Monoceros, the Unicorn, located near Sirius, the Dog Star.

> "The drawing may, of course, have been somewhat inaccurate. Yet, it did seem to single out some 'dark' star near Sirius. My attention was further drawn to Sirius the next a.m. in the office when I discovered a magazine, Sky and Telescope, that our company librarian had strangely decided to send me. It contained an article on Sirius and its binary companion, jocularly called Pup ... (Pup) is a white dwarf of about the same mass as our sun and makes an orbit around Sirius every 50.09 years. Located 8.7 light years away, Pup can be seen only when it is the farthest distance away from the main star... A peculiarity of white dwarfs like Pup is that they become 'degenerate.' Astronomers have now identified a number of dark (invisible) stars by radio astronomy." [100]

Well, if there is a dark star out there heading our way, it would certainly clean house in our area of the galaxy! If it were, as some scientists have conjectured, a neighbor that drops in regularly, sending herds of comets our way, I think I would be more willing to accept this explanation. But, there is nothing to say that we can't have a cyclical cause within our own system and a loose cannon too. Just because all the other dyings happened on schedule does not mean we have to stick to the schedule.

Vaughan remarks about the following quatrain that: "(this) seems to say that when the moon and the sun are eclipsed, then another celestial body will become visibly red..." [101]

> The moon shall be obscured in the deepest darkness,
> Her brother shall pass being of a ferruginous color,
> The great one long hidden under the shadows,
> Shall make his iron lukewarm in the bloody rain. I.84

Of course, the "great one long hidden under the shadows" could also be cloud-covered Venus and the blood-red brother could be Mars. On the other hand, the 'great one' could be Jupiter, long hidden in its gaseous envelope, which ejects a moon-sized 'brother,' Apollyon, during an eclipse of the Sun, which then passes close to the earth raining hot iron on us as it passes.

Nostradamus writes: *"When the eclipse of the sun shall be at noonday, the monster shall be seen..."* The next total eclipse of the Sun in the neighborhood of Paris will happen at 11:09 U.T., on August 11, 1999. So, we have a lot of variables to consider about the year 1999 in either July or August. Of course, something like this could be sighted in July but have no serious effect until August. And then we also have May of 2000 to think about.

Let's just look at Revelation again for a moment:

"Then the fourth [angel] emptied out his bowl upon the sun and it was permitted to burn humanity with heat. ... Then the fifth [angel] emptied his bowl on the throne of the beast, and his kingdom was in darkness, and people gnawed their tongues for the torment [of their excruciating distress and severe pain]... Then the sixth [angel] emptied his bowl on the mighty river Euphrates, and its water was dried up to make ready a road for the kings of the east... Then the seventh [angel] emptied out his bowl into the air, and a mighty voice came out of the sanctuary of heaven from the throne saying, It is done! And there followed lightning flashes, loud rumblings, peals of thunder, and a tremendous earthquake; nothing like it has ever occurred since men dwelt upon the earth... The mighty city was broken into three parts, and the cities of the nations fell. ... And every island fled and no mountains could be found. And great hailstones ... fell from the sky on the people, and men blasphemed God for the plague of the hail, so very great was the plague." [102]

And so, Nostradamus has given us a terrifying picture of cosmic upheaval, which matches almost exactly what we have found in the Bible. Jesus said in Luke, chapter 21:

"Be on your guard and be careful that you are not led astray; for many will come in My name, saying, I am He! and, The time is at hand! Do not go out after them. And when you hear of wars and insurrections (disturbances, disorder and confusion) do not become alarmed and panic-stricken and terrified; for all this must take place first, but the end will not come immediately. ...

Nation will rise against nation, and kingdom against kingdom. There will be mighty and violent earthquakes, and in various places famines and pestilences; and there will be sights of terror and great signs from heaven. ...

And there will be signs in the sun and moon and stars; and upon the earth distress of nations in bewilderment and perplexity at the roaring of the tossing of the sea, Men swooning away or expiring with fear and dread and apprehension and expectation of the things that are coming on the world; for the very powers of the heavens will be shaken and caused to totter. And then they will see the Son of Man coming in a cloud with great power and glory. Now, when these things begin to occur, look up and lift up your heads, because your redemption is drawing near.

... when you see these things taking place, understand and know that the kingdom of God is at hand. Truly, I tell you, this generation (those living at that definite period of time) will not perish and pass away until all has taken place. The sky and the earth (the universe, the world) will pass away; but My words will not pass away. But take heed to yourselves and be on your guard lest your hearts be overburdened and depressed with the giddiness and headache and nausea of self-indulgence, drunkenness, and worldly worries and cares pertaining to [the business of] this life, and [lest] that day come upon you suddenly like a trap or a noose; For it will come upon all who live upon the face of the entire earth. Keep awake then and watch at all times, praing that you may have the full strength and ability and be accounted worthy to escape all these things that will take place, and to stand in the presence of the Son of Man." [103]

I would like to point out that the explicit wording is that the faithful individual should be aware of the impending event by watching the signs, and that he should have the strength and ability to 'stand' in this presence which will come upon all who live on the earth. Strength and abilities of a very specific sort will definitely be required to survive the passing of the heavens and earth.

Chapter Eight

*"A great civilization is not conquered from without until it has
destroyed itself from within. The essential cause of Rome's decline lay
in her people, her morals, her class struggles, her failing trade, her
bureaucratic despotism, her stifling taxes, her consuming war..."*

— Will and Ariel Durant, *Caesar and Christ* (1944).

*Our lives are merely strange dark interludes
in the electrical display of God the Father.*

— Eugene O'Neill, *Strange Interlude* (1928).

After many years of attempts to sort out the prophecies of Nostradamus, the Bible, and other forecasters of 'Gloom and Doom,' the question naturally arises: Is prophecy an aspect of reality reflecting man's vulnerability to his own fears and desires? Do we create a fearful future by being fearful? Is prophetic fulfillment simply a congealing of quantum realities? Conversely, if we think positively and act benevolently, can we change the future to a more friendly evolutionary process?

By way of shedding some light upon this question, I want to paraphrase a story from II Chronicles, chapter 18:

400 Prophets

Once upon a time there were two kings of two small kingdoms who were related by marriage. The first king decided to pay a visit to his brother-in-law, the second king. When he arrived for his visit, he was welcomed by the second king who had prepared all sorts of goodies and entertainment.

After a great deal of feasting and merriment, the second king told his brother-in-law, the first king, that he was inclined to think of all of his possessions as mutual and he hoped the first king felt the same. This made the first king a bit nervous and he wondered what all of this was leading up to — and he was not long in finding out. The second king wanted to make war against one of his neighbors and take territory and spoil, but, in order to do this, he needed help. He knew that his brother-in-law had no such ambitions, and he and been softening him up to ask for his aid.

The first king was a bit taken aback at this request and asked if they could call in some prophets to find out if this plan was a wise course to pursue. The second king willingly called 400 prophets. All of them, to a man, commended the plan and praised the acumen and ambition of their king. But, the first king was still uneasy — something just did not feel right in his gut. He asked if there was not just one more prophet to consult. As it turned out, there was, but the second king warned the first king not to expect much from this fellow for there was hatred between them and this bad feeling made this last prophet prejudiced against then plan of the second king. Having thoroughly assassinated the last prophet's character, he then called him in.

Sure enough, the last prophet contradicted all 400 of the other prophets and told the second king that he would die if he went into battle. To punish this rudeness, the second king had the offending oracle cast into prison to think about his audacity until the return of the kings and the army. Insisting that his prophecy was true, the last prophet commented to the king that he would certainly be amazed at their return.

But, the wicked second king had a plan. Having persuaded his brother-in-law to accompany him, he arranged to go into battle dressed as a common soldier, while his relation went attired in his kingly robes.

As it turned out, the enemy soldiers had been instructed to immediately seek out and kill only the second king. During the course of the engagement, the enemy soldiers chased after the only man attired as a king, and, finding him to not be the man they were after, they turned in rage and frustration and killed the nearest common soldier — who happened to be the evil second king. Prophecy fulfilled.

There are several important lessons in this story. The first is that prophecy is inexorable unless fundamental alterations in activity and direction are made. You can't fool Quantum Reality! The second is: true prophecy very often manifests in the very same ratio depicted in this story — 400 to 1. A third, and no less important, lesson is, people seldom want to hear the truth because it is hard to give up the games and rationalizations. And, finally, the easiest way to avoid truth is to assassinate either the speaker or his character.

The story of Jonah illuminates the opposite side of the coin. As you may recall, Jonah had been called to prophesy destruction upon the decadent and sinful city of Ninevah. He did his job well (after being sufficiently motivated by an enforced meditation in the alimentary canal of a large fish). To Jonah's surprise, the Ninevites repented and changed their ways and, as a result, the disaster was called off. Instead of being overjoyed, Jonah was mortified. It seemed to him that he had been made out a fool. He was so humiliated that he stalked off to sulk in anger. God had a little chat with him and pointed out that there were other purposes for prophetic enlightenment — namely, repentance and change.

In the present we have modern day prophets — statisticians and various scientists — projecting trends and probabilities. In most instances, both in private and public affairs, decisions are based upon these types of data. Since these modern 'divinatory' methods rely on masses of statistics, which reflect purely material acts, the elevating quality of an ideal is neither considered nor projected. As a result, the predictions upon which our culture has framed its activities result in true evolution — which is an inexorable downward spiral of decline and decay.

In this respect, eschatological predictions can serve as a stepping-stone to awareness, which may serve to activate those higher aspirations, which then may act in a mitigating fashion upon future events. If enough people become convinced that something dreadful is about to happen unless we change our ways, it may create the necessary elevation in ideals, which would serve to alter quantum realities. This may have been what Jesus meant when he spoke about the shortening of the days of destruction for the 'elect's sake. The elect must be seen as those who espouse the ideals of love, truth, freedom, equality, and the brotherhood of man under the Fatherhood of God. The petty squabbles among the various religious denominations as to who is or is not 'elect' become meaningless in the light of the true interpretations of these prophecies.

Edgar Cayce

Edgar Cayce was a shining example of a seer who made use of his position to better the spiritual, as well as the physical, condition of mankind. Cayce never passed up an opportunity to reaffirm the unity of mankind and the omnipotence and love of the Creator-God.

The most famous of contemporary prophets, Cayce was, primarily, a healer. Cayce's clairvoyant abilities manifested while in trance state and were generally engaged to provide physical, mental and spiritual assistance to thousands of individuals who had exhausted the usual techniques of medicine and/or psychiatry. The 'sleeping' Edgar Cayce was a medical diagnostician, counselor, prophet and deeply spiritual advocate of the Bible and the 'law of the universe and God.'

Cayce's prophecies relating to the changing world conditions seldom reflected anything but hope for the higher principles of mankind to overcome those of the baser self, and create a society of true equality wherein no one would ever ask, 'Am I my brother's keeper?' For all would know within: I am my brother!

Yet, Cayce delivered some frightening material relating to changes both in society and on the terrestrial globe. When it first occurred to me that the eschatological prophecies might be identical to events of the past as interpreted by Velikovsky, incidents of normal atomic interaction exemplified by studies of the microcosm, I was struck by a statement made by Cayce in reading 1299-1:

> "... know that Life itself — to be sure — is the Creative Force or God, yet its manifestations in man are electrical — or vibratory. Know then that the force in nature that is called electrical or electricity is that same force ye worship as creative or God in action." [104]

This statement, in light of present day work in quantum physics makes plain the potential fulfillment of the Biblical prophecies in literal terms — the 'Vengeance of God' — the 'thunderbolts' of Odin and Jove.

Cayce predicted many earth changes, which were to begin gradually, gaining momentum and then...? He would not be pinned down as to times, quoting the Bible: *"The hour ye know not, and the time ye know not, not even the Son, but the Father."* He qualified some prophecies by the suggestion that the attitudes of individuals and groups could appreciably alter future events. By the same token, it could be seen that the events he predicted reflected the most positive aspects of cataclysms — the minimum event necessary to re-stabilize the planet in terms of electrical charge.

Cayce's view that mankind's application of spiritual laws determines the condition of the planet as well as the events in the solar system, is a reflection of the teachings of the Bible and is echoed by Nostradamus and other seers then and since. This position was beautifully expressed in a reading given November 28, 1939:

> "As in relationships to changes, these are indicated as not only through prophecies, but through astrological aspects, as well as the thought and intent of persons and groups in high places; bringing about these things, these conditions, in what might be said in the fullness of time.
>
> However, since the advent of the Son of Man in the earth, giving man an advocate with the Father, there has been indicated (things which) would come as retribution, or in filling the law of an evolution of ideas and the relationship of material things to the thoughts and intents of individuals and groups.
>
> Then, as to whether the hearts and minds of individuals or souls ... are fired with the thoughts of dire consequences or ... of the development of a spiritual awak-

ening, is still in keeping ... (with) an awareness of that which is in the making in the affairs of state, nation ... nations, and the universe as related to the conditions upon the face of Mother Earth... It depends upon which line is taken by an individual ... pessimistic or optimistic, positive or negative: (by negative we mean) one that sees the earth being damned irrespective of what (people) do about same, taking little or no account of the words, the promises ... of Him. He manifested in the earth ... the constructive influence... This may be seen according to the Book (Bible) — which is ... a guide to those who seek to know His ways... These interpretations of the promises must be taken in account." [105]

Up to this point, Cayce has expressed the positive view and has given a pattern for spiritual applications of prophecy. In his commentary on Revelation, this is the primary thesis: that these prophecies can be applied individually and expressed as a need to overcome the 'bestial,' or material aspects of our lives both individually and socially. The first portion of the Book of Revelation, the discussion of the natures of the seven churches, gives esoteric instructions for the elevating of the spirit through the seven glandular systems of the body; the link between body and spirit. However, in conclusion to the foregoing quoted passage Cayce adds:

"And then these (prophecies) indicate ... what is to come to pass ... through these periods of the earth's journey through space; catching up, as it were, with time." [106]

Here Cayce has interpreted the purpose of prophecy as both spiritual guide and descriptions of actual, literal, events. It is typical of his nature as a healer and teacher that he emphasized the former. One might be tempted to label Cayce's 'Pollyanna' point of view as ambiguous or even double-talk. Realistically, however, his mode of expression is truly diplomatic in the cosmic sense.

Typical of this manner is his response to the question asked prior to World war II: *"What is the outlook for war?"* His classic, *"If America acts as it prays,"* it would not be drawn into the war.[107] Apparently America didn't and was. So much for optimism!

Relating to Biblical predictions of 'tribulation' and Nostradamus' prophecies of war and famine and plague, Cayce made a very provocative statement in a reading given for himself:

"As this priest may develop himself to be in that position to be in the capacity of a liberator to the word in its relationships to individuals in these periods to come; for he must enter again at that period, or in 1998." [108]

What, one might say, will bring about conditions which would necessitate a liberator?

Many of Cayce's readings state that a large group of highly evolved beings were being incarnated in the thirties and beyond; their apparent purpose being to counterbalance the negative forces being brought to bear in the earth. Also, a great influx of former Atlanteans was noted; their primary characteristics being carnal self-indulgence combined with technical ability. These last were being given the opportunity to *correct or repeat* the errors of the past — a past characterized by materialism, pride and self-destruction. I think that, at this point in time, it is apparent which road has been taken. And, knowing the road, we can guess the destination. Quantum probabilities again!

Cayce predicted many destructive events to occur on the earth by the year 2000 to 2001. One of his most famous predictions was that Atlantis would emerge from the Atlantic around the area of Bimini and that this would be noted in 1968 or 1969. In actual fact, very unusual rock formations, indicating the work of human hands — pooh-poohed by the scientific community — were noted by divers off the island of Bimini at the predicted time. So, while Atlantis may not have broken the surface, it might be seen that it is waiting in the wings for a little push. And, Cayce did predict that these events would begin gradually. This idea is reflected in the Biblical prophecy about the earthquakes and tribulations in 'divers places' which would increase in frequency and severity similar to the pains of childbirth. A fitting allegory, for, at the expulsive moment of birth, all regard for self ends in the frantic and mindless need to be free of the source of the pain. An interesting idea considering the analogy of metamorphosis.

Cayce predicted a shifting of the terrestrial axis so that frigid or semitropical areas would become more tropical. He predicted oceans and bays where there is now land; new patterns of hurricane activity — stronger and more frequent storms which would tend to hit land more often than not; we can already see evidence that this prediction is coming to pass. A recent newspaper article quoted an eminent meteorologist as saying that an increase of the planetary temperature by just one or two degrees could increase hurricane activity as well as the intensity of the storms by about 50%.

Cayce predicted the sinking and rising of assorted land masses — not just islands, but entire coasts falling into the sea; most of Japan being inundated; the upper portion of Europe changed in the 'twinkling of an eye;' many changes in the United States — the east coast, west coast and central portion to be drastically altered, and the Great Lakes to empty into the Gulf of Mexico; Los Angeles, San Francisco and New York to go into the sea; portions of the Carolinas and Georgia to be inundated; upheavals in the Arctic and Antarctic; open waters in northern Greenland; new lands off the Caribbean, and more.

As with Nostradamus and the Bible, analysts of the Cayce material tend to interpret, once again, in Darwinian terms. Cayce did indicate some activity that would begin in a gradual way, but, for the most part, the timing and causes were vague and indeterminate. According to Cayce, the polar shift will occur around the year 2000 to 2001, and this is to be the culmination of all the preceding events.

This is right in line with Nostradamus and, as I will show later, the Book of Revelation. But, with the Cayce analysts, the pole shift is seen as a result of gradual crustal displacements rather than as the cause of same. In this instance, I think that we must realize that the only event which could result in a axial shift and a global game of 'musical lands' would have to be an extraterrestrial cosmic interaction.

A recent work, *Heading Toward Omega*, by Dr. Kenneth Ring, contains some interesting prophetic statements made in relation to the Near Death Experience, or NDE.

The effects of the NDE upon those who have had one are evidence of a transcendental event — a life-changing experience likened to being 'born again' in the truest sense of the words. The individuals who have had a NDE encountered a Being of Light which imparted to them knowledge of the future of the planet, in some cases, in addition to being infused with lasting feelings of love, joy, peace, patience, kindness, goodness, faithfulness, gentleness, self-control and loss of material motivations.

One fact of these experiences stands out: not one of the persons describing this event, regardless of religious affiliation, reported that he or she was questioned upon arrival in the other realm as to who or what they believed in, nor were they instructed to bear any such messages of doctrinal specifics back when they returned to the land of the living. Many of these individuals did describe an event of life review — a sort of judgment, during which the true import of events and attitudes was borne in upon them with the usual result of a comprehensive and fundamental value shift in their lives once recovery was achieved.

Dr. Ring prepared questionnaires that evaluated specific areas of conduct and philosophy both before and after the NDE. Where possible, he obtained other-party collaboration. Almost without exception, the individuals demonstrated shifts toward love, compassion, tolerance, firm belief in God and a total loss of the fear of death. The importance of this fine research cannot be overstated. In some cases, the NDE was experienced many years past with no loss of the validity of the event or its effects with the passage of time. Many of the individuals experienced heightened psychic perception and abilities and a turning to spirituality rather than 'religion.' It is noted that the NDE is, for the majority of those who experienced it, a catalyst for spiritual awakening. One of these individuals said:

> "I was raised Protestant... I gave it up in my early teens... I researched Catholicism. I found that was worse... Essentially, at the same time of my accident, I was a ranting, raving atheist. There was no God... He was a figment of man's imagination ... (Now) I know that there's a God. And that God is everything that exists, (that's) the essence of God... I have no question (that there is a God)." [109]

Now, while the orientation and consciousness of the people who have reported a NDE is important, we are mainly concerned with the prophetic elements within this thesis. A few of these people interviewed independently have had a vision of the planet's future in conjunction with the NDE. All of them had essentially the same vision. Additionally, they all seemed to agree on the year in which these changes were to begin — 1988. However, that the timing of the events was not set in stone was made abundantly clear.

One of Dr. Ring's subjects comments:

> "At one point I had complete knowledge of everything, from the beginning of creation to the end of time ... (but) I was told ... that I would remain unconscious for five days so that all the things I had been shown would not resurface, so they could be stored for future reference. ... When given this information, you are given ... the time ... when you can speak of it. If you were to ask me a question now ... (and) if the time wasn't (right) for me to answer, I couldn't give you the answer." [110]

What, specifically, are the visions of those who have had a NDE?

> "The vision of the future I received during my near-death-experience was one of tremendous upheaval in the world as a result of our general ignorance of the true reality. I was informed that mankind was breaking the laws of the universe and as a result of this would suffer. This suffering was not due to the vengeance of an indignant God but rather like the pain one might suffer as a result of arrogantly

defying the law of gravity. It was to be an inevitable educational cleansing of the earth that would creep up upon its inhabitants, who would try to hide blindly in the institutions of law, science and religion. Mankind, I was told, was being consumed by the cancers of arrogance, materialism, racism, chauvinism, and separatist thinking. I saw sense turning to nonsense, and calamity, in the end, turning to providence.

At the end of this general period of transition, mankind was to be 'born anew' with a new sense of his place in the universe. The birth process, as in all the kingdoms, was exquisitely painful." [111]

Further comments were more specific:

"The seismic activity is going to increase terribly; the United States is going to start suffering some great seismic problems." [112]

"There may be a pole shift ... there are going to be polar changes ... it's not going to kill all the races off, but we're going to have to start again from square one... There's going to be a larger land mass." [113]

This last comment is particularly interesting if one considers it carefully. Did the individual mean more total land area relative to ocean area? If so, there could be several reasons for an increase in landmass. The first could be an increase in the ice caps — taking up more of the planetary water. Or, there could be an actual addition of solid matter from an extraterrestrial contact and/or a suspension of some of the gases held in water in a canopy around the globe.

Further revelations include:

"They showed Florida breaking off from the mainland, land rising and becoming an island." [114]

"It (a higher being) said that there was going to be (environmental) stress. And I saw mudslides... I saw California... I saw water pouring. I saw quicksand. I saw things shifting... It looked like I was looking down on islands.... and I watched them tip and elongate and stretch and groan... I'm interpreting this now as probably an indication of this pole shift business." [115]

The 'pole shift business' is an oft-reiterated theme among the prophecies and there are many theories about its causes. Many interpreters believe that it will be a result of the alignment of the planets or a result of the melting of the polar ice cap and consequent planetary imbalance. This is entirely within the realm of possibility but the juxtaposition of 'heavenly' events with this terrestrial destruction makes it more likely that the two are intimately connected.

Those who experienced visions of the future as part of their NDEs also saw droughts, economic collapse, possible nuclear war. This nuclear war should be looked at particularly in light of the comments of Cayce, Nostradamus and the Bible relating to the 'Kings of the East.'

> *"I can see a magnetized target of some kind and all this energy is being focused on it... It's not like an explosion, it's like an implosion. And the result of this process is going to produce ... a tremendous amount of energy. But the important thing about this aspect ... well, it's a series of negativisms that are going on around the earth and (as a result) the human beings on the earth will experience rather extravagant things, happenings and disruptions, and so on, starting very shortly and through this period of time ... it will change everything."* [116]

It will change everything!

> *"For, behold, I create a new heaven and a new earth. And the former things shall not be remembered or come into mind. But be glad and rejoice forever in that which I create; for behold, I create Jerusalem to be a rejoicing, and her people a joy. And I will rejoice in Jerusalem, and be glad in My people; and the sound of weeping shall be no more heard in it, nor the cry of distress. There shall no more be in it an infant who lives but a few days, or an old man who dies prematurely; for the child shall die a hundred years old, and the sinner who dies when only a hundred years old shall be accursed. They shall build houses and inhabit them, and they shall plant vineyards and eat the fruit of them. They shall not build and another inhabit; they shall not plant and another eat. For as the days of a tree, so shall be the days of My people, and My chosen and elect shall long make use of and enjoy the work of their hands. They shall not labor in vain or bring forth for sudden terror or calamity; for they shall be the descendants of the blessed of the Lord, and their offspring with them. And it shall be that before they call I will answer; and while they are yet speaking I will hear. The wolf and the lamb shall feed together, and the lion shall eat straw like the ox; and dust shall be the serpent's food. They shall not hurt or destroy in all My holy Mount, says the Lord."* [117]
>
> *"Then I saw a new sky and a new earth, for the former sky and the former earth had passed away, and there no longer existed any sea. And I saw the holy city, the new Jerusalem, descending out of heaven from God, all arrayed like a bride beautified and adorned for her husband; Then I heard a mighty voice from the throne and I perceived its distinct words saying, See! The abode of God is with men, and He will personally be with them and be their God. God will wipe away every*

tear from their eyes; and death shall be no more, neither shall there be anguish (sorrow and mourning) nor grief nor pain any more, for the old conditions and the former order of things have passed away." [118]

So, again, we have metamorphosis.

That this change is to be more than a political and economic transformation is apparent to even a casual reader. Yet, a shadow is drawn over the actual event. The Bible refers to it as the 'Marriage of the Lamb' or 'The Great Supper of God,' which has an interesting sidelight that I will discuss at the end of this work. Nevertheless, as we have noted, a new heaven and a new earth is foreseen wherein the entire order of things is changed. What can be the nature of this change?

Supposing an extraterrestrial cataclysm occurs — the mechanics of which we can only conjecture — and the earth is changed in many ways; what would be the nature of the changes which would create all the benefits prophesied for us — long life, psychic powers, an end to sickness and disease, a drastic change in the entire order of things, even to the behavior of animals? I think it is a thought well worth contemplating.

Why do we repress such concepts and assign them to the realms of impossibility? I believe it is part and parcel of the meat of the next section. In this sense we must reexamine Jesus' words in Matthew 24:

"And many false prophets will rise up and deceive and lead many into error. And the love of the great body of people will grow cold because of the multiplied lawlessness and iniquity, But he who endures to the end will be saved. And this good news of the kingdom will be preached throughout the whole world as a testimony to all the nations, and then will come the end." [119]

Note that Jesus clearly intended to say that the 'Good News' would not be preached until just before the time of the end — and that prior to this many false prophets would arise and lead many into error, resulting in the loss of the love of the people. And, since he included it with the other signs of the end, we may assume that the truth has not been preached or taught or known up to the present time. There has been such confusion and error in the scope and identities of the various prophetic entities and it is with these identities I shall deal next. Once these entities are placed in their proper light and the scope of the events squared with actual happenings, many formerly confusing elements will become perfectly clear and logical.

In addition, by seeing when and how certain prophecies have already been fulfilled, we may know where we are on the prophetic timetable and, in this way, we might be able to tell exactly what is going to happen to us next.

Chapter Nine

If there is any fixed star in our constitutional constellation, it is that no official, high or petty, can prescribe what shall be orthodox in politics, nationalism, religion, or other matters of opinion, or force citizens to confess by word or act their faith therein... Those who begin coercive elimination of dissent soon find themselves exterminating dissenters. Compulsory unification of opinion achieves only a unanimity of the graveyard.

— Justice Robert H. Jackson, 1892-1954.

A popular book about the 'End Times' includes a chart listing the events preceding and including the 'Judgment.' An abbreviated list compiled from this timetable includes the following:

1. Israel regathers, signaling the beginning of the apostasy.
2. Signs in the sun and moon (eclipses, etc.). The 'Antichrist' is born.
3. Gentile rule ends in Jerusalem and the rebuilding of the temple is begun.
4. Atheistic Communism seeks world domination. Russia invades Israel.
5. Russia is destroyed and Israel saved; seven years required to bury the dead from this conflict.
6. Three and a half years after this war, the Antichrist emerges and forms a ten-nation confederacy.
   (This Antichrist to come from one of the divisions of Alexander's empire.)
7. The Antichrist is recognized by 'saved' individuals, but dupes the remainder of humanity. Antichrist institutes a worldwide pagan religion with government recognition in Rome.
8. The first stage of the Resurrection: the 'Stealing Away' of the saints — The Rapture.
9. The Holy Spirit, that which has 'hindered' the revealing of the Antichrist, having left with the 'Saints,' leaves the world wide open to oppression and Tribulation begins.
10. The Antichrist proclaims himself to be God and takes his seat in the temple in Jerusalem. Those who refuse to worship him will be decimated.

11. Plagues are poured on the kingdom of the Antichrist.
12. The Antichrist gathers a massive army and prepares to do battle with God.
13. Armageddon: the Antichrist loses; Jesus wins and returns to rule the world. Naturally, all those who were raptured out come back and rule with him.[120]

I truly hope that no one laughed. The foregoing was extracted from a book by an internationally known evangelical theologian who has more letters after his name than the average college professor.

Is this list of events what the Bible teaches? If not, how did this doctrine come to be so generally accepted?

Having set up the criteria, I will attempt to deal with them in order.

Israel regathers, signaling the beginning of the apostasy.

The regathering of Israel is not prophesied as the signaling of the beginning of apostasy.

That is a baseless assumption. Matthew says, referring to the regathering:

> "So also when you see these signs ... you may know ... that He is near, at the very doors."[121]

Paul declared that the 'Mystery of Lawlessness,' or the antichrist, was present in the early days of the Church.

Signs in the sun and moon (eclipses, etc.). The 'Antichrist' is born.

Signs in the Sun and moon are clearly prophesied to occur *after* the great tribulation and as the Son of Man approaches.

> "Immediately after the tribulation of those days the sun will be darkened, and the moon will not shed its light, and the stars will fall from the sky, and the powers of the heavens will be shaken. Then the sign of the Son of Man will appear in the sky..."[122]

Obviously these signs consist of more than eclipses. (Unless, of course, the literal interpreters wish to accuse Jesus of hyperbole.) So, if the Antichrist is to bring tribulation, it doesn't make sense that he would be just born as the signs appear in the heavens, which are prophesied to occur after the tribulation he institutes.

Gentile rule ends in Jerusalem and the rebuilding of the temple is begun. Luke says:

> *"They will fall by the mouth and the edge of the sword, and be led away as captives ... and Jerusalem will be trodden down by the Gentiles until the times of the Gentiles are fulfilled."* [123]

Daniel adds to this mystery:

> *"Then I heard a holy one speaking, and another holy one said to the one that spoke, For how long is the vision concerning the continual offering, the transgression that makes desolate, and the giving over of both the sanctuary and the host to be trampled under foot? And he said to him and to me, For 2,300 evenings and mornings (literal days: 6.3 years); then the sanctuary shall be cleansed and restored."* [124]

In 70 A.D., Jerusalem was sacked, the Temple destroyed, after being 'abominated.' This was the Abomination of Desolation spoken of by Daniel, which would occur after seventy weeks of years had passed. It occurred right on schedule and signaled the beginning of 'The Times of the Gentiles' relative to the Jewish people. However, when Jesus was asked about the destruction of the Temple and the consummation of the age, He answered both questions simultaneously thus making it clear that the former event was to be an archetype of the latter. However, the destruction of the Temple in Jerusalem, which occurred just as Jesus had predicted it, fulfilling Daniel's seventy weeks, related only to the small nation of Israel. Once the 'New Covenant' was established, the archetypal experience became a thing of global consideration, just as 'Jewishness,' or 'Chosenness' became a matter of spirit and not nationality. Thus, the event we are looking for is a global 'abomination' which will last for 6.3 years, during which time the temple of God's spirit, the human family, will be oppressed, abominated by fear and horror and the necessity of placing material survival above spiritual considerations. This must be the solution for, if we add 6.3 to 70 A.D., we have 76 A.D., at which time the restoration of the Temple was not accomplished. If we add the 6.3 to 1948, the time of the repatriation of the Jews, we have 1954 — and the Temple was not rebuilt nor in operation at that time either.

As noted, the timing and interpretation of these elements is based upon the assumed rebuilding of the Temple in Jerusalem and the restoration of the daily burnt offering. II Thessalonians speaks of the Antichrist taking his seat in the temple and this is where the idea of the necessity of the rebuilding of the Temple in Jerusalem had its genesis. The logic goes: How can the Antichrist take his seat in the Temple if it has not been rebuilt? Also, how can a seat be taken in a temple if it is not done by a single man?

In II Thessalonians Paul speaks of the temple of God. Many have been taught that this refers to the Temple in Jerusalem. However, Paul is addressing Christians about falling away from true Christian teachings. If Paul is addressing Christians about Christian concepts, the word 'temple' must refer to the body of man. For example: *"Do you not know that your body is a temple of the Holy Spirit Who lives within you, whom you have received from God?"* [125] *"For we are the temple of the living God; even as God said, I will dwell in and among them and will walk in and with and among them, and I will be their God, and they shall be my people."* [126] *"In Him the whole structure is joined together harmoniously, and it continues to rise into a holy temple in the Lord. In Him you yourselves also are being built [into this structure], to form a (dwelling place) of God in the Spirit."* [127]

The Greek word used for temple (*naos*) in the scriptures cited, which refer to man as the temple of God, is the same Greek word used in II Thessalonians 2:4 for temple. However, a completely different word is usually used when referring to the Temple in Jerusalem (*hieron*). Paul was not speaking of the Temple in Jerusalem in II Thessalonians; he was talking about mankind — the temple of God's spirit. And, though a man may claim to be following the standards of Christianity, he may, in reality, have set himself up as his own god because he exalts himself — his own interpretations and preconceived notions — against every so-called god or object of worship. This will become more meaningful as we go along.

Atheistic Communism seeks world domination. Russia invades Israel.

Atheistic Communism has long been associated with the Beast of Revelation 13 and the ideas related in Ezekiel 38 and 39. A careful reading of Ezekial will reveal that these chapters describe a cosmic catastrophe inflicted upon a nation known as Gog, long thought to be identified with Russia. It may have been true that there were political aspirations within Russia toward Israel, but there is so little organization left within this area of the globe, that I think we can count Russia out as a threat. In any event, the passages in Ezekiel make it clear that no battle will take place between the two nations. In Revelation, chapter 20, Gog and Magog are introduced as evil empires which attack the 'City of God' *after* the thousand year reign of Christ; *after* the Second Coming; *after* Armageddon; thereby indicating that all who survive the cosmic catastrophe may not be 'saved,' nor 'born again.' Or this could indicate a future deterioration following a long period of enlightenment.

Russia is destroyed and Israel saved; seven years required to bury the dead from this conflict.

See above.

Three and a half years after this war, the Antichrist emerges and forms a ten-nation confederacy.

This idea is drawn from an amalgamation of II Thessalonians and Revelation 13. The time element is drawn both from Daniel and from references in Revelation. It should be curious to anyone who considers these elements that if the 'Times of the Gentiles' and the trampling down of Jerusalem must end before the rebuilding of the Temple, how does it happen that the Soviets reenter and do further trampling and the Antichrist comes in and sets up shop? I assume that both could be considered Gentiles in strictly Jewish terms. Most confusing!

The Antichrist is recognized by 'saved' individuals, but dupes the remainder of humanity. Antichrist institutes a worldwide pagan religion with government recognition in Rome.

The Antichrist is supposedly recognized by virtue of the spirituality of the 'born again' believer and is assumed to be, somehow, connected with the Catholic Church, according to many Protestant doctrines. It should be obvious that if a great war were to be instituted by the invasion of Israel by the Soviets, or anyone else for that matter, the United States would not stand idly by, nor would most other treaty-bound nations. An invasion of Israel would institute a worldwide holocaust and few people would be left to care whether a pagan ruler took over or not. In any event, recent events in Russia make this point moot.

The first stage of the Resurrection: the 'Stealing Away' of the saints — The Rapture.

The Holy Spirit, that which has 'hindered' the revealing of the Antichrist, having left with the 'Saints,' leaves the world wide open to oppression and Tribulation begins. The 'Stealing Away' followed by 'Tribulation.'

The idea of 'Tribulation' comes from the word *tribulare*, which means 'to thresh.' This means that the useful parts of the wheat are separated from the chaff.

If we recall the parable of the wheat and the tares, it should be apparent what happens to whom. This parable is given as a description of the end times. The farmer plants wheat and in the night the enemy sows weeds which look like wheat in the field. The workers come and ask the owner of the field what to do. He instructs them to let all grow together and, at the time of the harvest, pull up the weeds and burn them first, then gather the wheat into the barn.

Theologians have endlessly distorted the last part of Matthew 24 to support an unfounded myth of being 'raptured' into the sky, as we have already discussed in a previous section. Only Christians who meet certain criteria based upon any number of variations in doctrine are eligible. The word *thief* was used to emphasize the need to watch and be prepared, not to indicate an absurdity called a 'Stealing Away.'

The idea of being raptured out of tribulation is, naturally, attractive, but this is not supported by the Bible nor does it stand to reason. As already pointed out, if the Soviets have invaded Israel, a great war has already erupted and we might assume this to be a very great tribulation. This doctrine is one of the most evil to have come out of the Christian religions for it places faith in an event that will never occur. And, when real tribulation begins to fall fast and hard upon the peoples who have adopted this concept, having placed their faith in an illusion, it is entirely likely that they will discard the entire attitude of Christianity, having been betrayed in that which pleased the flesh. For, it is apparent that this is a doctrine of flesh, for it caters to the abhorrence of physical dis-ease. The idea of enduring to the end, on the other hand, is mentioned not less than 13 times in the New Testament. The doctrine of the rapture is an assumption made by twisting scriptural references and is, in truth, a doctrine of men.

The Antichrist proclaims himself to be God and takes his seat in the temple in Jerusalem. Those who refuse to worship him will be decimated.

There has long been a tradition of the 'Secret Teachings' of Jesus, and any astute reader of the Bible can immediately perceive that much is alluded to, which was either never recorded or was later expunged. It is apparent that, since these things were hidden, they are the very meat of the matter — the foundational truths of Christianity. In at least sixteen passages in the Gospels, Jesus is described as 'teaching,' but the words he taught were never recorded. Mark wrote in his Gospel, that Jesus taught the multitudes only in parables and expounded and explained to his disciples only in private. Precious few of these explanations were included in the text. Some theologians have supposed that these 'deeper' truths are fully covered in the epistles, but a careful reading makes it apparent that this is not the case. Social commentary, mundane advice, allusions to deeper truths revealed in past conversations or promised in future conversations; this is the primary composition of these letters. And, as a result, most Christian denominations concern themselves primarily with such matters, believing that this is sufficient to ensure 'salvation.' But, we can determine that the fact that deeper teachings exist is supported by the Bible.

Why is this matter so generally ignored and these mysteries not sought by theologians (as a whole), in the obvious places where one could expect to find them — in the amplified teachings of supplementary ancient manuscripts; in parapsychological research; in new revelations; by studying other religions and finding the points of agreement? The findings in all of these are supportive of the cornerstones of the Christian worldview and offer scientific ground for movement away from the materialism and humanism that has so eroded Christian faith in this century.

Many Christians feel that whatever is revealed to them must come directly via the 'Spirit of Truth.' Yet, there are innumerable versions of doctrine dispensed, one would think, by this very same 'Spirit of Truth.' There has to be more to this fear of trading the traditional identity for a new and more enriching concept — and there is.

This circular argument relating to the a priori assumption of the infallibility of the Bible and the human doctrines that obscure the remaining truths of the scriptures themselves, and which has resulted in the multiplicity of denominations, is the fulfillment of a very important event prophesied in the scriptures themselves. The ultimate irony is that the forces operating through the individuals who have been responsible for the attempts to conceal the light of truth, have only served to set the stage for the playing out of the final act of the great cosmic drama.

The prophecy I refer to is to be found in II Thessalonians:

> "Let no one deceive or beguile you in any way, for that day (Judgment Day) will not come except the apostasy comes first [unless the great falling away of those who have professed to be Christians has come], and the man of lawlessness (sin) is revealed, who is the Son of doom, Who opposes and exalts himself so proudly and insolently against and over all that is called God ... proclaiming that he himself is God.

Do you not recollect that when I was with you I told you these things? And now you know what is restraining him; it is so that he may be manifested in his own time.

For the mystery of lawlessness (that hidden principle of rebellion against constituted authority) is already at work in the world, restrained only until he who restrains is taken out of the way. And then the lawless one will be revealed and the Lord Jesus will slay him with the breath of His mouth and bring him to an end by His appearing...
The coming (of the apostasy) is through the activity and working of Satan...
And by unlimited seduction to evil and with all wicked deception for those who are perishing because they did not welcome the Truth but refused to love it that they might be saved. Therefore, God sends upon them a misleading influence, a working of error and strong delusion to make them believe what is false, In order that all may be judged and condemned who did not believe in [who refused to adhere to, trust in and rely on] the Truth." [128]

One of the keys to this prophecy is the word *anthropes*, translated as *man of lawlessness*. This is the same Greek word Timothy uses in 3:17: *"That the man of God may be perfect."* It is also used similarly to mean many people in Hebrews 2:6. In I John 2:18—22, the term 'antichrist' is used to describe many people — not just those who deny Christ, but also those who claim to be Christians but, in fact, deny the true teachings of Christ.

"Beware of false prophets who come to you dressed as sheep, but inside they are devouring wolves. You will fully recognize them by their fruits. Do people pick grapes from thorns, or figs from thistles? ... A good tree cannot bear bad fruit... Not everyone who says to me, Lord, Lord, will enter the kingdom of heaven... Many will say to Me on that day, Lord, Lord, have we not prophesied in your name, and driven out demons in Your name and done many mighty works in Your name? (All sorts of miracles and signs and delusive marvels — lying wonders) And then I will say to them, I never knew you..." [129]

Organizing these prophecies and looking at them in the light of reason we find the following points:

1. A great many people are involved, not a single man; 'son of doom and Son of Perdition' must be seen as amplifying expletives added to *anthropes* (plural intent) of lawlessness.
2. They profess to be Christians — and, in fact, constitute the majority of Christianity.

3. They are self-righteous in their belief that they possess the only true knowledge — this is shown by the fact that they place this human judgment before all other evidence, assuming their view to be divinely inspired. In this way, they have taken the authority of judgment from God and placed their own will in its place — thus opposing and exalting themselves over God ... rebelling against constituted authority ... taking God's seat in the temple (the body); in short, proclaiming themselves to be God! *"For [although] they hold a form of piety (true religion,) they deny and reject and are strangers to the power of it [their conduct belies the genuineness of their profession]."* [130]

4. The principle of lawlessness was already active in the early Church. I have often wondered about the total absence of very early Christian documents and manuscripts. It has been explained that the originals were passed around until they were tattered, then copied and the copies passed until they were worn out also. By the time the canon was assembled, all that existed were copies of copies of copies of copies. Considering the reverence and awe the early Christians attached to relics and so forth, it seems far more likely that, say, a manuscript written by Peter himself would have been carefully preserved and copies taken from the original to be passed around. However, if the early Church leaders, anxious to strengthen their control over the masses, saw to it that all originals were destroyed and only carefully edited and altered copies remained, this would explain both the activity of the Mystery of Lawlessness as well as the loss of the Secret Teachings — if they had ever been written at all.

5. The word 'restrain,' (hinder in the KJV), is used in such a way that it can only mean 'hiding.' What is being hidden is the Mystery of Lawlessness, the Hidden Purpose of God, not the identity of a pagan world ruler who craves to be worshipped. This mystery is to remain hidden until just before the time of the end and then the Lord Jesus will slay 'the man (anthropes) of sin' with the breath of His mouth. *"From his mouth goes forth a sharp sword with which He can smite the nations ... and the beast was seized ... and with him the false prophet... Both of them were hurled alive into the fiery lake ... And the rest were killed with the sword that issues from the mouth of Him Who is mounted on the horse..."* [131] Who gets slain by the 'breath' or 'sword' from the mouth? Not the Beast nor the false prophet, long identified as 'The Antichrist' and his high priest. No, the clarifying sentence states that nations are slain.

6. The removal of the hindrance, or the revealing of the mystery of God is the breaking of the 'seal' on the prophetic truth — the pouring out of the Spirit of God — the Coming of the Spirit of Truth in the last days — to overcome the 'misleading influence sent by God,' which was in operation from the early days of the Church until just before the Day of the Lord. This misleading influence, the 'working of Satan,' sent by God, has been the spirit operating in all of the Christian churches as prophesied by Paul. The Hindrance to Truth. Thus, the traditions, the doctrines and dogma as taught until the present, are scripturally defined as predicated upon lies and deception. The prophesied coming of the 'Spirit of Truth,' taught by many to be the 'Baptism of the Holy Ghost,' in most instances, according to this prophecy, must be a delusion to error.

7. What event brings forth the Spirit of Truth? As described in Revelation, it is the 'Breaking of a Seal.' Understanding of the operation of angels and planets as described in a previous section, we may assume this to be an astrological event.

In *The Further Prophecies of Nostradamus*, Erika Cheetham translates:

> "*The great army will pass over the mountains when*
> *Saturn is in Sagittarius and Mars moving into Pisces.*" II.48 [132]

This astrological square is very rare. It last occurred in July, 1751 — that is, until it occurred again on December 16, 1986. Within 25 years of its previous occurrence, the United States was at war with Britain. The French Revolution followed soon after and the 1700's was a period of great change and turmoil due to the repercussions of the industrial revolution and the blossoming of Hu - manist philosophy.

Since no human army of global import passed over any mountain or breached any barrier at or around this time, I think we may assume that this quatrain has a cosmic significance. This may have been, in fact, the sign of the breaking of the seal of prophecy.

8. Many of this group will influence their followers with signs and marvels. I have noticed a tremendous increase in so-called faith healers who make fortunes off the trust and need of the poor and ignorant and who always keep their own health insurance paid up. Through mass hypnosis techniques, they control crowds while waving their hands and pronouncing 'magic' incantations. But, by and

large, their true successes are few and far between. Some permanent healings do occur from this type of activity, but reflect an action of faith within the individual. In general, these supposed healings can be ascribed to hypnotic symptom removal rather than a fundamental change in self-concept and this explains why so many of them are short-lived.

Suffice it to say that there is a Creative Force and this force can be tapped to energize and atomically alter matter, but this can occur spontaneously or within parameters other than the prescribed 'born again' experience as defined by the majority of Christendom. In this sense, we must observe that a Hindu holy man, or a spiritualist, or a New Age shaman who demonstrates this ability is condemned as 'Satanically deluded' by the 'born again' believer who experiences the exact same thing.

9. Being 'antichrist' or 'lawless' is equated with refusal to love, seek, and accept truth. As noted before, truth is very often defined as that which pleases a given individual or group. I have observed time and again that churches and church-goers are generally more interested in the material aspects of their religious practice than they are interested in working to effect permanent and proper growth in their spiritual being.

That is not to say that those who are, by their own definition, 'born again,' are not benefited by the experience, but, in general, they stop at this point and go no further. It is the old question of works versus grace. Most of them are involved in their religion in the manner of small children who fear severe punishment if they are not good. They are more interested in the games — the social and exclusivist aspects — of religious practice than the actual work necessary to follow the pattern of Christ. They have accepted the idea of salvation without the fulfilling of the law — they are lawless.

The loss of true knowledge within the Christian Church is foreordained and planned — for a purpose. And this purpose is now being revealed as the time draws near for the fulfillment of these prophecies.

These clues, when properly understood, make clear that the 'Antichrist' is, in part, the Christian churches. It is not, as the churches teach, a world taken over by Satanists, among whom they include everyone who doesn't believe as they do individually and collectively.

*Specifically defined, this Antichrist society will consist of those who claim
to be Christians or those who act in the name of Christ.*

Jesus' diatribe against the Scribes and Pharisees of His own time is a
prophetic injunction against the established churches of our time:

> *"But woe to you, scribes and Pharisees, pretenders (hypocrites)! For you shut the
> kingdom of heaven in men's faces; for you neither enter yourselves, nor do you
> allow those who are about to go in to do so. ... Woe to you scribes and Pharisees,
> pretenders (hypocrites)! For you travel over sea and land to make a single pros-
> elyte, and when he becomes one, you make him doubly as much a child of Hell
> (Son of Perdition) as you are. Woe to you blind guides, who say, If anyone swears
> by the sanctuary of the temple, it is nothing; but if he swears by the gold of the
> sanctuary, he is a debtor [bound by his oath]. You blind fools! For which is greater:
> the gold or the sanctuary...? You say, too, Whoever swears by the altar is not duty
> bound; but whoever swears by the offering on the altar, his oath is binding. You
> blind men! Which is greater: the gift, or the altar which makes the gift sacred?
> So, whoever swears by the altar swears by it and everything on it. And whoever
> swears by heaven swears by the throne of God and by Him Who sits upon it."* [133]

When one considers the elements of the foregoing passage, the deeper
truth emerges. Christendom has been rabid in its persecutions and attempts to convert 'heathens' who are considered by the Church to be
unsaved and on the road to hell. Jesus is the gift on the altar; the Christ
spirit, representing God on earth, is the altar. Jesus was the first-fruit
of the plan for resurrection and was, at the point of His baptism, the physical representative of the pattern that must be striven after in order to
partake of this resurrection/salvation.

The Christ Spirit, the Word, existed as the Root and Offspring of David
in this sense. To 'swear' by the altar and everything on it is an express
indication that grace is inextricably intertwined with the law. God is
not mocked — everything a man sows he will reap. He may be strengthened by grace to endure the reaping without further sin, but he will
reap nevertheless.

It should be made very clear that the law which is emphasized is the
Universal Law, not the hair-splitting Judaic law or modern Christian
dogma. Jesus came to demonstrate that one can fulfill the universal law
in spirit. He was accused by the holiest men of the day, those who would
not be caught dead breaking the 'rules of purity,' of consorting with the
lowest sort of people — drunkards, harlots, thieves, and publicans. Publicans were ritually 'unclean' because they were in the employ of the gen-

tile Romans. In fact, Matthew was a publican. Not only did Jesus consort with sinners, he ate heartily and drank wine.

In today's Christianity, the worship of the man, Jesus, has replaced the worship of God's Logos. Statements to the effect that Jesus is the only name by which a man may be saved, and that acceptance of this view is the key to God's plan of salvation, is the most grossly misrepresented teaching ever to come out of the Christian Church. *This amounts to worship of the offering while disregarding the altar.* For those of you who stumble over 'Jesus as the only name by which a man may be saved,' I ask you to seriously consider the *fruits of this doctrine* and the probable impetus for its propagation. Do not misunderstand me. I am not in any way denying the redemptive work of Christ in its true parameters.

Just consider the Crusades — in the name of Jesus only. Consider the Inquisition — in the name of Jesus only. Consider the annihilation of the American Indians — in the name of Jesus only. Consider of the murder of over 10 million fellow human beings in our own time — in the name of Jesus only.

* * *

In 1945 extensive Gnostic treatises were discovered in earthenware jars buried in a field at Nag Hammadi in Egypt. The fifty-two scriptures were in Coptic, translated from the Greek. Just as the discovery of the Dead Sea Scrolls at Qumran in 1947 gave us, for the first time, Essene scriptures, so the startling appearance of these Egyptian documents gave us the actual words of the Gnostics. But, the average person did not hear a lot about this particular group of manuscripts because the information contained in them was, in some cases, considered heretical.

These texts were known to the early Church Fathers, and were often referred to in a general way. It should be understood that these texts were excluded form the Canon primarily because of sectarian and political rivalries. It is also apparent from systematic study that the fundamental theological questions receive different emphases in these Gnostic texts. It is also interesting to note that many of the contradictions in the 'Textus Receptus' may be reconciled by critical analysis and comparison of these two sources. That is not to say that all problems vanish into the air, but a reasonable and acceptable theology can be derived which adequately accounts for the splintered and divisive beliefs of many of the world's most prominent religions, giving cohesiveness and unity to their primary notions. I think that this is what we must seek, for I don't think that anyone can argue the concept that 'God is not the author of confusion.' And, since there exists such diversity of beliefs around the globe, we may conclude that either somebody is right, excluding all others, or that nobody is right, including all.

In examining the expression of the various religious beliefs around the world, the Christian faith stands out as claiming to exclude all others on a fundamental point of doctrine. The Christian faith holds that belief in Jesus as the Son of God and Savior of the World and profession of this belief is the key to salvation. Any person, regardless of the conduct of their lives, is doomed to judgment (that is, some sort of afterlife punishment) if they do not make this confession.

The Epistle of James, in discussing faith versus works says: *"You believe that God is one; you do well. So do the demons believe and shudder!"* [134] The Gospel of John states: *"I assure you, most solemnly I tell you, the person whose ears are open to My words and believes and trusts in ... Him Who sent Me has eternal life. And he does not come into judgment, but he has already passed over out of death into life."* [135] The latter statement was made by Christ prior to his crucifixion and resurrection and clearly indicates that salvation is not hinged upon a belief in the man Jesus. Jesus referred to himself repeatedly as 'The Son of Man.'

On the other hand, there are numerous statements in the New Testament which declare that salvation hinges solely upon believing in the name of Jesus. Contradictory to this is Jesus' statement that *"Not every one who says to Me, Lord, Lord, will enter the kingdom of heaven, but he who does the will of My Father..."* [136] So, we have a fundamental doctrinal confusion and must find some criteria by which to reconcile this dilemma.

In describing false prophets, Jesus set up criteria for evaluation: *"By their fruits you shall know them."* Since these prophets were described as performing miracles and signs and wonders, we may assume that such are not to be considered fruits. What are fruits? A given plant or tree bears fruit after a period of time known as the growing season, so we may assume that fruit becomes evident after a period of time. Fruit also has the capability of propagating other fruit after its own kind. Galatians 5 says: *"But the fruit of the Spirit is love, joy, gladness, peace, patience, kindness, faithfulness; gentleness, self-control."* [137] So, it might be said that, by the criteria established by Jesus, himself, an individual who possesses these qualities must be 'saved' regardless of his religious affiliation.

The fact that God can work in and through all kinds of people of all faiths should be evidence that doctrines are creations of men and God is the only truth.

Yes, Jesus was the pattern in the flesh — the Way; yes, He bore our infirmities in that He was subjected to the weaknesses of the flesh over which he triumphed; and, yes, by His stripes and His death we are healed — but this healing is one of a change in understanding, thought patterns, knowledge of our true inner capabilities. When Jesus said: *"I am the Way, the Truth and the Life, and no man cometh unto the Father but by me"*, he spoke as the Christ, and His words are true. The Christ spirit is present in all who manifest the fruits of the Spirit. It doesn't matter who the messenger was, or the specific doctrine followed. If we follow the pattern of the life of Jesus, no matter who taught it to us, we are 'saved.' And this inner knowledge, this following of the pattern, is that which can change our lives and make all things new. Through faith we can align ourselves with the 'Waveform' of God — the Word, the Logos, the Christ — and receive power to perceive, through psychic potentials, truth relating to all those things necessary to pattern our lives after the Master — the Forerunner, the First-fruits — and thereby become Sons of God and Brothers of Jesus.

Jesus accused the Pharisees of shutting the door of the kingdom of heaven in men's faces, and this is a clue to how the Christian churches have accomplished their perversions of the truth. As noted, some of the teachings of Jesus may well have been withheld from the masses for fear of distortion. Others have, of a certainty, been expunged to make the masses more compliant and dependent upon the Church hierarchy. Many will blanch at this thought and mutter maledictions of heresy, but scriptural evidence can be seen to support this idea. The true teachings of Christ have never been fully expounded to 'all the nations.' This is due, primarily, to the 'anti-Christ' elements in the early Church, which sought to expunge all teachings that would not lead to the masses' dependence upon the Church hierarchy. They destroyed those manuscripts they could, banned those they couldn't destroy, and altered what was left. Fortunately the alterations were neither expert nor consistent. In this way, the very contradictions apparent in the Gospels and Epistles can lead us to a fuller understanding of the truth. But only if we love truth sufficiently to read, search, and accept.

If the kingdom of heaven is within, as Jesus suggested, how can the Church leaders prevent one from entering? The only answer is that the Church can do this by declaring all of the abilities, and expressions of the spirit of man, the seed of God's kingdom within, as evil manifestations or pathways, and dire consequences will fall upon any development or use thereof except under strict and narrow definitions as approved by some denominations. The truth is that the only dire consequences that will result are that the individual will grow beyond the need for outside direction, having established communication with God directly, and will no longer need or support the false prophet who has been attempting to hold him back.

There are many in the present who carry on the traditions of these ancient Antichrists, living well on the ignorance of the masses, but there are also many sincere and devout lovers of God who are prevented from experiencing the full truth and its concomitant benefits.

The standard argument against new knowledge and added revelation is based upon the last part of the Book of Revelation, which states, *"If any man shall add unto these things, God shall add unto him the plagues that are written in this book,"* [138] and is further amplified by the standard doctrine that, 'If an individual stands in opposition to the entire evangelical Christian doctrine as espoused through Martin Luther, he has to be without truth because the majority must be right.' Two points:

1. The Bible, as a book, did not exist at the time of the writing of Revelation. John's curse cannot possibly be construed to extend to the other documents assembled by very human hands some three hundred years (or more) after Christ.
2. The Bible itself prophesies that *"the love of the great body of people will grow cold because of multiplied lawlessness and iniquity."* [139] This can only be reference to those who formerly loved — the Christian Church — a majority in error!

The apostate condition of the established churches is also shown in the parable of the wheat and the tares. The common translations of today have left out a very important key word. The question is asked in the text: *"Sir, did you not sow good seed in your field? Then how does it have darnel shoots in it?"* [140] The original Greek translates: *"An enemy-man this did,"* but the *Amplified Bible* reads: *"An enemy has done this,"* [141] and is generally interpreted and taught as referring to Satan, losing the sense that the errors were initiated by men.

Jesus said, *"if you abide in my word [hold fast to my teaching and live in accordance with them], you are truly My disciples. And you will know the Truth, and the Truth will set you free."* [142] But we must consider this statement in light of the fact that there are literally hundreds of Christian sects espousing dozens of variations on different doctrines, some of which are diametrically opposed to each other. Each group believes that their own group has the one true interpretation and are invariably convinced that all others are in error. Most sects base their interpretations upon 'Revelation through the Spirit' as described in John 16. *"But when He, the Spirit of Truth comes, He will guide you into all the truth (the whole, full Truth)."* [143] The question arises: Among all these denominations who claim to possess the truth received by them from the Holy Spirit, who is telling the *truth?*

Some theologians admit to these problems, explaining that many teachings are just 'ideas of men.' These ideas however are taught as doctrine and accepted as doctrine, or truth, by the masses of adherents of any given group. If any one of them ever admits error to what was supposed to have been divine inspiration, what must we see in the spirit leading that group? I John 2 states: *"nothing false (no deception, no lie) is of the Truth."* [144] Further, James says: *"For wherever there is jealousy and contention, there will also be confusion and all sorts of evil and vile practices. But the wisdom from above is first of all pure; then it is peace-loving, courteous ... yield(s) to reason, full of compassion and good fruits."* [145]

Do the evolved doctrines of Christianity demonstrate absence of confusion? Purity of teaching? Peace? Courtesy? Yielding to reason? Compassion? Good fruits?

I would like to say that the great confusion of doctrine is an indication of the loss of purity that often leads to acts of discourtesy, absence of peace, and lack of compassion.

But what about yielding to reason? James said that wisdom yields to reason. Wisdom is defined as: *"the power of judging rightly and following the soundest course of action based on knowledge, experience, and understanding."* [146]

In 1985 there were over a billion professed Christians on the face of this planet. Christians outnumber any other single religion on earth. What are the fruits of this domination? What is the condition of the world?

The conclusion of this is that the Antichrist is the spirit of perverse Christianity, which prevails in most churches in our day and the teachings of most of them are the acts of men deciding what is true and thereby taking the seat in the Temple, and that this misconstruction of the Christian teachings began during the time of Paul and has continued down to this very day. It was part of a plan, and now that plan is being revealed.

This returns us to the foreordained and planned purpose of this lawlessness, this delusion to error — **it is so that sufficient electrical po-**

tential difference may be established so that metamorphosis may be accomplished. The ultimate purpose of the 'misleading influence' is described within the pages of the Bible itself:

> *"God sends upon them a misleading influence, a working of error and a strong delusion to make them believe what is false...* [147] *In order that they may look ... but not see and perceive, and may hear... but not grasp and comprehend, lest they should turn again, and it should be forgiven them.148In order that all may be judged and condemned who did not believe [who refused] the Truth ...* [149] *according to the revelation of the mystery of the plan of redemption which was kept in silence and secret for long ages,* [150] *... which God devised and decreed before the ages for our glorification.* [151] *... We shall not all fall asleep [in death], but we shall all be changed In a moment, in the twinkling of an eye, at the [sound of the] last trumpet call. For a trumpet will sound and the dead will be raised imperishable (free and immune from decay)* [152] *... (at) the maturity of the times and the climax of the ages to unify all things ... in heaven and things on the earth* [153] *... this mystery, which is Christ within and among you, the Hope of glory.* [154] *But that when the days come that the trumpet call of the seventh angel is about to be sounded, then God's mystery (His secret design, His hidden purpose), as He announced the glad tidings to His servants the prophets, should be fulfilled."* [155]

What is this Design?

Metamorphosis — the unity of spirit and matter — the ultimate alchemical event; matter vibrationally altered by atomic interaction between the bodies of the solar system. The earth and mankind returned to the Garden of Eden, literally.

But before that will happen, a Beast will arise...

Chapter Ten

The 'Beast' has been, in accepted theological theory, long associated with, and identified as, the One-Man Antichrist. This is due to a fundamental misunderstanding of the last verse of Revelation, chapter 13.

I first became interested in the book of Revelation well over twenty years ago through a series of unusual events which led me deeper and deeper into the present study. In those early days, I came into possession of a book written by a popular evangelist of the fire-and-brimstone-hold-on-I-feel-a-miracle-a-comin' ilk. This book was written as a serious theological study presented in story form. Actually, it was written in the fashion of one of Grimm's grimmer fairy tales.

The heroine was a pre-teenaged girl who is torn between her desire to be 'saved' and her doubts about the necessity for this 'confession of faith.' As it turns out, she hesitates one day too long. During the night, all the Christians disappear from the planet. (I assume that the same thing occurs in the daylight on the other side of the world, unless this particular theologian holds to the flat earth theory. He was pretty sure that it had to happen at night.) This event leaves empty cars in traffic, clothes dryers running, ovens baking and radios playing. Husbands and wives wake to find their spouses gone and children awake to empty houses. If I hadn't known the writer was serious, I would have laughed all the way through. As it was, I was horrified.

The story progresses through some two hundred pages of the most fantastic events ever concocted by the human mind. The heroine witnesses and suffers unimaginable horrors and torture (which she withstands with fortitude), as the globe is taken over by a pagan megalomaniac who chops the heads off of those who do not bite the dust in his presence.

Getting bored with this regimen, grueling by any stretch of the imagination, the Beast constructs a statue of himself, which is pulled by human slaves through the streets to accept the adulation of the masses by proxy. The young girl is finally, horribly, martyred, thereby having the opportunity to share, at least, in the Second Resurrection. Some comfort! This 'gothic' horror/fantasy had a profound effect on me. I re-read Revelation for the first time in many years and, though it was a scenario of stupendous cataclysm, I was sure that it was not describing what I had read in that awful book.

Many people who read Revelation assume that it is either the vision of a mystic which can only be understood by another mystic, or that it is the ravings of a spaced-out hermit who had eaten moldy bread. I must admit that I had such thoughts myself. I initially despaired of ever comprehending a word of it.

I began to study Revelation in earnest. I had no particular axe to grind except my own craving to know the truth spurred on by my natural tendency to love solving difficult problems. I began to read literally hundreds of books on every conceivable subject that seemed even remotely connected to these prophecies. My brain assimilated and stored massive amounts of data and, as I read, many pieces began to fall into place. By the time *Worlds in Collision* came into my hand, years of study had gone by and, while I felt I had solved the problem of the identity of the Beast, the remainder of the puzzle was still rather amorphous.

Reading Velikovsky was like finding a key to a Chinese puzzle box — suddenly the entire scope of the prophecy opened up and revealed itself to me. There were still annoying areas of obscurity, but these, too, cleared up as I separated and contemplated each portion. During this period of study, I lived, ate, drank and breathed Revelation. I took heart from the fact that the book was, after all, named Revelation, and not Concealment. I also began to understand that it was not meant to be fully understood until a certain point in time had passed. And, when the final pieces of the puzzle fell into place, I realized that time was, indeed, short.

One of the keys to unlocking the puzzle, as I mentioned, is the last verse of chapter 13. I had already figured out most of it but that last bit really had me stumped. I read the verse over and over and went back to the original Greek for clarification. I broke it down by syntax; rearranged it in numerous ways and went to bed exhausted by it one night. I awoke in the middle of the night with the word 'calculate' booming in my head and a vision of the word in large white letters against a black background. I jumped out of bed and grabbed my notes. Calculate was, indeed, the key.

Revelation 13, the chapter that describes the 'Beast,' begins:

"I stood on the sandy beach, I saw a beast coming up out of the sea with ten horns and seven heads. On his horns he had ten royal crowns and blasphemous titles on his heads." [156]

This first sentence tells us of a landing on a foreign shore; the Beast is to be found at a distance from the area of the previous chapter, which describes the nation of Israel, the birth of Christ, and the persecutions of the Church in Europe. To understand what John means by sea, we can look at chapter 17: *"The waters that you observed ... are races and multitudes..."* [157] (This is also interesting in light of the concept of people being waveforms of the divine source.) Examining all other references to beasts in the Bible, it is immediately apparent that, other than references to actual animals, this designation belongs to world empires.

Daniel's prophecies foreshadowed Revelation, and Daniel was told by an angel that a beast symbolized an empire. There is some interchangeability between 'king' and 'empire,' just as there is interchangeability between 'city' and 'nation.' This is also traditional since any king is considered diplomatically to be his country. I think that we can safely assume that John is not referring to a fantastic animal, so the only other supported interpretation we can give to this beast is that it is an empire.

John is most specific in describing the numbers of heads and horns and the placing of the crowns on the horns and not the heads. So, we must think this is to be of some import in describing the nature of this empire. Chapter 7 of Daniel describes his fourth beast as having ten horns and it has been determined that Daniel's fourth beast was the Roman Empire. The beast in chapter 12 of Revelation can also be identified, by its role, as the Roman Empire. The comparison can then be made that the crowns, in the case of the descriptions of the Beast representing the Roman Empire, are upon the heads and not on the horns.

The number '7' is sacred among the Jews, indicating perfection or completion. It was used very often in a symbolic manner for the 'whole' of a thing. Thus, seven heads would indicate an autonomous nation — not under the rule of any other empire. The placement of the crowns on the horns rather than on the heads indicates that this is not a totalitarian, monarchial or dictatorial regime. The horns symbolize strength and the assembly of the people, for the horn was used to call the people to pray and to hear the words of the prophets. We can see that on this beast they represent the strength of an empire in the diversity of its people. Ten is symbolic of testing, an earthly foreshadowing of divine principle: *"For since the law has merely a rude outline of the good things to come — instead of fully expressing those things — it can never ... perfect those who approach..."* [158] So, we can conclude that the ten horns represent the assembling of a large number of people who express an almost divine concept in government — since the rulership of the empire, symbolized by the crowns, is placed on the horns and not on the heads — government of the people, by the people, for the people.

The heads, on the other hand — the decision-making part of the Beast, the administrative or titular head of an empire — are represented as having blasphemous titles on their foreheads. The definition of blasphemy is 'profane usage of God's name.' Profane simply means that which is not connected with religion. The blasphemous titles on the heads inform us that the government of this nation will use the name of God and purported spiritual principles to lead the people and present its policies.

"And the beast that I saw resembled a leopard, but his feet were like those of a bear and his mouth was like that of a lion." [159]

Here we find that this new empire has many of the characteristics of former world empires as described by Daniel. The multiplicity of types also indicates the greater supremacy of this world empire. Possessing the military might of the Media—Persian empire, as exemplified by the bear; the speed and cunning of Alexander's empire, the leopard; and the kingly nobility of the lion. That the mouth is described as being like a lion denotes loud and boastful speech as well — self-aggrandizement and self-indulgence, and another meaning, as we shall see.

"And to him the dragon gave his might and power and his throne and great dominion." [160]

The dragon is, classically and in scripture, Satan. This sentence denotes the emerging character of this beast as well as establishes its position in the world. John says that the dragon gives his throne to the Beast. This means that this empire becomes the number one nation on the earth in all things material: industry, commerce, political influence, economic living standards, arts, science, technology, material goods of all sorts and fleshly pleasures; all things pertaining to the 'things of the world.' That is not to say that any of these things are evil in themselves — it is the attitude and ideal which is important as we will see further on.

There are characteristics of evil implied here that are not immediately apparent. Satan, as the average Christian conceives him, is a civilized devil — with his natty suit and elegant goatee and cute horns and pointed tail.

There is nothing wrong with wanting to have things, to experience physical pleasure, to eat well, laugh or be entertained. It may even be said that all of the benefits of 'the world' might be seen as desirable — as long as the spiritual orientation of the beneficiary is proper — as long as the emphasis is placed upon the spirit and not upon the object. To have more than is necessary while others do without is sin for it represents pride, gluttony, intemperance, possessiveness, selfishness, pettiness and sheer sensuality. A single individual or a nation that experiences abundance and asks: 'Am I my brother's keeper,' while one single other person on the planet suffers or does without, that nation, that individual, is Satan.

There is a fundamental evil in operation in this world which is perverting, twisting and making a mockery of people and governments — an evil so deep and wide that we cannot plumb its depths — an evil which has tended to lead man in the pathways of corruption so far-reaching that even his best attempts and intentions cannot stem this flow of decay and social vampirism. This evil is materialism.

John has informed us that the social structure of this end-time empire is controlled by a pervading principle of life that is antithetical to spirituality. The dragon exalts this empire far above all the other societies of the world in all the things that pertain to materiality. This society is one which has set itself up as arbiter of what is right and wrong as well as being excessively preoccupied with physical appearance and material wealth and goods.

> "And one of his heads seemed to have a deadly wound. But his death stroke was healed; and the whole earth went after the beast in amazement and admiration."[161]

This verse tells us that one branch or department of the administrative body suffers an attack. This attack is clarified in verse 14, which describes the wound as being inflicted by a sword — a military action. Note that the verse says 'seems' to have a deadly wound. This tells us that this event leads many to think that it is a death stroke and will finish the Beast. Yet, the empire/beast recovers quickly and goes on to lead, and be adored by, an admiring world.

"They fell down and did homage to the dragon, because he had bestowed on the beast all his dominion and authority; they also praised and worshipped the beast, exclaiming, Who is a match for the beast, and who can make war against him?" [162]

To do homage means to serve or venerate and this verse tells us that the benefits of Satan, materiality, as promulgated by the Beast, become the standard of the other societies of the world. In addition, this verse identifies the ascendancy of materialism as occurring through military actions.

"And the beast was given the power of speech, uttering boastful and blasphemous words, and he was given freedom to exert his authority and to exercise his will during forty-two months." [163]

Recall in the previous chapter where Jesus is described as slaying nations with the breath of his mouth? Well, here we have the Beast making war. 'Speaking' means war. And, having the mouth of a lion, we can be sure that this 'speech' will be proud, haughty, and declaiming noble ideals. But, that this war/speech is blasphemous tells us that there is something hidden here that we must find, and we will a bit further on. The authority during 42 months is identified in verses three and four as military. Thus, claiming to act in the will or name of God, this nation will lead the peoples of the earth in a war for 42 months.

"He was further permitted to wage war on God's holy people and to overcome them. And power was given him to extend his authority over every tribe and people and tongue and nation..." [164]

This verse describes the extension of authority after the military action has ceased. Once again this nation is described as having the top position, and to a greater extent than before, in all material aspects. The results of the military action have served to place the Beast in a position to 'wage war against God's holy people.' Contrary to popular theological opinion, I do not see these 'holy people' as members of any given denomination, 'born again' or otherwise. God's people must be understood to be those who are members of His kingdom and, since this kingdom has not been externally established, being described as being within, we must look for another meaning to this usage.

Deuteronomy describes the nation of Israel as God's holy people in its entirety. After the establishment of the 'New Covenant,' God's people are those who are 'circumcised in their hearts.' Thus, the 'holy people' must be seen as those who manifest spiritual values over and above materialism.

It might also be noted that Christ said, referring to little children, 'of such is the kingdom of heaven'; so we may include all of the children of the world among this group. The use of the word 'overcome' in this context, informs us that an actual military action is not involved — rather that the Beast uses some means of inducement to cause innocent and unsuspecting individuals to fall into the ways of materialism. This is a war of forces — materialism versus spirituality — a severe attack on spiritual values, leading many astray. It also indicates that those who place spiritual values above material considerations will have a difficult time dealing with life in general due to the fact that only those who know how to 'play the game' will be able to maneuver well in the society of the Beast.

"And all the inhabitants of the earth will fall down in adoration and pay him homage, everyone whose name has not been recorded in the Book of Life of the Lamb that was slain from the foundation of the world." [165]

This verse tells us that this empire will be victorious in propagating materialism over vast areas of the globe and that the ideals of independence from God, self-gratification and reliance on human wisdom and capabilities will come to be seen as the prevailing aspirations of the world. This does not mean that the entire world will attain these ideals, but that the economic, industrial, artistic, scientific achievements and living standards of this empire will be admired and emulated — idolized, in fact.

However, we must also see that there will be some who do not fall into the trap set by the Beast — those who retain their ideals of spiritual perfection and achievement — and that these people are foreordained to occupy this role.

"Whoever leads into captivity will himself go into captivity; if anyone slays with the sword, with the sword must he be slain. Herein is the patience and the faith and fidelity of the saints." [166]

This caveat is inserted at this point for several reasons. The first is to reassure those who have been 'foreordained' as well as those who have suffered actual death or loss, that what is sown is reaped. Not only will those who are faithful and patient be rewarded, but those who oppress will be destroyed. The Beast is warned that nations invoke karma also.

"Then I saw another beast rising up out of the land; he had two horns like a lamb and he spoke like a dragon. He exerts all the power and right of control of the former beast in his presence, and causes the earth and those who dwell upon it to exalt and deify the first beast, whose deadly wound was healed, and worship him. He performs great signs (startling miracles) even making fire fall from the sky to the earth in men's sight. And because of the signs which he is allowed to perform in the presence of the [first] beast, he deceives those who inhabit the earth, commanding them to erect ... (an image) in the likeness of the beast who was wounded by the sword and still lived." [167]

This second beast, must, once again, be an empire. However, it differs from the first beast in several ways, which John describes in great detail. The first detail is the number of horns. Two is a number that has several meanings. First, it represents a minority, for two is the smallest number by which testimony may be accepted. Also, we may look to Genesis for some esoteric clarification: *"And God said, Let there be a firmament in the midst of the waters; and let it separate the waters [below] from the waters [above]. ... And there was evening and morning, a second day."* [168] Here we see that the number two is related to a separating element, which divides waters below from waters above. Throughout the Bible, water represents spirit and humanity.

In applying this principle to two horns, we see that the horns represents a powerful minority, which acts in such a way as to separate mankind from his own spiritual heritage. This action comes about through things which appear harmless — *"appeared as a lamb"* — but are in actuality, propagating lies — *"speaks as a dragon"* — induces to material considerations. And, once again, speech refers to force, or violence so we may assume that this second beast has some relationship to making war.

"He exerts all the power and right of control of the former beast in his presence" tells us that this powerful minority acts through and is supported by, the established empire of the first beast — an empire within an empire. A minority, which takes control by force and deception.

"Causes the earth and those who dwell upon it to exalt and deify the first beast, whose deadly wound was healed, and worship him" indicates that this second beast was behind the initiation of the military action described as a deadly wound and that this event was planned to bring the first beast

into position to establish military supremacy and commercial world domination. This establishment of military supremacy is emphasized in the lines: *"He performs great signs (startling miracles) even making fire fall from the sky to the earth in men's sight"* which describes the use of atomic weapons in this military action which lasts 42 months. This display of power is so awesome to the peoples of the world that they submit to the political and commercial domination of the first beast.

> *"And because of the signs which he is allowed to perform in the presence of the [first] beast, he deceives those who inhabit the earth, commanding them to erect ... (an image) in the likeness of the beast who was wounded by the sword and still lived."*

The 'image' of the Beast has caused many a theologian to lose sleep. Understood in the context of this passage, we can perceive that this refers to the establishment of the principles of worldliness and materialism throughout the world. What is the image of the Beast? Military might, speed and cunning, exalted position in worldly possessions and technology — as described by John. That this ideal is extended around the earth through the lies, deception and force of the second beast, subverting other cultural ideals to materialism and using other nations politically, is what is being expressed by this verse — and that it is the end result of the war in which the Beast was wounded.

> *"And he is permitted to impart the breath of life into the beast's image, so that the statue of the beast could actually talk and to cause to be put to death those who would not bow down and worship the image of the beast. Also, he compels all, both small and great, both rich and the poor, both free and slave, to be marked with an inscription on their right hands or on their foreheads, So that no one will have power to buy or sell unless he bears the stamp, the name of the beast or the number of his name."* [169]

The dreaded 'Mark of the Beast.' The horror of totalitarian world government — tattoos, laser marks, implanted computer tapes — a host of interpretations! Yet, we cannot look upon this lightly for it contains the implications of the most horrific prophetic curse ever delivered in the pages of scripture.

Before delving into the 'Mark,' let's look at the first portions of this section. The 'breath of life' imparted to the image, or ideals of the Beast, coupled with 'speech' and 'putting to death,' express a repetition of the coupling of blasphemous speech and military action in the earlier verses. Thus we see that the Beast will initiate war with those nations that do not adhere to its image, or domination in military and commercial respects. This is further amplified by the implications of buying and selling — join the Beast or die!

The first mention of a mark in the Bible occurs in Genesis 4:15: *"And the Lord set a mark or sign upon Cain..."* [170] It must be remembered that Cain was the first individual who asked: "Am I my brother's keeper?"

Job lamented,

*"If I have sinned, what have I done You, O You Watcher and Keeper of men? Why have You set me as a **mark** for You, so that I am a burden to myself?"* [171]

Jeremiah cries:

*"I am [Jeremiah] the man who has seen affliction under the rod of His wrath. He has led me and brought me into darkness and not light. Surely He has turned away from me; His hand is against me all the day. My flesh and my skin has He worn out and made old; He has shattered my bones. He has built up against me and surrounded me with bitterness, tribulation, and anguish. He has caused me to dwell in dark places like those long dead. He walled me in so that I cannot get out; He has weighted down my chain. Even when I cry and shout for help, He shut out my prayer. He has enclosed my ways with hewn stone; He has made my paths crooked. He is to me like a bear lying in wait, and like a lion [hiding] in secret places. He has turned me off my ways and pulled me in pieces; He has made me desolate. He has bent His bow and set me as a **mark** for the arrow."* [172]

Ezekiel 9 says:

*"And the Lord said to him, Go through the midst of the city, through the midst of Jerusalem, and set a **mark** upon the foreheads of the men who sigh and groan over all the abominations that are committed in the midst of it. And to the others He said in my hearing, Follow through the city and smite: let not your eye spare, neither have any pity. Slay outright the elderly, the young man and the virgin, the infant and the women; but do not touch or go near any one on whom is the **mark**."* [173]

*"Then another angel, a third, followed them, saying with a mighty voice, Whoever pays homage to the beast and his statue and permits the stamp (**mark**) to be put on his forehead or on his hand, He too shall drink the wine of God's indignation and wrath, poured undiluted into the cup of His anger; and he shall be*

tormented with fire and brimstone in the presence of the holy angels and in the presence of the Lamb." [174]

"And the beast was seized and overpowered, and with him the false prophet who in his presence had worked wonders and performed miracles (the second beast, that which gives false testimony — LKJ) by which he led astray those who had accepted or permitted to be placed upon them the stamp (**mark**) of the beast and those who paid homage and gave divine honors to his statue. Both of the two were hurled alive into the fiery lake that burns and blazes with brimstone." [175]

"Then I saw a second angel ... Saying, Harm neither the earth nor the sea nor the trees, until we have **sealed** the bond servants of our God **upon their foreheads**." [176]

"Hear, O Israel: the Lord our God is one Lord [the only Lord]. And you shall love the Lord your God with all your heart, and with your entire being and with all your might. And these words which I am commanding you this day shall be in your own minds and hearts; You shall whet and sharpen them, so as to make them penetrate ... and shall talk of them when you sit in your house and when you walk by the way, and when you lie down and when you rise up. And you shall bind them as **a sign upon your hand**, and they shall be as **frontlets between your eyes**. And you shall write them upon the doorposts of your house and on your gates." [177]

So, now we have a much clearer idea of what John means by the use of the word 'mark' or 'stamp.' It is an ideological affiliation; a spiritual position; an attitude of mind, heart and action. Nothing more, nothing less. This attitude manifests in electromagnetic vibratory effects of either finer or baser degrees.

What is it that one wears upon their forehead as a frontlet and binds upon their hand? The laws of God. What is one supposed to do with the laws of God? Whet and sharpen them — use them and practice with them — make them penetrate; interpret all of reality in these terms; teach them and make them the focal point of existence. **This is the Mark or Seal of God.**

And, the Mark of the Beast? The antithesis of the Mark of God. The denial and rejection of the laws of God. The asking of the age-old question: Am I my brother's keeper? **The Mark of Cain.**

We should note, however, that John divides the Mark of the Beast into two categories: those who bear the 'stamp' — the name of the Beast or those who bear the number of his name. And here we come to the final solution: the identity of the Beast. For it is clear that those who occupy the geographical area of this Beast/empire are under sentence of doom as well as those who are marked by the esoteric significance of the number of the Beast.

"Here is discernment [a call for the wisdom of interpretation]. Let anyone who has intelligence (penetration and insight enough) **calculate** *the number of the beast, for it is a human number [the number of a certain man]; his number is 666."* [178]

1. CALCULATE — a mathematical operation.
2. Calculate what? — The number of the Beast.
3. Calculate how? —
   a) it is a human number;
   b) the number of a certain man.
4. The unfinished numerical form of the name of the Beast, the numbers that will give the mathematical result identical with the name number of the Beast, thereby affirming identity, is 666.

The companion to the Torah, the Jewish collection of scripture, is the Kaballah. The Kaballah consists of many occult and esoteric teachings, one of which is a system of numerology. (It also includes astrological information.) In Kabbalistic tradition, a name number is very significant. Numbers were so important to the ancient Jews that an entire book is named 'Numbers.' They understood, as physicists do today, that numbers represent the closest we can ever come to writing and understanding the laws of the universe. In the past, a man's name number was so important that his name was often changed, signifying some important accomplishment or change of life, thereby changing the numerical value as well as the intrinsic meaning. A striking example is the change God made in the names of both Abraham and Sarah; formerly Abram and Sarai.

Clue 3a is clarified by 3b which indicates that we are not to interpret the former in literal terms — the number of humanity being 6; but that we are to deal with a specific name just as if we were determining the name number of a certain (any given) man. In presenting these clues, John is telling us that we are to use numerology to find the name number of the Beast just as if it were a man. We may make this determination by matching our result with the result of the numerological application to the number 666. This will affirm our identification of the last great world empire — the Beast.

The symbology of these numbers is important in another way. The result of the rules of numerology applied to the number 666 is 9: 6 + 6 +

6 = 18, 1 + 8 = 9. Nine is not only the name number of the Beast; it is the product of 3 squared, or divine completion. We can also see in these numbers man's attempt to usurp the position of God — 6 repeated 3 times — or the number of man arranged as the divine trinity.

Symbolically nine signifies finality, completion, fulfillment. There are the nine beatitudes, nine gifts of the spirit, nine fruits of the spirit, and the words of Christ at the **ninth** hour: *"It is finished!"* This is echoed in Revelation: *"Then the seventh [angel] emptied out his bowl into the air, and a mighty voice came out of the sanctuary of heaven from the throne, saying, It is done!"* [179]

There are other clues to the meaning of the number nine. In the story of the ten lepers in Luke 17, only one, a Samaritan, turned back and thanked Jesus for his cleansing, and Jesus asked, *"Were not ten cleansed? Where are the nine? Was there no one found to return and to recognize and give thanks and praise to God except this alien?"* [180]

In Nehemiah 11, more light is shed upon the symbology of nine: *"Now the leaders of the people dwelt at Jerusalem; the rest of the people also cast lots to bring one of ten to dwell in Jerusalem, the holy city, while nine-tenths dwelt in other towns and villages."* [181]

We may also observe that 9 is an inverted 6 and, expressing the idea of the law of God, in the singular triad, acting upon man in the usurped multiple — or 3 × 666 — we get a most interesting product: 1998. This number is especially interesting in light of the prophecies of Nostradamus and Edgar Cayce.

Using this date as a stepping off point, we can add or subtract the 6.3 years of Daniel's prophesied tribulation. (The name 'Daniel,' by the way, is a nine — a coincidence? I think not, considering the many similarities of Revelation to Daniel.)

There is an even more esoteric meaning to the number nine, which I will describe only briefly because it is extremely complex and much study is required to understand the fundamentals behind it.

> *"(T)here is a certain symbol which takes the form of a circle divided into nine parts with lines connecting the nine points of the circumference in a certain order. ...*
>
> *The circle is divided into nine equal parts. Six points are connected by a figure which is symmetrical in relation to a diameter passing through the uppermost point of the divisions of the circumference. Further, the uppermost point of the divisions is the apex of an equilateral triangle linking together the points of the divisions which do not enter into the construction of the original complicated figure.*

This symbol cannot be met with anywhere in the study of 'occultism,' either in books or in oral transmission. It was given such significance by those who knew, that they considered it necessary to keep the knowledge of it secret. Only some hints and partial representations of it can be met with in literature. ... (This symbol) expresses the law of seven in its union with the law of three. The octave possesses seven tones and the eighth is a repetition of the first. Together with the two (additional elements) ... there are nine elements. ...

The isolated existence of a thing or phenomenon under examination is the closed circle of an eternally returning and uninterruptedly flowing process. ... The succession of stages in the process must be connected with the succession of the remaining numbers from 1 to 9. The presence of the ninth step filling up the interval ... completes the cycle, that is, it closes the circle, which begins anew at this point. ... Therefore every beginning and completion of the cycle is situated in the apex of the triangle, in the point where the beginning and the end merge, where the circle is closed, and which sounds in the endlessly flowing cycle... But it is the ninth step that closes and again begins a cycle." [182]

So, we can see that there are deep significances to the number nine. John was most likely perceiving some fantastic quantum probabilities and it should be quite apparent at this point that the laws of the universe are fairly fantastic, if not completely amazing.

In 70 A.D. the Jewish temple was polluted and then destroyed. This was an archetype of what was to come. In the present time, the Temple is the body of mankind — even the body of an individual. Our bodies are being polluted by materialistic attitudes and it is entirely likely that destruction will soon follow.

"Then I heard a holy one speaking, and another holy one said to the one that spoke, For how long is the vision concerning the continual offering, the transgression that makes desolate, and the giving over of both the sanctuary and the host to be trampled under foot? And he said to him and to me, For 2,300 evenings and mornings; then the sanctuary shall be cleansed and restored." [183]

Dividing 2300 by 365, we obtain the figure 6.3 years from that date, and, if that is the case, and the ending and beginning is 1998, then we subtract 6.3 years from 1998 and we find that the abomination that desolates will begin in late 1991. Or, on the other hand, the date could represent the beginning of destruction in which case we would add 6.3 years to 1998 finding that the end of tribulation would be in the year 2004. Only time will tell on this one.

What does Jesus say about the abomination that desolates?

"So when you see the appalling sacrilege, spoken of by the prophet Daniel, standing in the Holy Place — let the reader take notice and ponder and heed this — Then let those who are in Judea flee to the mountains; Let him who is on the housetop not come down and go into the house to take anything; And let him who is in the field not turn back to get his overcoat. And alas for the women who are pregnant (spiritually unformed souls — LKJ) and for those who have nursing babies in those days! (Those who are not yet ready for the meat of truth — LKJ) For then there will be great tribulation (affliction, distress and oppression) such as has not been from the beginning of the world until now — no, and never will be [again]. And if those days had not been shortened, no human being would endure and survive, but for the sake of the elect (God's chosen ones) those days will be shortened. ...

For just as the lightening flashes from the east and shines and is seen as far as the west, so will the coming of the Son of Man be. ... Immediately after the tribulation of those days the sun will be darkened, and the moon will not shed her light, and the stars will fall from the sky, and the powers of the heavens will be shaken. Then the sign of the Son of Man will appear in the sky, and then all the tribes of the earth will mourn and beat their breasts and lament in anguish, and they will see the Son of Man coming on the clouds of heaven with power and great glory [in brilliancy and splendor]." [184]

The prophecies of Revelation state that the Beast will be cast into the lake of fire along with the false prophet. This becomes meaningful when we remember Velikovsky's 'rains and rivers of fire,' or flaming naptha, which would be concomitant with an encounter with a comet of a certain type. Thus, those who have the name of the Beast (belonging to the empire and present in the geographical area), and the number of his name, (those who are doomed throughout the globe for their lack of spiritual growth), will be destroyed. And, considering the figure of Noah as well as the parable of the ten lepers along with the archtypal example from Nehemiah, we must understand that few will survive. One tenth, perhaps, of the earth's population of over five billion.

Now, you ask, who — or what — is the Beast?

Which world empire fits the descriptions of Revelation 13?

Which world empire began on a foreign shore, formed of many races and tongues (primarily people from the area of the old Roman Empire — the 'Little Horn' of Daniel, which made war with three of the ten divisions of the Roman Empire: England, France and Spain)?

Which nation on the earth rapidly became the richest and most powerful empire on earth, using the name of God as its motto?

Which nation suffered a military attack which seemed to be devastating, but was, in fact, a political manipulation designed to engender popular support for a war of greed — a wound which healed so quickly that one can't help but wonder if all preparations were made in advance?

Which nation rose up after such an attack and went on to lead an adoring world in a global war, winning on two fronts simultaneously? A war that involved this empire for a period of 42 months?

Which empire developed and used 'fire falling from the sky in the sight of men' — atomic weapons — to awe and intimidate the peoples of the world?

Which nation used such a blasphemous power on a people already defeated, after having deliberately drawn them into war?

Which nation, after this war, established, and still maintains, military presence and industrial outposts over all the globe and has made the world its marketplace — a financial bonanza — propagating materialism as though it were manna from heaven or the word of God in order to satiate its voracious appetite for money and power?

What nation on the earth is ruled from behind the political stage by the industrial-military complex — a group so powerful they can politically (or literally) assassinate public and private figures with impunity; a group of wealthy elitists who know no bounds to their greed; a group which foments social unrest, political strife, unstable economies, wars and revolutions; a group which stimulates technology and promulgates materialism, to keep their pockets full and the strings of power in their hands?

What nation on earth has been manipulated by the electronic media — under the control of the motivation masters hired by the industrial-military complex (the false prophets of materialism and technology) — so that they have lost sight of the spirit and meaning of those ideals which gave birth to their empire?

What nation's name number is NINE?

Chapter Eleven

To be a slave to pleasure is the life of a harlot, not of a man.

— Anaxadrides (died c. 520 B.C.).

No more deadly curse has ever been given by nature to man than carnal pleasure. There is no criminal purpose and no evil deed which the lust for pleasure will not drive man to undertake.

—Archytus of Tarentum (c. 400–350 B.C.).

The love of a harlot ... which arouses from mere external form, and absolutely all love which recognizes any other cause than the freedom of the mind, easily passes into hatred, unless, which is worse, it becomes a species of delirium and thereby discord is cherished rather than concord.

— Baruch Spinoza (1632–1677).

Years ago it occurred to me that it was most peculiar that the United States [185] was not taught as being included or mentioned in the great Biblical prophecies. Since it was apparent to me that it was the most powerful and influential nation on the face of the planet, I thought this rather strange. This was due, as it was explained to me, to the fact that the prophecies concerned, mainly, the Jews and, having been delivered through Jews, primarily concerned those events that affected the Jewish people. Yet, we are talking about prophecies that are global in import. If we are going to take, as a working hypothesis, the idea that prophetic abilities exist at all and that they can operate thousands of years into the future, then we must also accept that those same prophetic abilities will be able to perceive the major actors in the cosmic drama.

And, if the drama is played out on the stage of the entire globe, then we must understand that the discussion will, of necessity, involve the stars of the play.

The idea that the prophecies of the Bible relate only to the Jewish nation is not supported by the Bible itself if it is read and understood correctly.

In Genesis, Abram came out of Chaldea and God spoke to him one night under the tent of heaven saying:

"Look now toward the heavens and count the stars — if you are able to number them. ... So shall your descendants be." [186]

Abram had faith and God was pleased with him, and the covenant was renewed and expanded to include more than the Jewish people.

> *"As for Me, behold, My covenant is with you, and you shall be the father of many nations. Nor shall your name any longer be Abram [high, exalted father]; but your name shall be Abraham [father of multitudes]; for I have made you the father of many nations."* [187] (17:4-5)

God later renewed the covenant once again, through Moses, adding also the consequences of breaking the covenant, which was to lose all the benefits of 'election.'

It is on the strength of the Lord's oath that the Jews flatter themselves that they are secure, and present day theologians continue to regard prophecy strictly in relation to them.

In spite of the many assurances of God of an everlasting covenant, this is contingent upon the keeping of the covenant by the other party. John the Baptist said,

> *"And do not presume to say to yourselves, We have Abraham for our forefather; for I tell you, God is able to raise up descendants for Abraham from these stones! And already the ax is lying at the root of the trees; every tree therefore that does not bear good fruit is cut down and thrown into the fire."* [188]

Paul describes the New Covenant:

> *"Behold, the days will come, says the Lord, when I will make and ratify a new covenant ... with the house of Israel... It will not be like the covenant that I made with their forefathers ... for they did not abide in My agreement with them, and so I withdrew My favor and disregarded them... For this is the covenant that I will make with the house of Israel after those days, says the Lord: I will imprint My laws upon their minds, even upon their innermost thoughts and understanding, and engrave them upon their hearts; and I will be their God, and they shall be My people."* [189]

> *"Or is God merely of the Jews? Is He not the God of Gentiles also? ... Abraham believed in God and, it was credited to his account as righteousness. ... For the promise to Abraham or his posterity, that he should inherit the world, did not come through the Law... Therefore the promise (to be one of God's people — a 'new' Israel — LKJ) is the outcome of faith and ... guaranteed to all his descendants — not only to the devotees ... of the Law but also to those who share the faith of Abraham, who is the father of us all."* [190]

From this abbreviated study, we can understand the sense that after the establishment of the 'New Covenant,' all references to 'Israel,' 'God's people,' and 'Jews' (in application to prophetic events), become a matter of spirit.

The nation Israel was the archetype of God's people. The divisions of the twelve tribes refer to types and may be interpreted astrologically, rather than as material manifestations through lineage. In this way we can understand that prophecies of the end times refer to global events rather than the narrow applications of the small nation of Israel.

In a very real sense, then, the people of the United States can be seen as re-enacting the archetypal plan or pattern of Israel, in that individually and collectively they traveled to a promised land from a place of spiritual and actual bondage. And, just as the Hebrew people started their new nation based upon ten laws of God, the United States began as a loose confederation of free states. The Israelites rebelled and demanded a golden calf; the United States demanded a centralized federal government.

The entity known as the 'Beast' plays a large part in the end time prophecies and, considering the global implications, it is unwise to interpret in terms centered around the adherents of the Old Covenant. The interpretations must be centered around the spiritual manifestation of the type expressed in the story of Israel.

By the very fact of its global pre-eminence, these prophecies must be centered about the United States.

And, they are.

John, having brought the United States into his prophecy in Revelation 13, continues with his theme, describing the destructions of war and cosmic upheaval in chapters 14, 15, and 16. He then moves in for a close-up of an interaction that is very important for it further amplifies the roles of various participants in the end-time events. Chapters 17 and 18 deal with the identification and descriptions of destruction of an entity known as the 'Great Harlot.'

Many have interpreted this woman to represent the Catholic Church, all denominational churches, occultists, and so forth. However, careful analysis of this and related portions of scripture will show that this is neither appropriate nor in keeping with the global sense of the prophecy. (And, in a previous chapter, we described the apostate condition of the Christian churches.)

Scripturally, 'woman' means either the spiritual half of the human totality — the union of male and female — or, in an expanded view, 'woman' symbolizes the socio-cultural-political manifestations of a group, a city, or a nation.

Isaiah addresses the nation of Israel in a foreshadowing of John's prophecy:

> *"How the faithful city has become an [idolatrous] harlot, she who was full of justice! ... Your princes are rebels and companions of thieves; everyone loves bribes and runs after compensation and rewards. They judge not for the fatherless nor defend them, neither does the cause of the widow come to them."* [191]

Ezekiel uses the same terms and expands the theme:

> *"... you ate fine flour and honey and oil. ... your renown went forth among the nations for your beauty ... But you trusted and relied on your own beauty ... you have made your beauty an abomination ... You have played the harlot also with the Assyrians because you were unsatiable ... you multiplied your harlotry with the land of trade, with Chaldea, and yet even with this you were not satisfied. ... because of all the idols of your abominations, and for the blood of your children that you gave to them, ... I will gather all your lovers ... they shall throw down your vaulted place and shall demolish your high places ... they shall stone you ... and thrust you through with swords. And they shall burn your houses ... As is the mother, so is her daughter. ... Your mother was a Hittite and your father an Amorite. And your elder sister is Samaria ... your younger sister ... is Sodom ... you were more corrupt in all your ways than they were. ... the iniquity of Sodom: pride, overabundance of food, prosperous ease, and idleness were hers and her daughters'; neither did she strengthen the hand of the poor and needy."* [192]

Here we have a wealth of background for interpreting the 'Harlot' in John's prophecy. We may observe that **'harlotry' relates, in a well-defined sense, to materialism.** I also, at this point, want to call attention to an obscure reference in Revelation, which says: *"the great city which is in a spiritual sense called [by the mystical and allegorical names of] Sodom and Egypt, where also their Lord was crucified."* [193] It is obvious that Christ was not crucified in either Sodom or Egypt, but Jerusalem; and John makes it plain that this 'city' is re-enacting, in a spiritual sense, the sins of all three. Noting the 'sins' of Sodom and Egypt in the foregoing passages as well as the concept that the United States is taking the global role of Israel, and, understanding that the terms 'city' and 'nation' are very often interchangeable, we may arrive at a conclusion as to which nation this multiple reference applies.

Revelation 17 begins:

"One of the seven angels who had the seven bowls then came and spoke to me saying, Come with me! I will show you the doom of the great harlot who is seated on many waters, with whom the rulers of the earth have joined in prostitution and with the wine of whose immorality the inhabitants of the earth have become intoxicated." [194]

This passage gives us the clues that this 'harlotry,' or materialism, is worldwide and that the leaders of the earth are guilty of the specific sins of greed, perversion of justice, oppression of the poor and helpless, unfair trade practices, graft and governmental corruption as defined by Ezekiel. Sound familiar?

So, we see a socio-cultural-political condition of harlotry, which promulgates the idea of human technological achievement as the ultimate aspiration for mankind. This woman, or spiritual state of mankind, is further described as *"seated on a scarlet beast covered with blasphemous titles, with seven heads and ten horns. The woman was robed in purple and scarlet and bedecked with gold, precious stones, and pearls, holding in her hand a golden cup full of the accursed offenses and the filth of her lewdness and vice."* [195]

The nation, which is the seat, or foundation, of this corrupt spiritual ideal, described as a beast with seven heads and ten horns, harkens back to the beast of chapter 13. The colors are significant in that they represent government and religion — scarlet being the priestly color and purple being the governing color — and tell us that both the Beast and, to a greater extent, the woman are revered by the peoples of the earth.

Anyone who doubts that materialism has become a god in our society should try a little experiment: Try, for a period of twenty minutes each day, to clear the mind entirely and simply experience the quietness of the spirit. Nine people out of ten will have great difficulty quieting their thoughts and kicking them out, so to speak. Those thoughts that return to you most frequently, those ideas which are most persistent in holding your mind are, in truth, your god.

Some people think about sports, some people cannot stop thinking about their future plans in regards to making money, acquiring possessions, furthering relationships and rehashing past events. But, it will be seen, in the final analysis, that the main obstacle to meditation, or quieting the mind and contemplating spirit, is money — either the getting, keeping, or spending of it. Whatever the consciousness drifts to naturally is the individual's ideal.

The gold, the jewels and the pearls adorning the Harlot tell us that all the mental and spiritual achievements of the earth are centered upon materialism — this includes science, education, arts, culture, music and all other aspects of human potential — including religion.

"And on her forehead was inscribed a name of mystery [with a secret symbolic meaning]: Babylon the great, the mother of prostitutes and of the filth and atrocities and abominations of the earth." [196]

Babylon was the great city that arose in Chaldea, 'the land of trade.' This verse tells us that this harlotry — materialism — gives rise to unspeakable crimes, which individuals undertake to further their pursuit of sensual pleasure and acquisition of material goods. The deepest and most abominable sense of this description relates to warfare.

Many books have been written which expose the fact that governments do not wage war for moral or even ideological reasons — wars are simply acts of greedy materialism — but this is not commonly known among the masses for most of them do not read. Many still believe that the American Revolution, the Civil War, World Wars I and II were fought to defend noble ideals, and such people have been so thoroughly indoctrinated and duped on this subject that the mere mention of the actual facts causes them to close their ears and minds and live their lives in blissful ignorance, contaminating their children with unfounded patriotic zeal, and producing more fodder for the cannons.

One of the most abhorrent practices engaged in by ancient peoples, including, on occasion, the Israelites, was human sacrifice — in particular child sacrifice. It seems that we, in the present age, continue to pass our innocent offspring 'through the fire' with as little regard as did the ancients — only now we call it 'noble patriotism.'

I would like to suggest that governments and their industrial-military masters are fornicators and the 'Great Harlot,' the great, dark and evil system of materialism, is their mistress. Materialism is the mother of war, famine, disease, ignorance, drug addiction, murder, robbery, rape, and a host of assorted other evils of our day. Thus they are indeed drunk on the blood of martyrs.

"I also saw that the woman was drunk, with the blood of the saints and the blood of the martyrs for Jesus. And when I saw her, I was utterly amazed and wondered greatly. But the angel said to me, Why do you wonder? I will explain to you the mystery of the woman, as well as the beast having the seven heads and ten horns

that carries her. The beast that you saw was, but is no more, and he is going to come up out of the Abyss and proceed to go to perdition... This calls for a mind with wisdom and intelligence [it is something for a particular mode of thinking and judging of thoughts, feelings and purposes]. The seven heads are seven hills upon which the woman is sitting; And they are also seven kings, five of whom have fallen, one still exists; the other has not yet appeared, and when he does arrive, he must stay a brief time. And as for the beast that was, but now is no more, he is an eighth ruler, but he is of the seven and belongs to them, and he goes to perdition." [197]

A caveat is inserted into this explanation, which tells us that the answer is hidden and is in the form, once again, of a riddle. It is like the old conundrum: 'Down in the dark dungeon, I saw a bright light; all saddled, all bridled, all set for a fight. Now I've told you the answer three times in a row: what did I see?' And the answer? 'All.'

The first, and obvious, interpretation is that 'seven hills' relates to Rome — the 'City of Seven Hills' — and this is where most interpreters lose their way. Seven is also seven kings, or empires, five of which had fallen at the time John wrote Revelation. These can be identified as: Egypt, Assyria, Babylon, Media-Persia, and Greece. The sixth, Rome, was in power at the time of John's vision. The seventh *"has not yet appeared, and when he does arrive, he must stay but a brief time."* And, the eighth is *"of the seven and belongs to them."*

There is a very important transition indicated here in the number symbologies. Recall that the number seven is the number of perfection — the whole of a thing. We know that the sixth 'king,' or empire, is Rome; but who is the seventh, which completes the number, and how does the eighth fit in? This is why John said this was going to be tricky. The Beast which was, but is no more, and is going to come up out of the abyss is identified by seven hills (Rome), and is also the eighth — of the seven and belonging to them; eight being the number of regeneration — which identifies it as a reincarnation of the Roman Empire, but also connects it to Belshazzar in the Book of Daniel. If you recall, the king saw the handwriting on the wall and called for wise men and interpreters. Daniel interpreted the writing: *"O king, the Most High God gave Nebuchadnezzar your father a kingdom and greatness and glory and majesty; And because of the greatness that He gave him, all peoples, nations, and languages trembled and feared before him. ... But when his heart was lifted up and his mind and spirit were hardened so that he dealt proudly, he was deposed from his kingly throne, and his glory was taken from him; He was driven from among men, and his heart and mind was made like the beasts..."* [198] This is the 'beast' John meant when he spoke of the one which was cast into the abyss: Nebuchadnezzar and the empire he represented. This indicates that this beast which is to come will also have major aspects of the Babylonian influence, which is to glorify materialism.

However, John indicates that this is not as simple as it would appear. John is prophesying global events using archetypes familiar to him and, we have already conjectured that the United States is a cumulative reenactment of Israel, Sodom, Egypt and now, Rome and Babylon. This relates, in a sense, to the multiple animal identities of the beast of chapter 13. Just as that beast was composed of many aspects of various animals, so, now, we find the same concept expressed in terms of socio-cultural manifestations.

Every aspect of the United States is in agreement with these varied descriptions — from our government style (Roman), to our trade practices (Babylon), to our sensuality (Egyptian), to our pride, over-abundance, and prosperous ease and idleness (Sodom).

Additionally, we may observe that a nation which spends billions of dollars annually to fund warfare and space exploration while millions of its own citizens go without adequate food, clothing, housing and medical care, has, somehow, lost sight of the priorities which make an empire truly great.

The 'seventh' empire is Great Britain, which, as a truly great nation only lasted for a brief time. Great Britain was part of the original Roman Empire, and its subsequent conquerors and rulers were scions of Rome in fact as well as philosophy. The eighth is the present United Sates government, which 'belongs' to the seven in that it was a British Crown Colony and our form of government, language and social customs derive from England, which took them from Rome. The United States also belongs to the former 'seven' in that it embodies all the power and corruption of all the former empires put together and is the natural heir of them all.

John continues:

> "Also the ten horns that you observed are ten rulers who have as yet received no royal dominion, but together they are to receive power and authority as rulers for single hour, along with the beast. These have one common policy, and they deliver their power and authority to the beast. They will wage war with the Lamb, and the Lamb will triumph over them; for He is Lord of lords and King of kings — and those with Him and on His side are chosen and called and loyal and faithful followers." [199]

As noted in the previous chapter, ten is the number that represents an earthly foreshadowing of divine principle and, as such, exemplifies human law. In this passage, John amplifies the meaning of the ten horns — the ten rulers, or dominions, with no authority, which receive power along with the Beast — as representing the ten major divisions of the Roman Empire from which America drew its populace. John states that they ruled with the Beast and then delivered their power to the Beast, having one common policy — or, stated in more modern terms, created a democracy.

This verse reveals that, initially, the peoples, or horns, which constitute the nation of the Beast, had authority and power, but, at some point early on, delivered their authority over to the Beast — established a federal government. The term 'common policy,' prior to this event, describes a former state of true democracy — relinquished to the Beast. This point may be hotly disputed by those who have been stupefied by the media and believe that we have lived and continue to live, in a democracy set up by the Constitutional Convention of 1787.

To clarify this point, I find that I must digress again. The subject is history and the reader may find the facts I have gleaned from dozens of treatises to be quite interesting and informative.

We, in America, have grown up being spoon-fed a watered-down, tasteless gruel on this subject. Most college graduates suffer from mental-malnutrition in their concepts about American genesis. What is taught in our public school system is even worse. It is as though the government-controlled school system seeks to propagate the myth of the parthenogenesis of a secular 'Super State.' This is a dangerous and cunning slander.

The early settlers who came to America were, by and large, oppressed and desperate. Being outcasts in a despotic feudal system, they had little money to undertake such a venture. Most of them were funded by various European business interests who hoped to establish centers of trade so that they could benefit from the vast natural resources of the new land.

The colonists were brutally exploited and woefully unprepared for their ventures. Like the Israelites, they sought freedom from bondage and the only thing they had was faith.

The experiences of the early settlers soon taught them that mutual support and interdependence as well as industry and moderation were the keys to success. They worked long and hard and improved their lot individually and collectively. Soon the European business interests moved across the sea and set up shop on the graves of those they had used to pave the way. Greedy opportunists and upper-class land grantees followed and few found their dreams of riches or simple prosperity thwarted. It soon became apparent that the competition and greed of the business world of Europe was going to interfere with the wealthy elite of the New World, and a hue and cry was raised which has echoed over two hundred years.

As it happened, the philosophies being expounded in the European scientific and literary circles at the time came in handy as idealistic and inspirational extrapolations with which to underpin a spreading revolutionary spirit. And, for a single hour, the people and the government were united in their efforts to overcome despotism and oppression — the American Revolution.

Contrary to popular conceptions and teachings, the American Revolution did not create the American nation as we know it today. The Articles of Confederation actually bound thirteen new nations, each theoretically sovereign in its own right, into a loose confederacy. The Continental Congress could legislate but not enforce. However, the effects of the Revolution had been financially disastrous. The national and state debts went unpaid (monies owed to the wealthy elite who had financed the war), trade declined and credit collapsed.

Left to their own devices, the New Americans would have eventually sorted these problems out based upon emerging priorities and systems involving barter and mutually satisfying personal agreements. Democracy might have flourished.

Tradition teaches us that a group of 'noble patriots' called a Constitu - tional Convention to 'further the principles of democracy,' as spelled out in the Declaration of Independence. Nothing could be further from the truth. The Constitution actually checked the development of democracy.

In some of the states, a moratorium on debt was enacted to relieve the farmers who had fought in the war. But, in the largest and wealthiest states, the planters of Virginia, the manor lords of New York, and the merchants of Massachusetts and Connecticut, refused to give an inch. Massachusetts went so far as to prohibit barter, to which the impoverished returning soldiers had been forced to resort.

Daniel Shay, a Revolutionary captain who had been cited for bravery at Bunker Hill, had come out of the war, as had many others, with nothing. (General Lafayette had presented him with a sword, which he was soon forced to sell.) Seeing so many others like himself, he was filled with the injustice of the actions of the wealthy elite. He organized a force of

800 farmers and attempted to prevent the sitting of the courts that were foreclosing the properties of the returning soldiers. Shay's army was dispersed by the state militia but his action thoroughly frightened the upper classes.

Samuel Adams begged Congress for federal aid to protect 'property rights' and Congress authorized a force designed to prevent any further rebellion.

General Henry Knox wrote to George Washington in 1786:

> "The people who are the insurgents have never paid any, or but very little taxes. But they see the weakness of government; They feel at once their own poverty, compared with the opulent, and their own force, and they are determined to make use of the latter, in order to remedy the former. Their creed is 'That the property of the United States has been protected from the confiscation of Great Britain by the joint exertions of all, and therefore ought to be the common property of all. And he that attempts opposition to this creed is an enemy to equity and justice, and ought to be swept off the face of the earth.' In a word they are determined to annihilate all debts public and private and have agrarian Laws, which are easily affected by the means of unfortunate paper money which shall be a tender in all cases whatsoever." [200]

The insurgents may have paid very little taxes, but they paid much blood. Nevertheless, seized with fear that a democracy would actually be enacted, the wealthy classes murmured for a government by *"the rich, well-born, and capable"* (John Adams). Ezra Stiles and Noah Webster were vocal opponents of democracy. Webster claimed, *"The very principle of admitting everybody to the right of suffrage prostrates the wealth of individuals to the rapaciousness of a merciless gang..."* [201]

Taking advantage of the situation, Alexander Hamilton induced Congress to call a convention in 1787 to ostensibly revise the Articles of Confederation. Hamilton made no bones about his views that only the wealthy and educated were fit to rule.

> "It is usually stated that Hamilton's great achievement was to bring the men of wealth to the support of the new nation, but it could equally well be stated that he brought the new nation to the support of the men of wealth. Indeed it might be said that the new nation was created largely for that very purpose." [202]

Those who met for the Constitutional Convention were, and knew they were, the elite — wealthy, educated and intellectual. They believed that others like them must continue to rule for their own protection. The public good was a secondary issue. They meant to create a system in which this could be perpetuated, constitutionally, legally, and peacefully. Adopting strictest rules of secrecy, they proceeded to create the American Constitution.

M.L. Wilson wrote in *Democracy Has Roots*, that the Constitution was *"a remarkable achievement in the avoidance of majority rule."* [203]

It is not surprising that the ratification of this Constitution was popularly opposed. The conventioneers promised to amend it at the first regular session of Congress. These promised amendments came to be known as the 'Bill of Rights' and it is in these first ten amendments that Americans have their supposed 'Constitutional Rights.' A sobering thought when one considers that amendments have been repealed in the past. But for the 'Bill of Rights,' hundreds of years of bloodletting for personal liberty would have been tossed on the trash heap by the Federal Government, the Beast to whom the ten horns gave their authority.

This Beast, blasphemously using God's name to further its policies and plans, rapidly propagated the ideals of materialism and capitalism. And, in a process of unadulterated propaganda, these ideals have been inextricably linked with 'democracy' as though the two were identical.

The result of this has been a vast chasm between the 'haves' and the 'have-nots,' which grows wider and deeper every day, while the former continue to dupe the latter into believing and sacrificing for that which does not exist.

> *"And [the angel further] said to me, The waters that you observed, where the harlot is seated, are races and multitudes and nations and dialects. And the ten horns that you saw, they and the beast will hate the harlot; they will make her cheerless and they will strip her and eat up her flesh and utterly consume her with fire. For God has put it into their hearts to carry out His own purpose by acting in harmony in surrendering their royal power and authority to the beast, until the prophetic words (intentions and promises) of God shall be fulfilled. And the woman that you saw is herself the great city which dominates and controls the rulers and the leaders of the earth."* [204]

In order to get the correct sense of this portion of Revelation, we must organize the words in the correct order: *"For God has put it into their hearts to carry out His own purpose by acting in harmony in surrendering their royal power and authority to the beast, until the prophetic words — intentions and promises — of God shall be fulfilled. And the woman that you saw is her-*

self the great city which dominates and controls the rulers and leaders of the earth. The waters that you observed, where the harlot is seated, are races and multitudes and nations and dialects. And the ten horns that you saw, they and the beast will hate the harlot; they will make her cheerless and they will strip her, and eat up her flesh and utterly consume her with fire."

It is fairly simple to see the relationship between John's Great City — 'Babylon' — and Nostradamus' 'Great New City' and relate both appellations to New York, though in the greater sense it means the entire nation, just as Jerusalem means the entire nation of Israel.

I would like to digress again and pick up our history lesson where we left off.

At about the same time that the American Revolution was being fought, a man name Adam Weishaupt founded an organization in Europe dedicated to the idea that only the elite were fit to rule and it was the duty of these elite to band together and manipulate international affairs to this end. This organization was formed according to the format laid down by the Society of Jesus — circles within circles — and its code was expressed in Masonic terms. They were found out, raided and, supposedly, disbanded. However, there is evidence that they simply went underground. It might be conjectured that the framers of our Constitution were aware of and even participated in such ideological 'clubs.'

In the early part of the 20th century, certain members of this organization, affiliated with eminent European international banking families, emigrated to this country. Evidence exists that these individuals promoted the ideas and ideals of Weishaupt's 'Order of Illuminati' among the wealthy elite of America. Prior to this time, there were disorganized attempts to control the machinations of government by the wealthy elite.

This was deplored by Andrew Jackson, our seventh president, who wrote: *"I am one of those who do not believe that a national debt is a national blessing, but rather a curse to a republic; inasmuch as it is calculated to raise around the administration a moneyed aristocracy dangerous to the liberties of the country."* [205]

This brings us to the crux of the matter: Money. One of the downfalls of democracy in the early history of this country was money. Governments have always spent far more money than they could get from taxation. In order to finance their projects (including war, graft and corruption), they must issue bonds. A small percentage of these bonds are held by ordinary private citizens; the majority are held by international bankers. This is called the national debt.

When any given individual borrows money from a bank, they usually provide collateral. When a large business or corporation borrows money, they too, provide collateral — which usually consists in placing members of the lending institution on their board and permitting the lender to direct, or control, some of the corporate policies.

In this way, governments are like corporations — their policies are controlled by the moneylenders. The moneylenders have another means of assuring that the government keeps in line with its policies: by funding the enemy. In this way, political power is balanced and all power lies in the hands of the lender. Since it is evidently politic for enemies to be kept in a tense state to assure the bankers of their profits, it can be seen that political and social tensions are fomented for financial gain. This is exactly the case, and this is the game that has been played between governments for hundreds of years, with the bankers in the background pulling the strings.

On many occasions, this game has resulted in vast moneymaking operations called wars, which have taken literally millions of lives.

The group that formed among the wealthy elite in this country as a result of the propagandizing of the European Illuminati soon began manipulating the economy of the U.S. and a 'panic' ensued on Wall Street, which set the country up to accept 'banking reforms.' Since the wealthy elite were not popular among the masses, they realized that they must not openly advocate such reforms and, in fact, erected a smoke-screen of protest — feeling this to be the surest way of obtaining popular support. The ruse worked and the Federal Reserve System was enacted.

Henry Cabot Lodge, Sr., said:

> *"The bill as it stands seems to me to open the way to a vast inflation of currency. ... I do not like to think that any law can be passed which will make it possible to submerge the gold standard in a flood in irredeemable paper currency."* [206]

Our 'central bank' controls our money supply and interest rates. It can create inflation or deflation at will — recession or boom. And, the title of this system is misleading — no part of the federal government controls the Federal Reserve! This was admitted by Secretary of the Treasury, David M. Kennedy, in an interview, May 5, 1969.

The Federal Reserve has never been audited, either. How successful is the Federal Reserve system? When Woodrow Wilson took office, the national debt was $1 billion. Even considering our increase in population, a national debt in the trillions staggers acceptance. But, from the point of view of the bankers, this is progress, as they now own the county.

What is the ultimate goal of this group of wealthy elitists? A conspiratorial network is revealed in *Tragedy and Hope*, by Professor Carroll Quigley, Foreign Service School, Georgetown University, formerly of Princeton and Harvard:

> *"I know of the operations of this network because I have studied it for twenty years and was permitted for two years, in the early 1960's, to examine its papers and secret records. I have no aversion to it or to most of its aims and have, for much of my life, been close to it and to many of its instruments. I have objected, both in the past and recently, to a few of its policies ... but in general my chief difference of opinion is that it wishes to remain unknown, and I believe its role in history is significant enough to be known."* [207]

The professor goes on to describe the aims of the network as being nothing short of control of the entire world through the respective governments of individual countries by means of economics.

> *"In other words, this power mad clique wants to rule the world. Even more frightening, they want total control over all individual actions. As professor Quigley observes: '... his [the individual's] freedom and choice will be controlled within very narrow alternatives by the fact that he will be numbered from birth and followed, as a number, through his educational training, his required military or other public service, his tax contributions, his health and medical requirements, and his final retirement and death benefits.' It wants control over all natural resources, business, banking and transportation by controlling the governments of the world. In order to accomplish these aims the conspirators have had no qualms about fomenting wars, [economic] depressions and [international] hatred. They want a monopoly which would eliminate all competitors and destroy the free enterprise system. And Professor Quigley, of Harvard, Princeton and Georgetown approves!"* [208]

And, since 1945, where has this group of wealthy elitists centered their operation? New York — the marketplace and cultural center of the world. And, how far do their operations extend? Around the globe. And, who are the members? Over 1,500 members around the globe representing the lions of industry, communication, politics, economics, etc.

It may be apparent by this time that the Harlot is a creation of the 'second beast' of Revelation 13, and, because of the deceptive, controlling tactics of this entity, we may also understand the sense in which John addresses it as the 'false prophet.' However, up to the present, the propaganda of the 'false prophet' has been for 'materialistic capitalism.' There is a definite and sudden change noted in both Revelation 13 and 17.

In Revelation 13, John speaks of the 'worship' or 'reverence' given to the 'image' of the Beast. This act is connected with numbers and, in addition to the already discussed esoteric interpretation of these numbers, we must examine another facet.

The probability is that our government, as well as other governments of the earth will, in unity, move to a 'cashless' society, and that all financial transactions will be handled by computer based upon a number assigned to the individual at birth. In the U.S. we have, at the present time, the social security number, which is a series of nine digits. Quite recently, legislation was passed which made the obtaining of this number mandatory for income tax purposes. And, income tax is legally mandated. (It must be noted that a graduated income tax and a 'central bank' are two of the ten planks of the Communist Manifesto.)

If we view the instituting of the 'Mark of the Beast' as the onset of hidden totalitarianism, we must then see the destruction of the Harlot as popular opposition and revolution against same.

The materialism of the Harlot, as defined in Ezekiel, is that which oppresses the masses for the enrichment of the few. And, since the ten horns and the Beast, or the empire, 'eat up the flesh' of the Harlot at the time of the end, we may see this to be military or revolutionary actions within our own country. Additionally, the Harlot is seated on 'many waters' so we may infer that this indicates international reactions against totalitarianism and materialistic ideals.

Simply stated, at a certain point, the people of the United States will realize that they have been duped — stupefied and controlled by the machinations of the wealthy elitist government that uses the propaganda machinery of the media, which it owns and controls, and they will revolt. Daniel Shay's cause will finally achieve fruition.

However, that this is to be ultimately an international conflict, probably nuclear, is amplified in chapters 14 an 18. Chapters 14, 15 and 16 are a broad overview of the final conflicts leading up to the ultimate cosmic cataclysm. Chapter 18 is a close-up of the fate of the Harlot.

"Then another angel, a second, followed, declaring, Fallen, fallen is Babylon the great! She who made all nations drink of the wine of her passionate unchastity. Then another angel, a third, followed them, saying with a mighty voice, Whoever

pays homage to the beast and his statue and permits the stamp to be put on his forehead or on his hand, He too shall drink of the wine of God's indignation and wrath... Again I looked, and behold, a white cloud, and sitting on the cloud One resembling a Son of man, with a crown of gold on His head, and a sharp scythe in His hand. ... So he Who was sitting upon the cloud swung His scythe on the earth and the earth's crop was harvested. ... And another angel came forth from the altar, who has authority and power over fire, and he called with a loud cry to him who had the sharp scythe, Put forth your scythe and reap the fruitage of the vine of the earth, for its grapes are entirely ripe. So the angel swung his scythe on the earth and stripped the grapes and gathered the vintage from the vines of the earth, and cast it into the huge wine press of God's indignation and wrath. And [the grapes in] the winepress were trodden outside the city, and the blood poured from the winepress, as high as horses' bridles, for a distance of 1,600 stadia (about 200 miles)." [209]

There are several images here that lend credence to the idea of nuclear war. The first is the 'white clouds' which are described quite differently from the images of cosmic catastrophe. The second is the image of the angel with the scythe. One important thing to note is that the events are described as extending outside 'the city' for a distance of two hundred miles, which would fit models of nuclear destruction.

"She is fallen. Mighty Babylon is fallen! ... For all nations have drunk the wine of her passionate unchastity, and the rulers and leaders of the earth have joined with her in committing fornication, and the businessmen of the earth have become rich with the wealth of her excessive luxury and wantonness. ... Repay to her what she herself has paid and double in accordance with what she has done." [210]

This harkens back to Revelation 13: *"Whoever leads into captivity will himself go into captivity; if anyone slays with the sword by the sword must he be slain."* [211] And, considering the United States' use of nuclear weaponry upon the defeated Japanese people, this does not bode well for our nation. Also, we must consider the evils of the propagating of materialism that has seduced the nations into forgetting their priorities — spiritual development being the primary one. The scriptures say God is not mocked; whatsoever a man sows, that will he also reap — and we may assume this to apply to nations, as well.

"To the degree that she glorified herself and reveled in her wantonness [living deliciously and luxuriously], to that measure impose on her torment and anguish

and tears and mourning. Since in her heart she boasts, I am not a widow; as a queen I sit, and I shall never see suffering or experience sorrow... [212]

Edgar Cayce delineated these very things:

"Unless there is, then, a more universal oneness of purpose on the part of all, this will one day bring — here — in America — revolution! ... The ideals, the purposes that called the nation into being are well. It might be answered by saying that there needs to be on the part of each man, each woman, the adhering to those principles that caused the formulating of the American thought. Yet in the present (1943), there are seen many complex problems, many conditions that are variants to the First Cause (God), or first principles, not only among groups and individuals in high places, both from the political and economic situations, but the problems of labor-capital as well. ... That such is, and is to be, a part of the experience of America is because of unbelief!" [213]

The fate of the Harlot, the Beast, the False Prophet — all aspects of the same national entity — are cataclysmic as described by John.

"So shall her plagues come thick upon her in a single day, pestilence and anguish and sorrow and famine; and she shall be utterly consumed (burned up with fire), for mighty is the Lord God Who judges her. And the rulers and leaders of the earth who joined her in her immorality and luxuriated with her will weep and beat their breasts and lament over her when they see the smoke of her conflagration. They will stand a long way off, in terror of her torment, and they will cry, Woe and alas, the great city, the might city, Babylon! In one single hour how your doom has overtaken you! And earth's businessmen will weep and grieve over her because no one buys their freight any more. ... In one single hour (Babylon) has been destroyed and has become a desert!" [214]

Is this all John sees? The end of Babylon? We may recall at this time that Nostradamus predicted the coming of 'The Great King of Terror' in the sky, which then enabled the arising of the 'King of the Mongols.' Revelation describes a similar event in great detail, and it is described as occurring *after* the destruction of Babylon.

"Then I saw another wonder in heaven, great and marvelous: There were seven angels bringing seven plagues, which are the last, for with them God's wrath is completely expressed [reaches its climax and is ended]. Then I saw what seemed to be a glassy sea blended with fire... (Recall the rivers and rains of flaming pe-

troleum — LKJ) ... and the sanctuary of ... heaven was thrown open, And there came out of the temple sanctuary the seven angels bringing the seven plagues. They were arrayed in pure gleaming linen, and around their breasts they wore golden girdles. ... And the sanctuary was filled with smoke from the glory of God and from His might and power... So the first [angel] went and emptied his bowl on the earth, and foul and painful ulcers came on the people who were marked with the stamp of the beast and who did homage to his image." [215]

The fact that these plagues seem to be specific to a certain group, namely those 'marked' by the Beast, indicates that this is due to the adherence of ideology.

An individual who is so materialistic that he will not admit to the possibility of spiritual and prophetic truth, will do nothing to prepare for cataclysm and will, therefore, be unprepared to deal with it and will suffer the range of events unmitigated. Additionally, this idea seems to indicate that most of the destructive events will occur on the Western portion of the globe.

"The second [angel] emptied his bowl into the sea, and it turned into blood like that of a corpse [ill-smelling and disgusting], and everything that was in the sea perished. Then the third [angel] emptied out his bowl into the rivers and the springs of water, and they turned into blood. ... Then the fourth [angel] emptied out his bowl upon the sun, and it was permitted to burn humanity with heat. ... Then the fifth [angel] emptied his bowl on the throne of the beast, and his kingdom was [plunged] in darkness; and people gnawed their tongues for the torment... Then the sixth [angel] emptied his bowl on the mighty river Euphrates, and its water was dried up to make ready a road for the kings of the east." [216]

All of these effects describe the actions of a comet upon the earth. The 'drying of the Euphrates' probably indicates an alteration of the geography of the earth which will enable the peoples of the Orient to emerge as dominant which, by the implications of this statement taken with the foregoing passage relating to the destruction of Babylon, must be the military opponents of the Beast et al., at the time the comet heads their way, disrupting their conflict at least temporarily.

"And I saw three loathsome spirits like frogs, from the mouth of the dragon and from the mouth of the beast and from the mouth of the false prophet. For really they are the spirits of demons that perform signs. And they go forth to the rulers and leaders all over the world, to gather them together for war on the great day

of God the Almighty. ... And they gathered them together at the place which in Hebrew is called Armageddon." [217]

Now why, one must ask, in the name of all good sense, would the nations of the earth gather together for war in the midst of cosmic upheaval? We can note the similarity of the descriptions of the frogs as 'performers of signs' to the description of nuclear war in chapter 13: *"He performs great signs (startling miracles), even making fire fall from the sky to the earth in men's sight,"* [218] and thereby make the connection to nuclear armaments. But how are they being used? The connection with the 'dragon' relates to lies and deception and the false prophet relates to materialism and political manipulation.

Supposing the earth to be in a state of incredible turmoil due to war and now, cosmic catastrophe, the deceptive attitude of scientific materialism would be that something can be done to avert further disaster, assuming that a comet is, in fact, on a direct path toward the earth.

I believe that the description in this passage tells us that all the nations will assemble their nuclear armaments and attempt to use them to break the attraction between the earth and another cosmic body, or, deflect its path if it has not, in fact, made atmospheric contact. The implication of this passage is that the armies are gathered together to fight God, and this is reiterated in numerous other passages of scripture. The launching of all the warheads from the planet would serve a very beneficial purpose, assuming that nuclear war has not already gone too far. It would rid the earth of these dreaded objects, which would totally poison the globe if left to spill or seep after destruction by extraterrestrial contact.

Also, we must never lose sight of the fact that the actions of Satan, or the dragon, are part of the plan as explained in II Thessalonians.

Nevertheless, the effect of this effort is not clear. The result is clear, but whether it could turn out differently is not established. The result is global cataclysm:

"Then the seventh [angel] emptied out his bowl into the air, and a mighty voice came out of the sanctuary of heaven from the throne, saying, It is done! And there followed lightning flashes, loud rumblings, peals of thunder, and a tremendous earthquake; nothing like it has ever occurred since men dwelt on the earth, so severe and far-reaching was that earthquake. The mighty city (a usage which indicates the nation — LKJ) was broken into three parts, and the cities of the nations fell. And God kept in mind mighty Babylon, to make her drain the cup of His

furious wrath and indignation. And every island fled and no mountains could be found. And great hailstones, as heavy as a talent [between fifty and sixty pounds], of immense size, fell from the sky on the people; and men blasphemed God for the plague of the hail, so very great was [the torture] of the plague." [219]

This event is echoed in Revelation 18:

"Then a single powerful angel took up a boulder like a great millstone and flung it into the sea, crying, With such violence shall Babylon the great city be hurled down to destruction and shall never again be found!" [220]

And again:

"Then I saw a single angel stationed in the sun's light, and with a mighty voice he shouted to all the birds that fly across the sky, Come, gather yourselves together for the Great Supper of God, That you may feast on the flesh of rulers, the flesh of generals and captains, the flesh of powerful and mighty men, the flesh of horses and their riders, and the flesh of all humanity ... both small and great! Then I saw the beast and the rulers and leaders of the earth with their troops mustered to go into battle and make war against Him Who is mounted on the horse (a celestial event — LKJ) and against His troops. And the beast was seized and overpowered, and with him the false prophet who in his presence had worked wonders and performed miracles by which he led astray those who had accepted or permitted to be placed upon them the stamp of the beast and those who paid homage and gave divine honors to his statue. Both of them were hurled alive into the fiery lake that burns and blazes with brimstone." [221]

Each of these passages is about the same event; each adding layers of color and detail. If we recall that angels were used to symbolize the planets in Jewish traditions, and considering all the related references to comets and other prophesied extraterrestrial destruction, particularly that found in the writings of Nostradamus, I think that it is reasonable to assume that these passages describe just such an event.

The common elements of all the prophetic excerpts I have compared and analyzed in this thesis are:

1. Wars, pestilence, famine.
2. Visible changes in the appearance of the Sun.
3. Rains of fire and meteorites.
4. Global earthquake.

5. Destruction of nearly the entire human race, particularly those inhabiting the geographic area of the 'Beast.'
6. Horrifying signs and events in the heavens.

All of these, taken together, point to one event — the contact between the earth and another celestial body or bodies.

Chapter Twelve

It is better to debate a question without settling it
than to settle a question without debating it.

— Joseph Joubert (1754—1824).

We have discussed the idea that prophecy is the ability to see the All and to see the probable direction we are heading. In this sense, I feel that at the present time we are facing a quantum change that is inexorable in terms of accomplishment, but variable in terms of specifics. It will be cataclysmic — there will be extraterrestrial interactions — but the severity and the timing are still in the realm of probabilities. It would take tremendous interaction on the part of every human being presently on the planet to change this destiny. In fact, I think that the only kind of change that could be manifested at this point is a spiritual elevation, which would make material cataclysm a moot issue.

An understanding of quantum physics makes it comprehensible that the slight electrical current that manifests through the individual, increased by great emotional responses such as anger or hatred, could appreciably alter the flow and placement of sub-atomic particles. Multiply this by the multiplied billions of people on the planet, and you have a very great Contact Potential Difference. Add to this the deliberate manipulation of the atomic structure of the earth through nuclear testing activities, and the affect is increased exponentially. The consequence is the establishment of a massive state of electrical usage. As long as the Sun remains quiescent, this difference results only in terrestrial disturbances such as earthquakes and volcanic eruptions, changing weather patterns, etc.

The continuing deterioration of human relations across the globe increases this Contact Potential Difference in two ways: On an individual basis through improperly controlled and inadequately developed brain wave functions; on a global basis through the use of nuclear energy either in tests, power plants or actual military actions. There is also another way we must consider.

"There is an Eastern tale which speaks about a very rich magician who had a great many sheep. But at the same time this magician was very mean. He did not want to hire shepherds, nor did he want to erect a fence about the pasture where his sheep were grazing. The sheep consequently often wandered into the forest, fell into ravines, and so on, and above all they ran away, for they knew that the magician wanted their flesh and skins and this they did not like.

At last the magician found a remedy. He hypnotized his sheep and suggested to them first of all that they were immortal and that no harm was being done to them when they were skinned, that, on the contrary, it would be very good for them and even pleasant; secondly he suggested that the magician was a good master who loved his flock so much that he was ready to do anything in the world for them; and in the third place he suggested to them that if anything at all were going to happen to them it was not going to happen just then, at any rate not that day, and therefore they had no need to think about it. Further the magician suggested to his sheep that they were not sheep at all; to some of them he suggested that they were lions, to others that they were eagles, to others that they were men, and to others that they were magicians.

And after this all his cares and worries about the sheep came to an end. They never ran away again but quietly awaited the time when the magician would require their flesh and skins." [222]

This accurately describes the condition of the great masses of humanity at the present time. In order to awaken, first of all one must realize that one is in a state of sleep. And, in order to realize that one is, indeed, in a state of sleep, one must recognize and fully understand the nature of the forces which operate to keep one in the state of sleep, or hypnosis. It is absurd to think that this can be done by seeking information from the very source that induces the hypnosis.

"Theoretically (a man can awaken), but practically it is almost impossible because as soon as a man awakens for a moment and opens his eyes, all the forces that caused him to fall asleep begin to act upon him with tenfold energy and he immediately falls asleep again, very often dreaming that the is awake or awakening." [223]

It is in the awakening of mankind that the hope of mitigating the prophesied disasters lies. In order to bring a halt to the conditions that have operated to bring humanity to the present deplorable conditions, they must be exposed and understood. The False Prophet — the strong delusion to error — must be overcome.

"Beware of false prophets who come to you dressed as sheep, but inside they are devouring wolves. You will fully recognize them by their fruits. Do people pick grapes from thorns, or figs from thistles? ... A good tree cannot bear bad fruit, nor can a bad tree bear excellent fruit." [224]

While everyone will readily admit that there is probably too much violence on television and that the ads are probably pure balderdash, very few people have a real conception of the precise nature and extent of the hypnotic influence of the media. Still fewer have any idea of the purposes behind this inducement.

"After World War II, television flourished... Psychologists and sociologists were brought in to study human nature in relation to selling; in other words, to figure out how to manipulate people without their feeling manipulated. Dr. Ernest Dichter, President of the Institute for Motivational Research made a statement in 1941 ... 'the successful ad agency manipulates human motivations and desires and develops a need for goods with which the public has at one time been unfamiliar — perhaps even undesirous of purchasing.

Discussing the influence of television, Daniel Boorstin wrote: 'Here at last is a supermarket of surrogate experience. Successful programming offers entertainment — under the guise of instruction; instruction — under the guise of entertainment; political persuasion — with the appeal of advertising; and advertising — with the appeal of drama.'

... programmed television serves not only to spread acquiescence and conformity, but it represents a deliberate industry approach." [225]

Aside from the fact that television has been shown to be extremely detrimental to children and that it is now thought that most of the deteriorating aspects of society can be attributed to the decaying values portrayed on television, there is a deeper and more insidious effect upon the human psyche. As quoted, it is a planned and deliberate manipulation to spread acquiescence and conformity and to hypnotize the masses to submit to the authority of the television.

Allen Funt, hose of a popular show, Candid Camera, was once asked what was the most disturbing thing he had learned about people in his years of dealing with them through the media. His response was chilling in its ramifications: *"The worst thing, and I see it over and over, is how easily people can be led by any kind of authority figure, or even the most minimal kinds of authority. A well dressed man walks up the down escalator and most people will turn around and try desperately to go up also ... We put up a sign on the road, 'Delaware Closed Today.' Motorists didn't even question it. Instead they asked: 'Is Jersey open?'"* [226]

A picture is forming of a deliberately contrived society of televised conformity, literate and creative inadequacy, and social unrest and decadence. It is apparent that the media is in charge of propagating these conditions.

It would seem that the motivation masters would, in the interests of their industrial clients, plan programming to bring about beneficial societal conditions — which they could, in fact, do. It is apparent that the final authority on televised programming is in the hands of the advertisers, backed by the industries whose products are being sold. With all the psychological input to which they have access, it would seem that they would force programming to correct societal conditions which cost them money. Over 25 billion dollars a year is spent to teach workers to read and write, after graduating from the combined effects of a public school system and the television. It is accepted that the burgeoning crime rate, which also costs these industrial giants vast sums of money, is mostly attributable to the frustrations and dissatisfactions engendered by the false view of reality presented over the television. Why don't they use their financial resources to back the motivation masters to figure out how to present programming that could effect positive changes? Can it be that the conditions of society, including the programmed response to 'minimal signs of authority' are planned? Would anyone care to suggest that the figures and studies relating to the detrimental influence of programming is not available to them and that they don't realize that it is costing them money? If that is the case, then they are too stupid to be arbiters of our values and we should disregard them entirely in any event. If it is not the case, then we must assume that there is an object to this manipulation.

There is much evidence to support the idea that this purpose, or the object of this manipulation, is to create psychological and social disunity sufficient to permit the instituting of a totalitarian government at the behest of the people. It is further theorized that the 'wealthy elite' seek to control the entire world from behind the scenes and it is to this end that they mastermind and fund the various actions that appear to the masses as political and international 'accidents.' F.D.R. allegedly said: *"Nothing in politics ever happens by accident; if it happens, you can bet it was planned!"* And he was in a position to know.

There is much evidence to support the notion that wars are fomented and fought to redistribute these balances of financial power behind the scenes and that, though our fathers, brothers, grandfathers, uncles, cousins and sons die in these actions, they are merely games of 'international relations' played by those whose money and position give them little else with which to occupy their time or intelligence.

There is, however, a consequence to this game of global chess, which is apparent to neither the players nor the pawns of the game.

The level and types of energy created by the societal conditions that exist today are of such a nature that at the point in time when the Sun expresses its atomic nature in its regular and periodic pulsation, the conditions will be ripe for the inflow of a vast surge of electromagnetic energy far beyond our ability to comprehend or measure.

In like manner did the former 'Dyings' occur, and deterioration of atomic particles increased or accelerated so that the fossil record shows this event to have been in the past millions of years rather than the actual thousands of years. In those times, similar societal conditions created the Contact Potential Difference, but we have something they didn't have — nuclear weapons and five billion people. And, so, it is prophesied that this will be the worst cataclysm the earth has ever known.

And here we have the hidden purpose, the Mystery of God — the release of energy potentials, the feeding of the cosmos by the destruction of humanity — the Marriage Supper of the Lamb.

*"... as it was in the days of Noah, so will it be in the time of the Son of Man. [People] ate, they drank, they married, they were given in marriage, right **up to the day when Noah went into the ark**, and the flood came and destroyed them all.*

*So also [it was the same] as it was in the days of Lot. [People] ate, they drank, they bought, they sold, they planted, they built; But on the [very] **day that Lot went out of Sodom**, it rained fire and brimstone from heaven and destroyed [them] all. That is the way it will be on the day that the Son of Man is revealed.*

*On that day let him who is on the housetop, with his belongings in the house, not come down [and go inside] to carry them away; and likewise let him who is in the field not turn back. **Remember Lot's wife! Whoever tries to preserve his life will lose it, but whoever loses his life will preserve and quicken it.***

*I tell you, in that night there will be two men in one bed; one will be taken and **the other will be left**. There will be two women grinding together; one will be taken and **the other will be left**. Two men will be in the field; one will be taken and **the other will be left**.*

Then they asked Him, Where, Lord? He said to them, Wherever the dead body is, there will the vultures or eagles be gathered together." [227]

The disciples asked specifically where those people would be taken. Being 'taken' clearly does not mean being 'raptured,' according to the response given. The last sentence above is repeated in Matthew:

> "For just as the lightning flashes from the east and shines and is seen as far as the west, so will the coming of the Son of Man be. Wherever there is a fallen body, there the vultures will flock together." [228]

The meaning of the flocking of the vultures is clarified in Revelation:

> "Then I saw a single angel stationed in the sun's light, and with a mighty voice he shouted to all the birds that fly across the sky, Come, gather yourselves together for the great supper of God, That you may feast on the flesh of rulers, the flesh of generals and captains, the flesh of powerful and mighty men, the flesh of horses and their riders, and the flesh of all humanity, both free and slave, both small and great." [229]

As for those who are 'left behind:'

> "By faith we understand that the worlds were framed by the word of God, so that what we see was not made out of things which are visible. ... by faith Noah, being forewarned of God concerning events of which as yet there was no visible sign, took heed and diligently and reverently constructed and prepared an ark for the deliverance of his own family. By this [faith] he passed judgment and sentence on the world's unbelief and became an heir and possessor of righteousness." [230]

This faith is the Noah Syndrome.

Notes

1 Bertrand Russell, *Why Men Fight: A Method of Abolishing the International Duel* (New York: Century Co., 1917), p. 178.

2 Nick Herbert, *Quantum Reality: Beyond the New Physics* (Garden City, NY: Anchor Press/Doubleday, 1987), p. 58.

3 Ibid., p. 61.

4 P. D. Ouspensky, *Tertium Organum: A Key to the Enigmas of the World* (New York: Vintage Books, 1982 [1920]), p. 194.

5 Romans 1:19—20. Unless noted, all Bible quotations come from *The Amplified Bible* (Grand Rapids: Zondervan, 1987).

6 R. P. Feynman, R. B. Leighton, and M. Sands, *The Feynman Lectures on Physics*, Vol. 3 (Reading: Addison-Wesley, 1965), p. 1.

7 Ouspensky, *Tertium Organum*, op. cit., pp. 84—85.

8 Ibid., p. 28.

9 Ibid., p. 29.

10 Ibid., pp. 30—31.

11 Ibid., p. 31

12 Ibid., p. 31.

13 Ibid., p. 33.

14 Ibid., p. 235.

15 John 1:1, 3—4 (King James Version).

16 David Wallechinsky and Irving Wallace, *The People's Almanac*, Vol. 2 (Garden City, NY: Doubleday, 1975), p. 1270.

17 *Scientific American* 7:298 (June 5), p. 1852.

18 Fred Warshofsky, "When the Sky Rained Fire: The Velikovsky Phenomenon," *Reader's Digest* (Feb. 1976), p. 156.

19 Immanuel Velikovsky, *Worlds in Collision* (New York: Pocket Books, 1977 [1950]), p. 174.

20 Ibid.

21 Adapted from: Immanuel Velikovsky, *Ages in Chaos I: From the Exodus to King Akhnaton* (London: Sidgwick and Jackson, 1977 [1953]), chapter 1.

22 Velikovsky, *Worlds in Collision*, op. cit., p. 69.

23 Ibid., p. 104.

24 Ibid., p. 86.

25 Ibid., p. 118.

26 Wallechinsky and Wallace, *The People's Almanac*, op. cit., p. 930.

27 Luman H. Long (ed.), *The 1972 World Almanac and Book of Facts* (Newspaper Enterprise Association, 1972), p. 216.

28 Quoted in: Arthur Holmes, *Principles of Physical Geology* (New York: Ronald Press, 1965), p. 44.

29 Jonathan Weiner, *Planet Earth* (New York: Bantam Books, 1986), p. 14.

30 Velikovsky, *Worlds in Collision*, op. cit., pp. 36—37.

31 Ibid., pp. 37—39.

32 Ibid., pp. 39—40.

33 Robert T. Bakker, *The Dinosaur Heresies* (New York: William Morrow and Co., 1986), pp. 27, 38, 39.

34 Ibid., p. 44

35 *Mysteries of the Unexplained* (Reader's Digest, 1985), p. 37.

36 Ibid., p. 38.

37 Genesis 6:4 (KJV).

38 Clark R. Chapman, *Planets of Rock and Ice: From Mercury to the Moons of Saturn* (Scribner, 1982).

39 Weiner, *Planet Earth*, op. cit., p. 200.

40 Velikovsky, *Worlds in Collision*, op. cit., pp. 387—88.

41 Ibid.

42 Wallechinsky and Wallace, *The People's Almanac*, op. cit.

43 Nils O. Jacobson, *Life Without Death? On Parapsychology, Mysticism and the Question of Survival* (New York: Dell, 1974), p. 281.

44 I Corinthians 15:21—23.

45 I Corinthians 15:45—56 (excerpts).

46 David Vaughan, *A Faith for the New Age* (Regency Press, 1967).

47 Ibid.

48 Ibid.

49 Frank C. Tribbe, *Portrait of Jesus: The Illustrated Story of the Shroud of Turin* (1983).

50 Matthew 24:28.

51 J. B. S. Haldane, *Possible Worlds and Other Papers* (London: Chatto & Windus, 1927), p. 227.

52 Genesis 1:14.

53 Ecclesiastes 3:1.

54 Psalm 19:1—4.

55 Isaiah 13:12 (KJV).

56 Exodus 7:21.

57 Revelation 16:3.

58 Exodus 8:17.

59 Exodus 8:24.

60 Exodus 10:14.

61 Velikovsky, *Worlds in Collision*, op. cit., pp. 192—93.

62 Revelation 9:3—11.

63 Exodus 9:3, 9.

64 Revelation 16:2.

65 Revelation 16:10—11.

66 Exodus 9:23-24.

67 Velikovsky, *Worlds in Collision*, op. cit., pp. 69—70.

68 Revelation 9:15—18.

69 Exodus 10:19, 22.

70 Revelation 16:8—12 (excerpts).

71 Velikovsky, *Worlds in Collision*, op. cit., p. 78.

72 Revelation 16:17—21.

73 Daniel 12:4.

74 Daniel 12:1, 3.

75 Matt. 24:21— 22, 27, 29—31, 33.

76 J. Trachtenberg, quoted in Velikovsky, *Worlds in Collision*, op. cit., pp. 295—96.

77 Ibid., p. 297.

78 Revelation 2:26, 28.

79 Matthew 24:30.

80 Matthew 24:37—40.

81 I Thessalonians 5:2—3.

82 I Thessalonians 5:4, 9, 8.

83 II Corinthians 5:4, 10.

84 Revelation 3:17—18.

85 Matthew 24:17—18.

[86] II Peter 3:3—7, 10, 13—14.

[87] William Steuart McBirnie, B.A., B.D., M.R.E., Ph.D., F.R.G.S., Th.D., L.H.D., O.S.J., *The Antichrist* (Dallas: Acclaimed Books, 1978).

[88] Acts 2:17—18.

[89] Daniel 12:4.

[90] Matthew 24:44.

[91] Matthew 24:34.

[92] Matthew 24:32.

[93] Matthew 24:6—7, 21—22.

[94] Editor's note: In 2005, Joseph Ratzinger chose the name of Benedict XVI after St. Benedictine, whose crest consists of an olive branch.

[95] Revelation 26:12.

[96] Reading #3976-15, quoted in Lytle Robinson, *Edgar Cayce's Origin and Destiny of Man* (New York: Penguin, 1983), p. 163.

[97] Revelation 8:7—12.

[98] Alan Vaughan, *Patterns of Prophecy* (New York: Hawthorn Books, 1973).

[99] Ibid.

[100] Ibid.

[101] Ibid.

[102] Revelation 16:8—21 (excerpts).

[103] Luke 21:8—10, 25—28, 31—36.

[104] Quoted in Mary E. Carter, *Edgar Cayce on Prophecy* (New York: Castle Books, 1968).

[105] Reading 1602-5, quoted in ibid.

[106] Ibid.

[107] Reading 1598-2.

[108] Reading 294-151.

[109] Quoted in Kenneth Ring, *Heading Toward Omega: In Search of the Meaning of the Near-Death Experience* (New York: William Morrow and Co., 1984), p. 151.

[110] Ibid., p. 196.

[111] Ibid., p. 198.

[112] Ibid., p. 199.

[113] Ibid., p. 200.

[114] Ibid.

[115] Ibid., p. 201.

[116] Ibid., p. 202.

[117] Isaiah 65:17—25.

[118] Revelation 21:1—4.

[119] Matthew 24:11—14.

[120] Adapted from McBirnie, *The Antichrist*, op. cit.

[121] Matthew 24:33.

[122] Matthew 24:29—30.

[123] Luke 21:24.

[124] Daniel 8:13—14.

[125] I Corinthians 6:19.

[126] II Corinthians 6:16.

[127] Ephesians 2:21—22.

[128] II Thessalonians 2:3—12.

[129] Matthew 7:15—16, 18, 21 23.

[130] II Timothy 3:5.

[131] Revelation 19:15, 20—21.

[132] Erika Cheetham, *The Further Prophecies of Nostradamus: 1985 and Beyond* (New York: Perigee, 1985).

[133] Matthew 23:13—22.

[134] James 2:19.

[135] John 5:24.

[136] Matthew 7:21.

[137] Galatians 5:22.

[138] Revelation 22:18 (KJV).

[139] Matthew 24:12.

[140] Matthew 13:27.

[141] Matthew 13:28.

[142] John 8:31.

[143] John 16:31.

[144] I John 2:21.

[145] James 3:16—17.

[146] *Webster's New World Dictionary* (Cleveland: World Publishing, 1970).

[147] II Thessalonians 2:11.

[148] Mark 4:12.

[149] II Thessalonians 2:12.

[150] Romans 16:25.

[151] I Corinthians 2:7.

[152] I Corinthians 15:50—51.

[153] Ephesians 1:10.

[154] Colossians 1:27.

[155] Revelation 10:7.

[156] Revelation 13:1.

[157] Revelation 17:15.

[158] Hebrews 10:1.

[159] Revelation 13:2.

[160] Revelation 13:2.

[161] Revelation 13:3.

[162] Revelation 13:4.

[163] Revelation 13:5.

[164] Revelation 13:7.

[165] Revelation 13:8.

[166] Revelation 13:10.

[167] Revelation 13:12—14.

[168] Genesis 1:6, 8.

[169] Revelation 13:15—17.

[170] Genesis 4:15.

[171] Job 7:20.

[172] Lamentations 3:1—12.

[173] Ezekiel 9:4—6.

[174] Revelation 14:9—10.

[175] Revelation 19:20.

[176] Revelation 7:2—3.

[177] Deuteronomy 6:4—9.

[178] Revelation 13:18.

[179] Revelation 16:17.

[180] Luke 17:17—18.

[181] Nehemiah 11:1.

[182] Gurdjieff, quoted by P. D. Ouspensky, In Search of the Miraculous (New York: Harvest/HBJ, 1977), pp. 285—88.

[183] Daniel 8:13—14.

[184] Matthew 24:15—22, 27—30.

[185] UNITED STATES (of) AMERICA =

$(3 + 5 + 9 + 2 + 5 + 4) + (1 + 2 + 1 + 2 + 5 + 1) + (1 + 4 + 5 + 9 + 9 + 3 + 1) = 72$; $7 + 2 = 9$.

[186] Genesis 15:5.

[187] Genesis 17:4—5.

[188] Matthew 3:9—10.

[189] Hebrews 8:8—10.

[190] Romans 3:29, 4:3, 13, 16.

[191] Isaiah 1:21, 23.

[192] Ezekiel 16:13—15, 25, 28—29, 36—37, 39—41, 44—47, 49.

[193] Revelation 11:8.

[194] Revelation 17:1—2.

[195] Revelation 17:3—4.

[196] Revelation 17:5.

[197] Revelation 17:6—11.

[198] Daniel 5:18—21.

[199] Revelation 17:12—14.

[200] Letter to George Washington (October 28, 1786), quoted in: The Writings of James Madison: 1783—1787, volume II, ed. Gaillard Hunt (New York: Putnam & Sons, 1901), p. 408 (footnote).

[201] Ernest Sutherland Bates, American Faith: Its Religious, Political, and Economic Foundations (New York: W.W. Norton & Co., 1940), p. 289.

[202] Ibid.

[203] Milburn Lincoln Wilson, Democracy Has Roots (New York: Carrick & Evans, 1939), p. 98.

[204] Revelation 17:15—18.

[205] Printed in the Raleigh Star (May 28, 1824).

[206] Quoted in Gary Allen, None Dare Call It Conspiracy (1971), p. 50.

[207] Ibid., p. 12.

[208] Ibid., p. 13.

[209] Revelation 14:8—10, 14, 16, 18—20.

[210] Revelation 18:2—3, 6.

[211] Revelation 13:10.

[212] Revelation 18:7.

[213] Reading 3976-24, quoted in: Carter, *Edgar Cayce on Prophecy*, op. cit.

[214] Revelation 18:8—11, 19.

[215] Revelation 15:1—2, 5—6, 8, 16:2.

[216] Revelation 16:3—4, 8, 10, 12.

[217] Revelation 16:13—14, 16.

[218] Revelation 13:13.

[219] Revelation 16:17—21.

[220] Revelation 18:21.

[221] Revelation 19:17—20.

[222] Gurdjieff, quoted by P. D. Ouspensky, *In Search of the Miraculous*, op. cit., p. 219.

[223] Ibid., p. 220.

[224] Matthew 7:15—16, 18.

[225] Wallechinsky and Wallace, *The People's Almanac*, op. cit., pp. 805, 807.

[226] Quoted in ibid.

[227] Luke 17:26—37; my emphases.

[228] Matthew 24:27—28.

[229] Revelation 19:17—18.

[230] Hebrews 11:3, 7.